School of American Research
Advanced Seminar Series

DOUGLAS W. SCHWARTZ, GENERAL EDITOR

SCHOOL OF AMERICAN RESEARCH
ADVANCED SEMINAR SERIES

Reconstructing Prehistoric Pueblo Societies
EDITED BY WILLIAM A. LONGACRE

New Perspectives on the Pueblos
EDITED BY ALFONSO ORTIZ

Structure and Process in Latin America
EDITED BY ARNOLD STRICKON AND SIDNEY M. GREENFIELD

The Classic Maya Collapse
EDITED BY T. PATRICK CULBERT

Methods and Theories of Anthropological Genetics
EDITED BY M. H. CRAWFORD AND P. L. WORKMAN

Sixteenth-Century Mexico
EDITED BY MUNRO S. EDMONSON

Ancient Civilization and Trade
EDITED BY JEREMY A. SABLOFF AND C. C. LAMBERG-KARLOVSKY

Photography in Archaeological Research
EDITED BY ELMER HARP, JR.

Meaning in Anthropology
EDITED BY KEITH H. BASSO AND HENRY A. SELBY

The Valley of Mexico
EDITED BY ERIC R. WOLF

Demographic Anthropology
EDITED BY EZRA B. W. ZUBROW

Demographic Anthropology

Advanced Seminars are made possible
by a gift in recognition of
Philip L. Shultz
for his efforts on behalf of
the School of American Research

DEMOGRAPHIC ANTHROPOLOGY

Quantitative Approaches

EDITED BY

EZRA B. W. ZUBROW

A SCHOOL OF AMERICAN RESEARCH BOOK

UNIVERSITY OF NEW MEXICO PRESS · Albuquerque

Library of Congress Cataloging in Publication Data

Main entry under title:

Demographic anthropology.

(Advanced seminar series)
Papers of a seminar sponsored by the School of American Research and held in Santa Fe, Jan. 14–20, 1973.
"A School of American Research book."
Includes bibliographical references and index.
1. Demographic anthropology—Congresses. I. Zubrow, Ezra B. W. II. Santa Fe, N.M. School of American Research. III. Series: Santa Fe, N.M. School of American Research. Advanced seminar series.
GN33.5.D45 301.32 75–40840
ISBN 0-8263-0413-3

 Library of Congress Catalog Card Number 75-40840. International Standard Book Number 0-8263-0413-3.
First Edition

Foreword

The world's population will increase by two hundred thousand people today and again tomorrow, and every day for the foreseeable future. This growth rate has prompted a recent United Nations report to warn that "the magnitude of the new population boom surpasses all earlier expectations. The longer the high tempo persists . . . the more precarious will be prospects for a healthy life on this planet." We have all become accustomed to doomsday predictions concerning the relationship between population growth and economic disaster, made popular first by Malthus over one hundred years ago and recently reinforced by the publications of the Club of Rome. But gradually this litany has grown to include discussions of the effect of population growth on other cultural phenomena. A *Wall Street Journal* article referred, for example, to the ominous prospect of the rise of reactionary regimes and a worldwide growth in the number of conflicts resulting from future demographic pressures.

This rather spectacular leap from population statistics to cultural explanation implies a great deal more knowledge of causal links than presently exists. While the study of demography reaches back into the second half of the nineteenth century, only recently have anthropologists begun to realize the heuristic value of viewing the culture context of population structure and trends and of attempting to understand the causal routes from population statistics to cultural explanation. It was our desire to examine such connections more critically and to isolate demographic variables and their cultural consequences that led first to a seminar on demographic anthropology and then to this publication.

The volume begins with Ezra Zubrow's well-reasoned and precise essay on demography and anthropology, interacting variables and propositions, current trends, and an introduction to the other papers. Seven articles follow, each an excellent illustration of contemporary interests and levels of analysis. The authors explore various aspects of demography and anthropology, emphasizing cultural or biological structures and processes in relation to population trends. They examine more accurate indirect measures for estimating prehistoric population, the dynamics of a prehistoric community's demography, the effect of sedentism on fertility, socioeconomic correlates of biological processes, the significance of cultural values to demographic structure, Malthusian and neo-Malthusian assumptions regarding changes in fertility, and a number of economic models applied to regional demography.

Clearly this kind of detailed and broad-gauged analysis is quite different from the awesome quantitative leap directly from data to determinism. The anthropological view of demography, with its use of small cultural laboratory situations, provides a much more controlled approach to these complexities. For this reason, *Demographic Anthropology* is certain to be an important contribution to contemporary anthropological and demographic thought.

Douglas W. Schwartz

School of American Research

Preface

The fifteenth in a series of advanced seminars sponsored by the School of American Research was held January 14–20, 1973, in Santa Fe, New Mexico. The topic of the seminar was demographic research in anthropology.

The participating scholars were Lewis R. Binford (Department of Anthropology, University of New Mexico); L. Luca Cavalli-Sforza (Department of Human Genetics, School of Medicine, Stanford University); Eugene A. Hammel (Department of Anthropology, University of California, Berkeley); William A. Longacre (Department of Anthropology, University of Arizona); James N. Spuhler (Department of Anthropology, University of New Mexico); Arthur P. Wolf (Department of Anthropology, Stanford University); and Ezra B. W. Zubrow (Department of Anthropology, Stanford University). E. Z. Wrigley (Peterhouse College, Cambridge University) prepared and circulated a paper but was unable to participate in the seminar.

Eight papers were prepared in advance of the seminar, forming the basis for discussion during the five-day session. Seven of the papers were revised in the light of the discussions and form the core of this volume. Several of the papers were joint efforts to varying degrees. Although A. Ammerman (Stanford University), W. J. Chasko, Jr. (University of New Mexico), D. Hutchinson (University of California, Berkeley), K. Wachter (St. Catherine's College, Oxford University), and D. Wagener (Harvard University) did not attend the conference, their contributions were important to the papers and to the success of the conference.

Demographic anthropology has been of growing interest to anthropologists for the last two decades. It incorporates a wide range of theoretical issues, for it concerns two human universals, culture and population. The problems tend to be integrative, and in this domain of research the contributions of scholars from the various anthropological and ancillary disciplines are particularly relevant to each other. Methodologically, population may be studied "etically" or "emically" across time and space. Since the data are quantitative, verifiable, and replicable, they are particularly conducive to some of the most sophisticated testing procedures and manipulation being used in anthropology today.

The seminar focused on cultural structure and demographic process through quantitative analysis, the term quantitative being used in its widest sense, meaning "potentially measurable." Emphasis was on the overlap of demographic processes with ecological, social, biological, and economic systems, respectively, as well as on a series of related methodological problems. Specific topics included the demographic implications of sedentism, kinship, childhood marriage association, and stable and unstable economic growth. In addition, the socioeconomic correlates of inbreeding and indirect techniques for estimating population size and detecting migration were explored.

Most important, the seminar provided an opportunity for discussion in depth of common research problems encountered by scholars from different geographic areas and disciplines. In the interchange of information, the participants discovered the existence of previously unknown methodological solutions to problems and new sources of data. New directions for research and research topics of high priority were proposed, and it is gratifying to see that work is beginning along these lines. The interchange of ideas among various participants has continued since the conclusion of the seminar.

The advantages of isolating demographic variables were clear throughout the conference. Because a statistical population is interdisciplinary, one may examine physical and social phenomena using a common unit. This enables one to combine such diverse interests as ecology, economics, and kinship within a single anthropological study. One advantage of a generic concept of population is that it provides the common focus for viewing a universe of recognizable individual elements collectively. It is concerned with such group attributes as number, composition, distribution, and change, and thus is highly amenable to quantitative analysis.

The seminar is particularly grateful to Douglas W. Schwartz, Director, the members of the Board of Managers of the School of American Research, and the School's members for making the seminar possible. We are indebted to Mrs. Douglas Schwartz and to Ella Schroeder and the SAR staff for their assistance and hospitality. By now the School has a long tradition of exciting and stimulating seminars in anthropology. We are gratified to be participants in that tradition and hope that the School will be able to continue these seminars for many years to come.

Ezra B. W. Zubrow

Contents

Contents

Figures

Tables

1
Demographic Anthropology: An Introductory Analysis

EZRA B. W. ZUBROW
Department of Anthropology
Stanford University

Introductions are preliminary, synoptic, and incomplete, particularly when a book's scope is broad. The articles collected in this book may be seen from many perspectives: methodologically, as emphasizing quantitative approaches; thematically, as emphasizing demographic and cultural structure or process; or as disciplinary examples of archaeological, physical, and cultural anthropological research. This introduction places the articles in an even broader context.

I wish to introduce an overview of some aspects of ongoing demographic research in anthropology by examining what I believe are four fundamental questions: What is the relationship between demography and anthropology? Why pursue demographic research in anthropology? What are some of the major propositions and interacting variables? What trends seem to be emerging? I will then briefly summarize each chapter according to a series of comparative criteria—excerpting subject, proposition, techniques, data base, and relevance to related disciplines. Finally, I will review some general themes which integrate not only this particular conference but the individual articles with the fundamental questions.

WHAT IS THE RELATIONSHIP BETWEEN DEMOGRAPHY AND ANTHROPOLOGY?

The fields are related by definition, history, and methodology as well as conceptually and theoretically. Demography is defined as the study of human populations, anthropology as the study of the human development and culture of these same populations. In order to analyze a human population in such a manner that its demographic characteristics may be understood, such anthropological criteria as cultural boundaries, family types, and regional organization must be utilized. Conversely, if an anthropologist wishes to study the development of man or a particular culture, demographic parameters such as population size, age and sex structure, mortality, and fertility are indispensable.

Historically, the two fields derive from similar origins, although they have developed in different directions with only spasmodic interchange over the last four centuries. Both demography and anthropology result from the attempt by the scientific forerunners of the philosophes to apply natural history to human society. In approximately 1566, two decades after Copernicus and Vesalius were revolutionizing the concepts of the heavens and the human body, the *Relación de las cosas de Yucatán* was being written by Bishop de Landa. An ethnographic classic, it changed the European conception of society. Between Bacon's "Novum Organum" (1620) and Newton's *Mathematical Principles of Natural Philosophy* (1687), Graunt published the first noteworthy empirical demographic study, entitled "Natural and Political Observations upon the Bills of Mortality" (1662).

Both fields have descriptive origins. De Landa attempted to describe and reconstruct the social, religious, economic, and material bases for the postcontact Maya. Graunt observed the quantitative variation in migration and mortality in greater London and speculated upon socioeconomic causes.

The genesis was not only empirical; methodologically, description preceded theory in both fields. Bacon had argued that knowledge should be reorganized on inductive principles, and early scholars interested in anthropological and demographic problems complied. Both required fieldwork; both were usually undertaken to satisfy other needs by individuals whose locations and interests made the research feasible. The later development of data collection techniques, however, took very different directions in the two fields. Ironically, demography has moved away from its geographically localized beginnings toward the collection of data on a regional and national scale. Anthropologists, who initially examined major, even national, non-Western cultures, tend now to collect data from marginal, localized primitive isolates. Sophisticated censual data collection today is a priori and not problem specific, not being gathered with a specific researcher's problem in mind. Anthropological data collection, in contrast, tends to be more problem specific. Most demographic data collection requires large teams of enumerators, in contrast to the individual character of most anthropological fieldwork—with the exception of archaeology. Censual data are, of course, quantitative, verifiable, and often comparable. Anthropological data are far more variable, ranging from the quantitative and cross-culturally comparable to culturally specific, qualitative data that are not verifiable but interpretive.

Conceptually, culture and population are subtle concepts, similar in several aspects. Both provide a common focus for viewing a universe of phenomena comprising recognizable individual elements but concerned with group attributes such as number, composition, structure, distribution, and change; both have generic and specific uses. Each is superorganic and holistic, transcending social roles or the individual organism. Culture and population are everywhere and nowhere simultaneously. Academically, the biological, sociological, economic, historical, and geographical aspects of anthropology and demography may be studied simply as parts of the disciplines concerned. Theoretically, the existence of population and culture is often assumed and otherwise ignored. Analytically, culture and population are constructs. Descriptively, they are difficult to measure since the boundaries are fuzzy and the critical variables elusive.

Theoretically, anthropology and demography have often intertwined and overlapped but usually not too explicitly. Anthropologists have been interested in examining the demographic determinants and consequences of cultural processes. Demographers have looked for the cultural causes and effects of demographic processes. Thus it should not surprise the reader that both fields have imported and exported theory and data to each other—a type of intellectual international trade. For example, one can cite such anthropologists as Leslie White, Julian Steward, and Ludwik Kryzwicki for demographic determinants of cultural processes and Herbert Spencer, W. H. R. Rivers, and Meyer Fortes for demographic consequences. Or one may note Thomas Malthus, Frank Lorimer, and T. H. Hollingsworth for cultural causes of demographic processes or Jean Fourastie and F. W. Notestein for cultural effects. Needless to say, such lists could be expanded enormously.

This volume, reflecting the editor's choice and the interests of the conference participants, selectively emphasizes the anthropological perspective.

WHY PURSUE DEMOGRAPHIC RESEARCH IN ANTHROPOLOGY?

There are many reasons to undertake demographic research in anthropology, ranging from the metascientific to the practical, from national needs to personal interests. Obviously, I cannot recapitulate all the motivations of all the scholars, but I can discuss briefly some general rationales.

It is a domain suited for theoretical analyses and tests. At the most abstract level anthropologists are concerned with the discovery, classification, and explanation of mankind. The growth of anthropological knowledge is dependent upon recognizing generalizations about society and recognizing the limited uniformity of the human condition. This ability to abstract generalities from specifics is particularly important, for the large variability of human patterns has severely restricted the numbers of generalities discovered. In this context culture and population, as two of the few human universals, represent one area of anthropological research with many implications and applications within the discipline. All cultures consist of populations, and all populations consist of one or more cultures. Cultures are regulators; populations are regulated.

In addition to its universality, population is one of the few domains that is both etic and emic. In other words, it is observable, replicably quantifiable, and cross-culturally comparable. Yet simultaneously it is conceived differently by members of various cultures, classes, and ideologies. In short, part of the exploding interest in demographic research in anthropology is the recognition by theorists that it represents one of the few areas within anthropology that is favorable for the testing of theory against the course of events.

It is focused upon a series of important problems. Researchers themselves are often unaware of what is or will become significant within a field. However, demographic research in anthropology appears to be directed toward a series of fundamental scientific and social problems with ramifications far beyond anthropology. One set of issues involves problems related to the potentially anomalous nature of human systems. To what extent are the principles governing human populations subsumed under general biological principles? Does culture modify basic population ecology for human populations? Theoretical and empirical answers require demographic research in anthropological societies.

A second set of problems concerns the complexity of human systems. These problems require factorial answers based upon the recombination of relatively simple solutions. For example, an analysis of industrialized urbanization requires an attempt to isolate the effects of demographic processes (such as increasing density and migration), social processes (such as developing stratification and kin network contraction), and economic processes (such as intensifying technology and extensifying labor). Then, reuniting these factors synthetically, one approaches an explanatory estimate of the more sophisticated problem. For such problems demographic research in anthropology is simply one of a set of factors.

A third set of problems pertains to the characteristic properties of populations. Rather than requiring synthetic techniques, these issues call for an analytic methodology that allows cultural and demographic attributes to be recognized. For example, are there cultural attributes that distinguish members of demographic categories, such as potential "outmigrants," from other members of a society? Such attributes might include differences in ethnicity, socioeconomic status, or distance to nearest kin. Conversely, are there demographic attributes distinguishing such cultural categories as social class? Among these might be size, age-sex structure, and differential fertility and mortality. Such attributes may be but need not be causative.

Finally, a fourth set of problems exists in the realm of policy and application. Demographic research in anthropology is relevant to problems of growth, underemployment and unemployment, birth control in various cultural settings, and family structure, to mention only a few. Any of the following questions could be considered internationally significant by governments, world organizations, and numerous academic disciplines. Are maximal, minimal, and optimal populations viable concepts cross-culturally, and, if so, what is the variation in acceptable levels? How should various population policies be implemented in different cultures in order to disrupt other cultural patterns minimally? What is the cross-cultural significance of pro and antinatalist policies? Are there mechanisms to relieve class-specific mortality, one of the worst forms of human injustice based upon cultural factors?

Demographic research in anthropology is relevant to other areas of research. Although we have previously alluded to areas of overlap, it is useful to specify some of the other disciplines for which demographic research in anthropology is relevant. These are presented in Table 1.

TABLE 1
DISCIPLINES RELATED TO DEMOGRAPHIC RESEARCH IN ANTHROPOLOGY AND EXAMPLES OF OVERLAP

Discipline	*Areas of Mutual Interest*
Economics	Cross-cultural regularities and variations in the growth of labor, consumption, and other population-related variables in market and nonmarket economies
Sociology	Comparative data on the effects of population upon social patterns in complex Western and anthropological societies
History	The importance of population pressure and size in the development of particular historical events for differing types of societies
Geography	The variation in the type, size, and distribution of settlements for differing cultures
Medicine	The effects of culture on disease and mortality patterns
Biology	The effects of culture on general biological and ecological processes as well as its importance for a synthetic general theory of human evolution
Political Science	The size of population necessary for efficient cross-cultural operation of differing political systems

There are numerous miscellaneous rationales. A variety of other rationales for demographic research in anthropology exists. Some scholars pragmatically suggest that it is a research topic whose time has come. Baker and Sanders (1971) have pointed to the increase in the availability of descriptive data as well as the increased interest in human ecology. These ecological interests have been broadened and their popular base deepened by a series of poliscientific movements. Crusades for zero population growth, conservation, and the "green revolution" are all manifestations of a general interest in evaluating and improving upon the success of varying human adaptations. Far too often a modern nation's economic policy impinges upon "anthropological populations" with detrimental demographic and cultural consequences. Frequently such populations are the first to be starved or culturally battered. Funds for applied research on such topics are becoming available as the political and social consciences of national and international organizations are awakened.

In conclusion I might note that the rationales for demographic research in anthropology vary, but ultimately the researcher believes the work is interesting, satisfying, and useful.

WHAT ARE THE INTERACTING VARIABLES AND PROPOSITIONS?

Underlying any social science that attempts quantitative analysis is the ability to delimit and measure relevant variables. For demographic anthropology, a series of caveats should be noted. It is difficult to catalog the interacting demographic and anthropological variables for four reasons: (1) demographic research in anthropology is incomplete and limited; (2) anthropological variables are not as standardized as demographic variables; (3) anthropological variables, unlike demographic variables, do not have common units; and (4) anthropology and demography both incorporate variables from other disciplines. Therefore, the interacting variables presented in Table 2 should be viewed as a first and incomplete attempt that will be refined as more work is completed.

A considerable number of recent studies concern the interaction of demographic and anthropological variables. A quick review of the literature may be found in Baker and Sanders's "Demographic Studies in Anthropology" (1971) and Sherburne F. Cook's *Prehistoric Demography* (1972a). More detailed studies include Stephen Polgar's *Culture and Population: A Collection of Current Studies* (1971) and the very important revision of the United Nations' *Determinants and Consequences of Population Trends* (1973). However, it is not my intention here to provide even a cursory review of the literature. Instead I wish to examine the scope of the quantitative data for demographic studies in anthropology. Most current anthropological research uses data from communi-

TABLE 2
INTERACTING DEMOGRAPHIC AND ANTHROPOLOGICAL VARIABLES

Demographic Variables

Static Variables

1. Population size
2. Number of births
3. Number of deaths
4. Number of migrants

Dynamic Variables

1. Mortality (general or age specific)
2. Fertility (general or age specific)
3. Natural increase
4. Rate of growth of total population
5. Emigration rate or velocity
6. Immigration rate or velocity
7. Net migration (international or cross-cultural)
8. Net internal migration
9. Net migration rate or velocity
10. Internal migration rate or velocity

Structural or Distributional Variables

1. Population density
2. Internal distribution of population total
3. Age composition of population
4. Sex composition of population
5. Differential mortality (intergroup differences in mortality)
6. Differential fertility (intergroup differences in fertility)
7. Differential internal migration (intergroup differences in internal immigration)
8. Qualitative composition of population (genetic, educational, etc.)
9. Qualitative composition of a component of the population

Life-Table Variables

1. Age in completed years
2. Probability of death between age X and X + 1
3. Probability of survival from age X to age X + 1

Anthropological Variables

Environmental Variables

1. Location
2. Ecotype
3. Climate

Economic Variables

1. Subsistence type
2. Net societal or national product
3. Net societal or national income
4. Net societal or national product per capita
5. Net societal or national income per capita
6. Land per capita
7. Resources by type per capita
8. Terms of trade
9. Income by type (e.g., wages, interest)
10. Consumption
11. Investment
12. Capital or income producing wealth
13. Savings
14. Division or occupational composition of labor
15. Composition of consumption
16. Composition of investment
17. Index of fullness of employment
18. Producer and consumer ratio
19. Technology
20. Distribution system

Social Variables

1. Political organization
2. Social complexity
3. Social stratification
4. Economic stratification
5. Social specialization
6. Community organization
7. Inheritance
8. Kinship
9. Contact
10. Administrative specialization
11. Legal specialization
12. Medical specialization

TABLE 2 CONT'D.

Demographic Variables	*Anthropological Variables*
4. Probability of survival from age X to age X + t	*Ideological Variables*
5. Number of dying at age X last birthday	1. Type of religion
6. Number living at age X	2. Religious specialization
7. Number living at age X last birthday	3. Values
8. Expectation of life at age X	4. Philosophical and psychological modalities
9. Complete expectation of life at age X	*Linguistic Variables*
10. Central death rate at age X	1. Number of languages per capita
11. Force of mortality at age X	2. Total number of languages
	Physical Variables
	1. Incest
	2. Population isolation
	3. Race
	4. Mutation rate
	5. Drift rate
	6. Selection rate
	7. Gene flow

ties, cultures, or regions. It is not surprising that syntheses are rare, for the problems are complex and most research is recent.

No one would question the importance of increasing the size of the quantitative domain by looking for global cross-cultural demographic regularities. Unfortunately, the data for this type of study are incomplete and uneven in quality, comparability, and analysis. An examination of existing data does show the potential for limited generalization. For example, consider the data presented by Textor in *A Cross-Cultural Summary* (1967), an analysis based upon a 400-culture sample from some 38 sources. Textor cross tabulated and calculated chi-square and phi tests on over 500 dichotomous variables, producing more than 20,000 significant correlations. Using only the most highly conservative test of significance, a probability level of .001 or less, it is possible to relate average population size of local communities to various cultural variables, as shown in Table 3.

An examination of Table 3 shows that as average population size of local communities increases, the number of significant correlations with the specified cultural variables increases. Too much importance should not be placed upon this pattern, as it is impossible to suggest the direction of the causal arrow or the mechanisms operating. For that matter, the changes in the variables might be caused by "outside" variables. Some of

TABLE 3
SELECTED ANTHROPOLOGICAL VARIABLES THAT CORRELATE WITH AVERAGE POPULATION SIZE OF LOCAL COMMUNITIES

Variable	*Textor Variable Number*	*Average Population Size of Local Communities*				
		50>	50≤	200≤	5,000≤	50,000≤
1. Located inside circum-Mediterranean area	4				+*	+
2. Located outside South America	9					+
3. Environment is not harsh	33				+	+
4. Environment is not harsh, subtropical bush	36					+
5. Fixed settlement pattern	44		+	+	+	+
6. Subsistence based on food production, not gathering	51		+	+	+	+
7. Subsistence based on intensive agriculture	53					+
8. Subsistence based on simple or intensive agriculture	54		+	+	+	+
9. Subsistence based on intensive rather than simple agriculture	55				+	+
10. Metallurgy present	71		+	+	+	+
11. Weaving present	73		+	+	+	+
12. Pottery present	74		+	+	+	+
13. Alphabetic writing	77				+	+
14. State political integration	84				+	+
15. High societal complexity	91			+	+	+
16. Hierarchy of national jurisdiction	94				+	+
17. Hierarchy of national jurisdiction has 2 to 4 levels	95				+	+
18. Class stratification	102		+	+	+	+
19. Class stratification not based on wealth	106				+	+
20. Class stratification based on occupational status	107				+	+
21. Full-time occupational specialization present	116				+	+

TABLE 3 CONT'D.

Variable	*Textor Variable Number*	50>	50≤	200≤	5,000≤	50,000≤
		Average Population Size of Local Communities				
22. Judicial and medical agencies highly differentiated	152				+	+
23. Individual volition is cause of crime	163				+	+
24. Individual volition is not the cause of illness	164				+	+
25. Community is structured on agamous, nonclan basis	182					+
26. Individual rights to real property and rules for inheritance are present	196		+	+	+	+
27. Inheritance does not follow sexual "lines"	197					+
28. Eskimo or Hawaiian cousin terminology	234				+	+
29. Monogamous marriage patterns	242				+	+
30. Wives obtained without major cost (i.e., no dowry)	263					+
31. Full-time religious specialists	424				+	+
32. No active ancestral spirits	436					+
33. Games of strategy	458				+	+
34. Games of chance	459					+
35. Frequent cross-cultural contact	468				+	+

* + indicates a significant correlation at .001 level.

the correlations may be over or understated. Also, average population size of local communities is far from being an ideal demographic variable because of the likelihood of estimation errors and specious coding. It may be conservatively argued, however, that for some 234 cultures the variables interact in a recognizable fashion. Clearly, one high priority for future research is the development of comparable cross-cultural demographic data. This set of data would provide an alternative to the national and transnational censuses for the development and testing of theories and models.

Propositions relating demographic and anthropological variables abound in the literature. Their testing varies: some have met rigorous testing procedures; some remain totally untested; others have been rejected. They range from formal mathematical treatments such as Kenneth M. Weiss's *Demographic Models in Anthropology* (1973) to insightful generalizations drawn from ethnographic or archaeological experience.

Part of the problem clearly lies in the quality of anthropological demographic data. I have already alluded to the comparability-of-data problem, which has two aspects: (1) different analysts collect different types of data, and (2) when similar types of data are collected, the methodologies of collection or analysis differ.

The accurate testing of propositions is additionally limited by what seem to be systematic biases in the data. For example, infant mortality and infanticide appear to be systematically underreported, while age for the elderly is often exaggerated in age-oriented societies.

Nonsedentary societies, or sedentary societies whose labor or social schedules entail high mobility, present similar demographic problems. The difficulties of accurately counting or representatively sampling the entire population for these cultures are far greater than for sedentary, fixed populations. The effects of stochastic fluctuation on small populations may be considerable, suggesting to the demographer the pressure of nonexistent forces. Most census taking for anthropological societies is primarily synchronic, corresponding to the anthropologist's single field season. This is often interpreted in the literature to suggest a stability in the population that may or may not be there.

Let us now turn to the propositions, cognizant of their range of verification as well as the limitations of the variables and the data. Following is a selected set of propositions compiled from a variety of sources; they are neither hierarchically arranged nor mutually exclusive, neither complete nor necessarily verified cross-culturally.

Selected Propositions Relating Demographic and Anthropological Variables

Population and Resources

1. If the population-to-resource ratio is stable, there is cultural stability.

2. If the population-to-resource ratio is variable, then cultural adaptation by changes in social structure and resource distribution are necessary to bring population-resource ratio into balance.
3. If population is greater than resources, then (a) land tenure and marriage restrictions increase; (b) migration to urban areas increases; (c) the importance of kin networks increases; (d) the use of marginal roles and marginal ecotypes increases; and (e) social mobility decreases.
4. If resources are greater than population, then (a) the importance of marriage restrictions decreases; (b) kin networks decrease in importance; (c) use of marginal roles and marginal ecotypes decreases; and (d) social mobility increases.

Family and Kinship

1. The nonindustrialized agrarian family is the reproductive, residential, productive, and consuming unit, and for most societies membership in the four coincides.
2. The industrialized family is the reproductive unit but need not be a residential, productive, or consuming household.
3. The ratio of nonindustrial agrarian families to industrialized families is proportional to producer-dependent ratio.
4. The number of family types is increasing and not being replaced by the nuclear family as usually assumed.
5. Clans function to aggregate and distribute resources.
6. Clans are independent of the fertility rate today.
7. Fertility rates are independent (dependent)* of polygamy.
8. If a family has marginal resources, then the probability of a female head of household increases.
9. For families with marginal resources, the stability of male income is a function of the probability of a female head of the household.
10. The stability of the marriage union is directly proportional to increasing (decreasing)* fertility, depending upon cultural area.
11. If labor composition shows an increasing female/male labor composition, then fertility decreases.
12. Female labor is a cross-cultural norm and not an exception.

---

* Both positions are held.

13. If the child/adult ratio increases, then dependency increases and fertility decreases.
14. Cultural extension of the family is a direct function of the probability of a child being prematurely biologically parentless.
15. With increasing economic development, the reproductive period of a family is increasingly restricted.

Migration

1. The probability that an individual will migrate is directly proportional to the ratio of the size of his kin network in the donor community to the size of his kin network in the recipient community, as well as to the ratio of the depth of his kin network in the donor community to the depth of his kin network in the recipient community.
2. The amount of migration between two communities is directly proportional to the amount of overlap between kin networks and to the amount of perceived and real economic advantage of the recipient community.
3. The amount of migration between two communities is inversely proportional to a distance function between the communities (i.e., any "gravity" model).
4. The effect of kinship networks upon migration is greatest for the upper and lower socioeconomic classes and least for the middle class.
5. If migration is sex specific, then fertility is affected.
6. In immigrant-recipient societies, marriages occur between older males and younger females, and vice versa in emigrant societies.
7. Migration changes the producer/dependent ratio.
8. Migration changes ethnic boundaries and dialects.
9. Migration is a direct function of the population/resource ratio.
10. With increasing economic development, the geographic distribution of the population becomes increasingly uneven.

Fertility and Mortality

1. Economic development need not depress fertility.
2. Fertility is a direct function of the demand for labor and the family's demand for capital.

3. Low mortality and fertility increase aging in the society and increase the dependency ratio.
4. The "green revolution" has decreased labor demand by increasing mechanization, thereby decreasing fertility, deferring marriage, and changing marriage patterns in a predictable manner.
5. Child spacing is a direct function of amount of lactation.
6. Age of menarche is an inverse function of nutrition.
7. Fertility is limited by sexual access, which in turn is a function of cross-culturally varying social, ritual, and economic restrictions.
8. Mortality is an inverse function of socioeconomic class, that is, "social mortality."
9. If mortality is high, the nuclear family is not viable.
10. As mortality decreases, the economic functions of the extended family are transferred to the society as a whole.
11. Birth-control measures increase the probability of inbreeding within a population.
12. Fertility is a function of marriage (i.e., frequency of marriage, age at marriage, divorce rate, frequency of intercourse, mortality of spouse), conception (fecundity and contraception), and gestation (fetal mortality).
13. Increased dependency, decreased savings, and decreased societal expenditure are functions of increased fertility.

Aging

1. For most societies the aging of a population is a function of decreasing fertility rather than lengthening of life.
2. The younger the population of a society, the greater the investment of power, prestige, economic wealth, and other similar roles to the elderly.
3. Increased life expectation tends to increase a society's age grading.
4. Increasing conservatism and declining geographic and economic expansion are functions of increasing age of the population.
5. In nonindustrial societies under and unemployment are functions of the youth of a population.
6. Increasing recruitment into age grades by cooption is a function of the increasing age of the population.
7. Emigration ages a population.
8. Immigration rejuvenates (opposite of ages) a population.

WHAT ARE THE TRENDS IN DEMOGRAPHIC RESEARCH IN ANTHROPOLOGY?

There appear to be at least seven major easily discernible trends, some of which we have already touched upon in other contexts:

1. the increasing amount of demographic research in anthropology;
2. the recognition of the importance of collecting and analyzing subnational groupings of data in cultural, ethnic, and racial categories;
3. the development and application of new techniques of quantitative analysis;
4. the questioning of such established theories as the Malthusian doctrine or transition theory;
5. the inadequacy of existing demographic data for anthropological societies;
6. the recognition of the necessity for increasingly sophisticated field studies of the anthropological variables that are concomitant with demographic processes; and
7. the recognition of the responsibility of anthropologists to influence national and transnational demographic policy as it affects anthropological societies.

In this section I wish to focus on only two of these trends, namely, the theoretical challenge (4) and the question of policy (7). Such distinguished demographers as Ansley J. Coale, director of the Office of Population Research at Princeton University, and Paul J. Demeny, vice-president of the Population Council, have argued in print as recently as September 1974 for the reality of transition theory. Transition theory is a major descriptive statement that has been found to be empirically useful. Prior to development (as exemplified by the Industrial Revolution) population is either not growing or growing slowly. High fertility rates are almost balanced by high mortality rates. With the initiation of development, parity between births and deaths is disturbed, and mortality decreases as a result of a wide variety of interlinked causes including advances in medicine, technology, and available resources. Later the rate of population growth declines to a new "steady level" as the birth rate decreases. This decrease in the birth rate is caused partially by higher consumption expectations and the development of new social values.

There have been several problems with the concept of the demographic transition. The first has been determining the reality—usually assumed by demographers—of the lower asymptotes where high mortality and fertility are roughly equal. Anthropologists who have actually tried to find such societies have not been particularly successful according to a report published in August 1974 by the Advisory Committee on Cultural Factors in Population Programs of the American Association for the Advancement of Science (AAAS). Paleoanthropologists have been showing that the transition between hunting and gathering and agriculture has been a gradual process characterized by societies with moderate fertility and mortality rates, not uniformly high rates as presumed by the theory. Ethnographic data indicate a wide variety of mortality and fertility rates for present-day nonindustrialized societies.

A second problem is that transition theory was originally formulated to explain data from Western Europe. The characteristic stages or rates need not be universal. Anthropologists have been showing that demographic characteristics are neither geographically nor temporally uniform. They conclude that the availability of resources seems to determine population size and characteristics. This appears to be a better, more general explanation of the known variation than the a priori high fertility and mortality stages of transition theory.

Third, transition theorists argue that mortality drops as a result of the diffusion of new medical techniques, and that fertility declines after industrialization. It is now clear, however, that even in Western Europe the decline in mortality preceded medical technology while the decline in fertility preceded industrialization. From the Advisory Committee's viewpoint, the decreases in preindustrial populations appear to be the result of culture contact with Western civilization and the consequent epidemics, wars, and slave trades. They analyze the rise of the Third World population as a response to new economic opportunities, that is, labor traded for cash goods, rather than as a transition. High fertility is a family response to the new demand for labor by colonial powers. This demand for labor is matched by the family's increased demand for cash and manufactured products.

The fourth problem concerns the upper asymptote of the transition, where low mortality and low fertility should once again be approximately equal. Demographers such as Harold Dorn have had trouble finding quantitative support for the upper asymptote. Transition theorists have tended to look toward modern industrial societies with capital-intensive economies. Anthropologists, however, have now pointed out numerous examples of "primitive isolates" which are neither industrial nor capital intensive but which meet the transition theorists' criteria of low fertility and mortality.

It is clear from the above four problems that anthropologists have presented a challenge to the transition theorists. This is not to imply that transition theory should be totally rejected or even that the concept of the demographic transition has been proved wrong. Rather, the concept has certain clear advantages: parsimony, simplicity, and predictability. It still summarizes a huge body of data. It does, however, have numerous exceptions and leaves major questions unanswered. One of these has been termed the paradox of posttransition societies: it is philosophically disquieting that in those societies where life is best protected from danger and so highly valued, it is given so grudgingly.

Similarly, there have been major challenges to the neo-Malthusian arguments. The neo-Malthusian position is essentially a "food pull" argument. Briefly, man cannot be isolated from his environment because population size is restricted by subsistence. This has been stated in both economic and ecological terms. Given the biological tendency of our species to reproduce and the fact that resources are ultimately finite, population growth must end through decreasing fertility or increasing mortality. An increase in utilizable resources (the "pull") resulting from new discoveries, technology, or organization will lead to an increased standard of living or to an increased population. When the resource increase is sufficiently large, it is possible for both population and standard of living to rise simultaneously. Malthus's error of assuming that man's capabilities for production and redistribution could never exceed population has been avoided by such neo-Malthusians as Kenneth Boulding.

Many anthropologists alienated by the economic and ecological determinism of the neo-Malthusians have recently been interested in the more culturally compatible "population push" argument of Ester Boserup. She suggests that the size of the population pushes economic development until subsistence needs are met. Given population increase and flexibility in scheduling leisure and labor, stresses on production may be resolved through territorial expansion, technological advance, and/or intensification. In agricultural societies intensification occurs, since expansion is limited and innovation decreases per capita output. For example, by decreasing the amount of time land is left fallow, one may increase production without innovation or expansion. Such intensification, however, requires more labor per capita at the cost of less leisure per capita. In other words, population pressure intensifies the utilization of existing resources and labor.

At the most theoretically general level, anthropologists see a potential conflict between increases in the supply of the means of subsistence and increases in the efficiency or ease by which subsistence may be gained. Demographic and economic theorists have tended to ignore this conflict or relegate it to that catchall phrase "the quality of life." The diversity of existing societies reveals the variation in social values regarding the ease of production. One group of anthropologists has argued that hunting and gathering groups with low population densities and limited technologies have the widest choice of resources; that is, a wider variety of resources is potentially capable of adequately supporting their populations. The choice among potential resources is based upon ease of acquisition and ease of processing. Those items found in the environment closest to the native state are preferred. This is Sahlins's "original affluent society" or what I term the "happy hunter" interpretation. This same group of anthropologists sees agricultural societies, in contrast, as being under greater demographic and economic pressure, inevitably faced with increasing cost and increasing demand for labor. Thus their agricultural societies are composed of "pessimistic peasants."

Another group of anthropologists follows a more traditional neo-Malthusian viewpoint. The more advanced technologies of agricultural societies provide an increased resource base, which implies larger populations and/or the potential for a higher standard of living with less labor. The demographic arguments—and their economic implications—between the two schools of thought have not yet been resolved. Thus today, depending upon one's theoretical interpretation, one believes in the Malthusian "grim gatherer" or Sahlins's "happy hunter." For the former interpretation, economic development results in the Malthusian "adequate agriculturalist"; for the latter, Boserup's "pessimistic peasant."

Let us turn briefly to the increasing interest of anthropologists in problems of demographic policy. Traditionally, anthropologists have provided only minor and sporadic input for demographic policy decisions, responding to occasional requests from the Bureau of Indian Affairs or colonial administrators. Recently anthropologists have begun their first real foray into transnational demographic policy.

The United States delegation to the United Nations World Population

Conference in Bucharest (1974) brought the AAAS study *Culture and Population Change* to the conference, in part to make it clear that cultural factors impinging on population matters would not be ignored. This report, prepared under the auspices of a 15-member committee of whom 9 were anthropologists, reflected the viewpoints of more than 100 interviewed scholars in the fields of population, comparative development, and cultural change, 64 of whom were anthropologists. Indicative of the increasing interest of anthropologists in policy was Margaret Mead's attendance at the conference as president-elect of AAAS.

At a more politically pragmatic level, the committee suggested additions, changes, and substitutions for parts of the wording of the "World Populations Plan of Action." Only a few will be noted here due to limitations of space. They include such points as:

> III.A.3.27.a . . . ensure the emancipation of women from the constraints of involuntary reproductivity . . .
> III.A.3.27.d . . . for contraceptives, explore nonclinical means of distribution . . .
> III.A.3.37a . . . recognition should be given of the many different types of family in the contemporary world . . .
> III.A.3.37.c . . . both partners should be permitted to exercise comparable choice in marriage. . . .

It is clear from the preceding that although anthropologists are continuing their more passive consultant roles they are also beginning to take a more active position by initiating proposals on demographic policy issues. For the first time they are utilizing international bureaucracies to attempt to effect changes. As the rate of information exchange among societies increases and the necessity for rapid decision making by national and transnational organizations becomes critical, one can expect more problem-specific task forces composed of anthropologists asking questions of and contributing to policy.

THE ARTICLES

The articles in this volume are a sampling of recent demographic research in three of the four subdisciplines of anthropology. Cultural anthropology, physical anthropology, and archaeology are represented—linguistics is omitted. It is a sample of interesting and innovative work but should not be construed as a comprehensive survey.

The seminar demonstrates a wide range of quantitative techniques. At one end of the continuum are descriptive statistics, while at the other are careful mathematical deductions and simulations. In between are various correlations, estimations, and regressions.

The quantified data correspond to some of the most basic demographic, cultural, and biological concepts. Population size, space and age distribution, growth, migration, fertility, and mortality are all measured. From the cultural side, marriage relationships and kinship are given quantifiable reality, while biological processes such as the biological opportunity for selection are examined.

Let us examine the seminar and the following papers as a totality and then narrow our focus reiteratively. Three important themes crosscut the entire seminar. First, there was an emphasis on demographic and cultural structure and process. Second, greater importance was given to diachronic changes and causal mechanisms than to synchronic description. Third, a strong interest in the operationalization of theory and in methodological problems underscored the articles and the discussion.

Organizing the papers in groups reveals several areas of overlap. The relationships between aspects of social organization and demographic processes were best brought out by Hammel's and Wolf's contributions. Those between ecological systems and demographic processes were considered by Binford both theoretically and in his presentation of Nunamiut data and by Longacre in his in-depth analysis of a single prehistoric Pueblo community. The relationships between economic systems and demographic processes were emphasized by Zubrow's examination of the implications of stable and unstable economic-growth models for population growth. The relationships between population genetics, demographic processes, and social organization were incorporated into Spuhler's cross-cultural study of the economic and social correlates of Crow's index of inbreeding. This was augmented by numerous discussions by Cavalli-Sforza, Spuhler, and Binford. Methodological problems and innovations were broached with the Ammerman, Cavalli-Sforza, and Wagener estimator; Hammel's, Longacre's, and Binford's simulations; and Longacre's abutment and burial data.

The contents of the papers that make up this volume have been summarized below on the basis of a set of standardized criteria: general subject, theoretical or methodological propositions, data base, techniques employed, and relevance to ancillary disciplines.

Synopsis of Articles

Authors: Ammerman, Cavalli-Sforza, Wagener

General Subject: Estimators for prehistoric population growth
Proposition: The adequacy and limitations of a variety of traditional population estimators are discussed in the context of both the development of a new "packed house" estimator and the problems of the growth heterogeneity and contemporaneity.
Data: Near Eastern (6000 B.C.–A.D. 0 approximately)
Techniques: Calculations; fitting of curves; literary search
Relevant to: Archaeology; anthropology; demography

Authors: Binford and Chasko

General Subject: Nunamiut demographic history
Proposition: The growth of population coincident with the development of sedentism is a result of a rise in the birth rate rather than decreased mortality.
Data: North-central Alaskan Nunamiut (1880–1970 approximately)
Techniques: Fieldwork (ethnographic); literary search; calculations; simulations
Relevant to: History; ecology; economics; anthropology; archaeology; demography

Author: Hammel

General Subject: Matrilineal implications of structural cross-cousin marriage
Proposition: Nonkinship biases in the selection of mates have implications for the relative proportions of types of consanguineal relationships.
Data: Predominantly theoretical
Techniques: Calculations; literary search; simulations; modeling
Relevant to: Ethnography; demography

Author: Longacre

General Subject: Population dynamics at Grasshopper Pueblo
Proposition: Normal growth of the founding population of less than

1 percent was insufficient to account for the community's ultimate population, which must have been augmented by immigration.
Data: A single prehistoric southwestern pueblo—Grasshopper
Techniques: Fieldwork (archaeological); simulations; calculations; burial analysis; room distributions
Relevant to: Archaeology; demography

Author: Spuhler

General Subject: Opportunity for natural selection of human populations
Proposition: There is a trend toward lower maximum opportunity for genetic change by differential mortality in much of the world's population; the maximum opportunity today for natural selection by differential fertility is significantly greater than zero in all peoples and has increased during the last century.
Data: Worldwide (ethnographic present)
Techniques: Mathematical deduction; calculations; literary search
Relevant to: Physical anthropology; ethnography; genetics

Author: Wolf

General Subject: Childhood association and fertility in Taiwan
Proposition: Intimate and prolonged childhood association lessens sexual attraction and thereby reduces the fertility of couples who are raised in the same family.
Data: Taiwan (1880–1916)
Techniques: Fieldwork (ethnographic); analysis of household registers; calculations
Relevant to: Demography; ethnography; sociology; psychology

Author: Zubrow

General Subject: Stable and unstable economic and regional demographic growth
Proposition: Models of stable and unstable economic growth predict stable and unstable regional demographic growth patterns simultaneously occurring in each of two regions.

Data: Approximately 1,500 southwestern archaeological sites in the Hay Hollow Valley and Wetherill Mesa regions (A.D. 0–1300)
Techniques: Fieldwork (archaeological); calculations; curve fitting
Relevant to: Archaeology; demography; economics

The seminar consisted of a small group of scholars interacting intensively on related subjects over a short period. They brought to bear on the issues ideas developed separately over considerable periods of time, so it is not surprising that there were several disagreements on—among other matters—the value of simulation versus analytical techniques, the utility of Crow's index, the comparative roles of sedentism and agriculture as causes of population growth and migration, the validity of archaeological regional surveys, and logical problems in the various models. It is clear from my perspective as organizer of the symposium and editor of the papers that areas of agreement far outweighed those of disagreement and that each paper presented here in its revised form profited from the discussion.

How do the general themes of the conference integrate these articles with the four fundamental questions? Each author examines different related aspects of demography and anthropology. Their concerns range from the socioeconomic correlates of inbreeding to the effects of marriage patterns upon fertility. Each paper emphasizes aspects of demographic and cultural structures and processes. Hammel focuses on social structure, Binford on cultural processes, and Wolf on demographic structure; Longacre considers demographic growth and migration processes. Each recognizes the importance of structure and process in demography and anthropology for meaningful operationalization of theory.

Their motivations for doing demographic research in anthropology vary. Longacre wants to understand a specific community, Binford an event—sedentism. Spuhler is looking for socioeconomic correlates to biological processes; Zubrow wants to develop explanatory models. Hammel wishes to know the consequences of cultural rules, while Ammerman, Cavalli-Sforza, and Wagener are looking for more accurate indirect measurements of prehistoric populations. Although the motivations vary, there is a remarkable consistency: five of the seven papers are diachronic, and most of the authors used similar techniques.

The variables and propositions may differ, but the papers share similar methodological characteristics. Longacre's rooms, Zubrow's communities, Wolf's numbers of marriages by age, Binford's populations by time, Spuhler's Crow's indices, Hammel's distributions of relationships, and Ammerman, Cavalli-Sforza, and Wagener's estimations are measurable, quantifiable, and replicable. This gives to demographic research in anthropology the potential for testability, for more sophisticated information manipulation, and for more adequate explanations and predictions.

Finally, it is possible to see in these articles some of the trends in demographic research in anthropology. Of the six trends discussed previously, only one is not touched upon by the articles—the increasing participation in policy. (Nevertheless, three of the seven participants were part of the AAAS group of interviewed scholars.) The increasing interest in policy is, I believe, obvious. The importance of collecting data on the subnational level is indicated by the fact that none of these articles are concerned with national-level data except Spuhler's, in which such data are only a small part of the totality. The attack upon established theory is stated directly in Binford's anti-Malthusian position. The inadequacy of existing data for anthropological societies is implied in Ammerman, Cavalli-Sforza, and Wagener's cogent criticisms of prehistoric censuses as well as in the paucity of societies from which Spuhler could gather information. Hammel and Wolf both show the importance of a more sophisticated reexamination of our understanding of cultural processes in the light of refined demographic data.

The potential for understanding human and cultural variability through their demographic aspects is just beginning to be realized. It is hoped that this and subsequent seminars will help the process.

2
Toward the Estimation of Population Growth in Old World Prehistory

ALBERT J. AMMERMAN
Program in Human Biology
Stanford University

L. L. CAVALLI-SFORZA
Department of Genetics
Stanford University

DIANE K. WAGENER
Museum of Comparative Zoology
Harvard University

INTRODUCTION

Estimates of population growth are needed if we are to evaluate some of the hypotheses that have been advanced during the last few years about the role of population dynamics in certain developments in prehistory. In this chapter, an attempt will be made to consider two lines of archaeological evidence—settlement data and skeletal data—that can be used to obtain population estimates.[1] The characterization of patterns of population growth will be examined both in terms of the methodology of estimation procedures and through worked examples drawn from Europe and the Near East. One of the aims of the chapter is to indicate the kinds of data that need to be collected in the field if further progress is to be made toward the estimation of population growth.

Our interest in the subject stems in part from previous work on the spread of early farming and the emergence of early Neolithic cultures in Europe (Ammerman and Cavalli-Sforza 1971). A model that we have recently put forward would see much of the spread over Europe as resulting from processes of population growth and local migratory activity (Ammerman and Cavalli-Sforza 1973). Population growth has also been cited as an important factor in the related but somewhat different problem of the origins of food production in the Near East. According to the Flannery-Binford model (Wright 1971), cereal domestication in the Near East arose as a consequence of population growth in "optimal" ecological zones, which produced migrations to adjacent "marginal" zones where population pressure in turn called for new kinds of adaptations or innovations in subsistence strategies. Population growth is also viewed by Smith and Young (1972) as playing a major role in subsequent cultural developments in the Near East. No attempt will be made here at a more extended discussion of these and other models that point to the potential importance of growth estimates.

It may be useful at this point to take a brief look at the current state of prehistoric demography with special reference to the Old World. With few exceptions (e.g., Braidwood and Reed 1957), it has only been during the last ten years or so that active interest has been taken in questions of population size and growth in Old World prehistory. A review of the literature indicates that there are still few cases where demographic reconstructions have been assigned a primary place in research designs or field strategies. Interest in the subject has remained for the most part at the level of either general statements of an interpretive nature (where estimates are usually not given) or specific and often apologetic statements about population size at a given site (where the methods used are often not explained). There are still relatively few cases where a survey of regional population trends over time has been attempted (Trigger 1965; Adams 1965; Hole et al. 1969; Renfrew 1972b; Angel 1972). Most of these represent attempts to get estimates on the board and display a practical orientation toward doing one's cautious best with the data available (in most cases collected originally for other purposes). What would seem to be called for, in general, is a wider view of prehistoric demography and the development of methods of estimation.

Population Growth in Old World Prehistory

Perspectives on Population Growth

A few general considerations about population growth deserve attention before we turn to questions of estimation. It is possible to look at population growth in terms of various levels of resolution with respect to both time and space. On the one hand, there is the level of detail of historical demography, where population trends can be followed generation by generation and which is probably beyond the scope of existing archaeological methods for most of prehistory. At the other extreme, we can adopt a long-term evolutionary perspective where time is measured in thousands of years. For those interested in the explanation of cultural developments during the last 10,000 years, it is probably most useful to think in terms of a middle-range perspective (that is, events falling for the most part in a 250-year to 2,500-year time range). In order to avoid semantic arguments about whether growth in a given situation is to be regarded as rapid or slow, it is important to have a sense of the time scale of various rates of growth.

Table 4 lists several rates of growth, ranging from 3 percent per year, which represents more or less an upper bound to growth for human populations, to 0.1 percent per year, a figure that has been mentioned as a probable rate of growth during the Neolithic period in the Near East (Carneiro and Hilse 1966). Also listed are the population doubling times and the amounts of time required for a tenfold population increase associated with the various rates, assuming an exponential mode of growth. Two points are especially worth noting here: (1) it is unreasonable to expect the population of an area to continue growing at a rate of 1 to 3 percent per year over a period as long as one thousand years, and (2) even such an apparently low rate of growth as 0.1 percent per year will lead to major changes in population size and probably to socioeconomic changes as well if it is maintained over periods on the order of two thousand years. Another factor to consider is that growth in a given area may well occur with heterogeneous rates over time. Phases of active growth may alternate with phases exhibiting little or no growth, as is shown for some of the regions in Figure 1. An overall or average rate taken over long periods of time for such a region may not provide an adequate description of patterns of growth. Instead, it would probably be more useful to try to characterize growth in terms of a sequence of distinct phases rather than as a single overall trend.

TABLE 4
RATES OF POPULATION GROWTH AND THEIR RESPECTIVE TIME SCALES UNDER AN EXPONENTIAL MODEL OF GROWTH.

Growth Rate (% per Year)	*Doubling-Time (Years)*	*Tenfold-Increase (Years)*
3.0	23	77
1.0	69	230
0.5	139	461
0.2	347	1151
0.1	693	2303

The question of levels of resolution in terms of space is no less important. Figure 1 gives a hypothetical example of the course of population growth in four adjacent regions and also in the superregion that would result if the four were lumped together. Here the curve for the superregion includes a combination of heterogeneous rates from the various regions. This is a situation that is probably quite common during the last ten thousand years or so of prehistory and that we may in fact be dealing with when we consider growth patterns on the Mesopotamian Plain in a later section. It is apparent that what is happening in one of the regions is not clearly seen at the level of the superregion and that the two levels cannot readily be used to characterize one another. This example points up the need for trying to adopt a spatial framework that is appropriate to patterns of growth and their associated cultural developments. Finding such a regional framework will not necessarily be easy; in some cases it may be useful to characterize growth over a series of nested levels. It will be noted that growth rates for a superregion will tend on the average to be slower and appear less variable than those in particular regions.

Another point worth making here concerns the interrelated questions of the form and rate of growth.[2] It is usually necessary to have an idea of the form that growth takes before meaningful rate estimates can be made. It would be unsatisfactory, for example, to adopt an exponential model of growth and try to fit an exponential curve to the initial and final population sizes of the superregion in Figure 1. An exponential form of growth does not really describe the basic pattern of growth here and the use of such a model in this case could easily result in misleading expectations

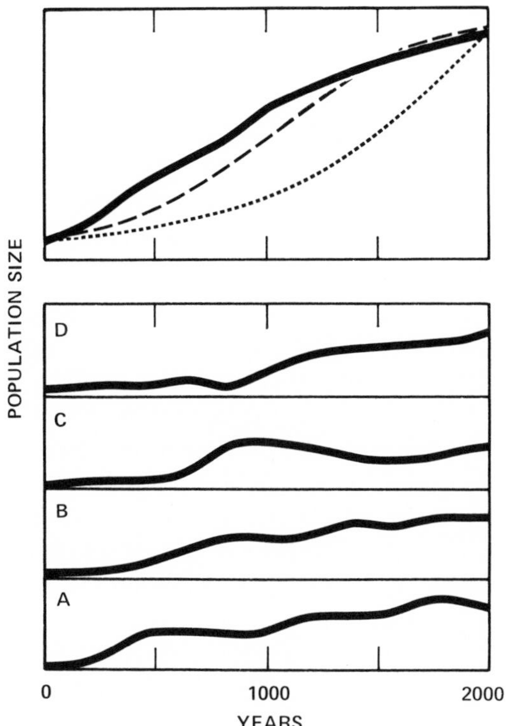

FIGURE 1. Curves of population growth in four adjacent regions (A–D) and in the superregion (top), where the four are considered together. Also shown in this hypothetical example are curves which have been fitted to the initial and final population sizes of the superregion according to exponential (lower broken line) and logistic (upper broken line) models of growth.

about how population densities change over time and also about the timing of cultural events (see, for example, Carneiro 1972). In this case, a logistic model would be somewhat better, although even the logistic curve shown in Figure 1 provides only a rough approximation of actual patterns of growth. While it is desirable from many points of view to try to use standard forms of growth such as the exponential and logistic, it may be necessary to consider more complex forms in certain situations.

Archaeology as Census Taking

It does not take profound insight to realize that there is some degree of correspondence between the number of people living at a given time and place and the number of objects used by a group or population. What is not all that clear, however, is the nature or structure of this relationship.

The archaeologist as census taker is confronted with the problem of trying to discover how sets of material remains—flints, pots, houses—can be translated into human population sizes. Certain methodological problems deserve particular attention here. In modern census practice, the aim is to count all of those people living over a brief period of time or even ideally at a given point in time. In contrast, the archaeologist normally has to deal with material remains that from a census point of view have accumulated over a substantial time period. An estimate of the length of the period of accumulation as well as information on rates of accumulation are needed if useful statements are to be made about the number of objects in circulation (and, by extension, the number of people living) at a given point in time. In this respect, estimates of population size and chronological control are very closely linked. As we shall see later, a dependence on data in accumulated form tends to complicate the whole business of making estimates of population size.

There is at present relatively little evidence to indicate the existence of universal relationships between numbers of things and numbers of people that hold over wide ranges of time and space. For the time being at least, such relationships, if they can be identified, have to be established more or less empirically for various regional and chronological cases.[3] Once a sufficient number of case studies is available, patterns of variability can be analyzed and results may help to streamline estimation procedures, especially those aimed at the level of first approximation. There is also a need to consider patterns of variability within the context of particular case studies. This is a lesson that archaeologists have recently learned along various lines of investigation (e.g., Binford 1971). In a given case study, we may be dealing with two or more essentially different modes of household occupation. For example, one group of families may occupy single-room structures, while other families at the same settlement live in three- and four-room structures. This kind of situation would call for the analysis of data in the form of statistical distributions if meaningful estimates are to be made of such things as the number of persons per room. Variability within a sociocultural tradition is likely to complicate the analytical problems involved in the estimation of population size.

Before proceeding, it is worth considering the question of the level at which we want to try to measure population growth, since this will in some ways determine the kinds of archaeological evidence to which we want to turn. While it is possible to consider population size at the level of individual sites, a given site may not accurately reflect patterns of local or regional growth. A site with a growing population and a fair amount of emigration to nearby areas may appear to have a stationary population. One way to control for the factors of immigration and emigration would be to work on a global scale; however, this is neither practical nor necessary in most prehistoric contexts. Normally, it will be satisfactory to consider population growth in terms of geographical area or region, notwithstanding the difficulties that may be involved in defining such entities. Once the problem is framed in this way, certain kinds of archaeological evidence can be seen as more appropriate than others. A regional context means that we usually have to deal with a fair number of sites located through survey work and that only a small proportion of these sites have been excavated on even a moderate scale. In this situation, there are definite limitations on what can be done with various classes of portable artifacts in providing a basis for population estimates. Instead, the main line of attack would seem to lie in what has been called "habitation space" (Cook 1972a), taking advantage of information on the spatial characteristics of rooms, houses, and settlements. This approach is most likely to be productive in the context of a sedentary way of life and in those cases, such as mound sites, where the size of settlements can be determined with some degree of accuracy from survey work.

SRP AND SARP

One way of estimating population on a regional basis is through what can be called the *SRP* approach. Here the population of a region is given by the product of the following three quantities: *S*, the number of settlements in the region, *R*, the number of rooms per settlement, and *P*, the number of persons per room. This approach has been used with some degree of success in the American Southwest. While the first two quantities can be derived from observations in the field, it is much more difficult to estimate the number of persons per room. Even in cases where the study of different classes of artifacts may lead to information on such things as household composition or average family size, problems may still remain when it comes to deciding upon the relationship between "families" and rooms. One solution, used by Longacre (1964), is simply to drop *P* and use *SR*, the total number of rooms in a region, as an index of population size.

In practice, the *SRP* approach usually entails what might be termed the

SARP approach. Here, the variable A represents the area per settlement and is commonly used at settlements that have been only partially excavated (or not excavated at all) in determining the number of rooms dating to a given period at the site. According to the more general *SARP* formulation, the population of a region is given by the product of *S*, the number of settlements in the region, *A*, the area per settlement, *R*, the number of rooms per unit area of settlement, and *P*, the number of persons per room. If we consider a region where population growth is taking place, there will be tangible expressions of change in one or several of the four *SARP* variables. It is possible to obtain estimates of the first three quantities by more or less direct observation. If need be, these estimates (and the errors associated with them) can be checked and refined by further fieldwork. Again, the fourth quantity is likely to be the most difficult to estimate.

There is at present no region in those parts of the Old World of immediate interest where information is available on all four of the *SARP* variables. Evidence related to individual variables is, however, available for certain areas. It may be instructive at this point to examine the patterns of change taking place in terms of individual variables. As mentioned earlier, it will be necessary to consider both rates of growth and the closely related question of the form that growth takes. The following examples are put forward mainly to give an idea of how estimation proceeds when we turn to the analysis of actual data. No attempt will be made here to develop the examples in detail or to consider sampling questions related to the different sets of data as done, for example, by Renfrew (1972b).

Number of Settlements

While the S variable is probably the easiest one to measure through survey work, there are still relatively few examples of such regional estimates in the Old World literature. Two regions where information of this kind has been collected are the Aegean (Renfrew 1972a) and the Lower Diyala area of Iraq (Adams 1965). Renfrew (1972a: Fig. 14.2) has recently examined the number of settlements occupied in various parts of the Aegean during several periods of time between 4000 B.C. and

1200 B.C. The rate of growth in the number of new settlements between 4000 B.C. and 2500 B.C. ranges between about 0.11 percent per year for the Cyclades and 0.02 percent per year for Central Macedonia, if one assumes an exponential mode of growth (a more refined chronological framework is really needed in order to decide here between different kinds of growth curves). The six Aegean regions together have a mean rate of increase of 0.06 percent per year, lasting over a period of about fifteen hundred years.

For the Lower Diyala region (Adams 1965), there is information on the number of settlements existing in various periods going back to about 4000 B.C. (see Table 7). A growth curve of the number of settlements in the Lower Diyala region between 4000 B.C. and 1600 B.C. is shown in Figure 2. A logistic fit is used here since the number of occupied settlements apparently reaches a maximum value in the period between about 2000 B.C. and 1500 B.C. (there is, if anything, a decline between 1500 B.C. and 500 B.C.). The actual technique used for obtaining the fitted curve is given in the appendix to this chapter. The initial rate of growth for the curve in Figure 2 is 0.15 percent per year, which is somewhat higher than the rates for the Aegean at a comparable time. Probably the main source of systematic error in the Diyala data is that early phases of settlement are buried and difficult to recognize at mounds where there is occupation on a large scale in later phases. The implication here is that growth in the number of settlements may have actually been somewhat faster in the first part of the curve.

Area of Settlements

The recent excavations at Knossos in Crete (Evans 1971) provide one of the few cases where information on the size of a Neolithic settlement is available for a sequence of chronological phases. In Figure 3, the settlement area *(A)* at Knossos is shown at various times between about 6000 B.C. and 3000 B.C. Again, a logistic curve has been fitted to the data, since the area of the site does not continue to increase significantly after about 3000 B.C. Using the curve in Figure 3, the initial rate of growth of settlement area is 0.22 percent per year. This rate is relevant to the earliest phases of a food-producing economy in the area.

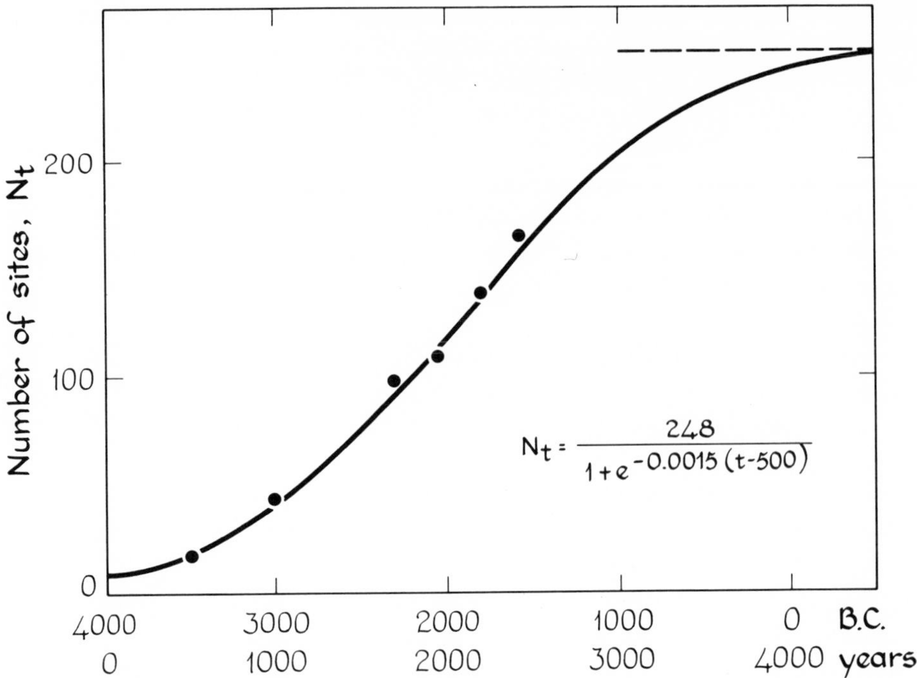

FIGURE 2. Growth in the number of settlements in the Lower Diyala region over the period between c. 4000 B.C. and 1600 B.C. Here a logistic growth curve has been fitted to data published by Adams (1965).

FIGURE 3. Growth in settlement area at the site of Knossos during the period between c. 6000 B.C. and 3000 B.C. Here a logistic growth curve has been fitted to estimates put forward by Evans (1971); note that time is plotted on a log scale.

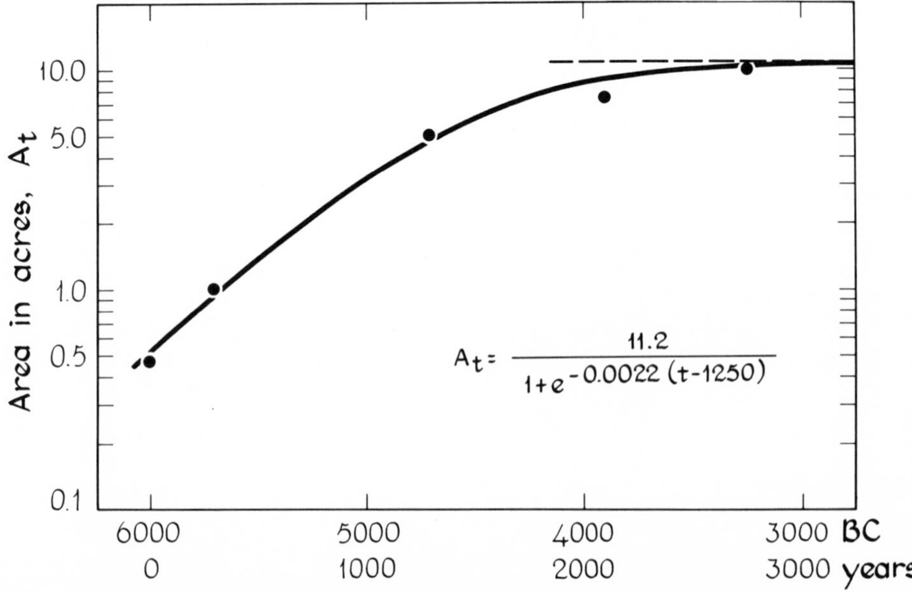

Rooms per Settlement Area

The density of rooms or dwelling units in relation to settlement area (*R*) is a variable that has seldom received much attention in either quantitative or nonquantitative statements about population growth. One of the few cases where it has been mentioned is the early Neolithic site of Nea Nikomedeia in Macedonia, where an increase through time in the number of "houses" in relation to settlement area has been suggested (Rodden 1965). Until detailed site plans for Nea Nikomedeia are available, no attempt can be made to describe the pattern of change in quantitative terms. Where the internal layout of houses at a settlement takes a closely packed form (e.g., Çatal Hüyük), there will be relatively little opportunity for growth in these terms, as long as room or house size remains basically the same. This can, however, be an important factor at sites with a more dispersed pattern of internal arrangement.

In those cases where significant changes in room size occur during the time period over which growth is being examined, it may be useful to expand the *SARP* formulation to *SARFP*. Here the dimensions of the *RFP* variables would be *R*, rooms per unit area of settlement, *F*, floor space (area) per room, and *P*, persons per unit area of floor space. The reason for this variant is not, as it might seem, to make the estimation of population size impossibly difficult but rather to control the potential range of variation of *P*, the variable least subject to direct archaeological observation.

At this point, it may be worth mentioning still another *SARP* variant that has actually been used in various studies in the Near East. This is the *SAP* approach, where *S* is the number of settlements in a region, *A* represents the area per settlement, and *P* is the number of persons per unit area of settlement. While this method appears to offer a shortcut to population estimates, it does so at the cost of placing a heavy reliance on the last variable. In fact, the difficulties involved in making actual estimates of *P* would seem to explain the assumption commonly made that *P* is constant over time and also between sites for a given region. However, data on fifty-three villages in Khuzestan (Adams and Nissen 1972: Fig. 15), while indicating a mean density of 231 persons per hectare, suggest quite a wide range of variation in the number of persons per hectare between settlements. Considerable variation in this quantity (but interestingly not in the average number of persons per house, where values range between 5.6 and 7.3) is also reported by Wright (1969:23) for four modern Iraqi settlements. It is also worth noting here that, in their study of aboriginal populations in California, Cook and Heizer (1968) were not able to find all that clear or consistent a relationship between settlement area and population size. The weakness of the *SAP* approach can perhaps be seen most clearly from an analytical point of view. If *P*, as defined in the *SAP* approach, is assumed to be constant in a study covering a long period of time, the implication turning to the *SARP* formulation (where *P* is defined in different terms) is either that both of the last two variables (*RP*) are constant over time or that the two vary together in such a way as always to yield a constant product. Both of these alternatives imply a rather static image of the past and would seem to run counter to normal expectations. While the *SAP* approach may produce approximations of some interest, the basic problem here would seem to be that we are assuming values—through the use of modern and historical analogies—of just those quantities that we should be trying to measure through archaeological means.

Persons per Room

As mentioned above, *P* is the variable least subject to direct observation. Estimates will usually have to be made on the basis of inferences drawn from the various lines of archaeological evidence at hand. This is the factor that would appear to justify pessimism about ever being able to make sound estimates of population size and growth in prehistory. But much depends on how the problem is set up: it may be easier, contradictory as this may sound, to estimate population growth in some cases than population size itself. What is called for is to have (1) growth reflected as much as possible in variables (sites, rooms, etc.) that can be directly counted or measured, and (2) good control over the expected range of variation of *P*. If there are grounds for thinking that *P* in a given archaeological context can at most double over a reasonably long period of time, then the maximum potential growth rate of *P* may be quite small.[4] For example, if *P* were to increase from an average of three to six persons per room over a period of 700 years, there would be an average growth rate of 0.1 percent per year for this variable. In situations where population growth is actively taking place, the maximum potential rate of change of *P* itself may turn out to be negligible in comparison with the rates for other variables, which can then be used to describe the basic pattern of growth. It should be stressed that this approach represents a practical solution; whenever possible, it would be preferable to include this term in growth estimates.

A point worth adding here is that short-term changes in population size may well find expression in temporary changes of *P* rather than in the more tangible variables of habitation space. In some cases, *P* may be seen as acting as a buffer that allows minor or short-term changes in population size to occur without leaving more tangible expression in the archaeological record. The implication here is that actual estimates of *P* may be called for if we want to describe short-term population trends (this may be relevant in the case of the Grasshopper site discussed by Longacre in Chapter 5).

Bringing the Individual Rates Together

The task of trying to combine the growth rates of individual variables is by no means an easy one. The rate obtained for one of the *SARP* variables on its own is likely to represent an underestimate of the overall rate of population growth. This indicates one of the potential shortcomings of an index approach to the estimation of population size and growth. No doubt the simplest case to deal with would be one where the growth rates of individual variables could be combined directly. For instance, if each variable followed an exponential form of growth, the overall rate of population growth could be described by a fairly straightforward mathematical function incorporating the rates for individual variables. A major problem that arises is that growth is unlikely to take the same form over each of the *SARP* or *SARFP* variables. Some may grow according to an exponential form, others according to a logistic form, and still others in more complex and perhaps irregular ways. This means that there is usually no straightforward way of combining the individual rates to describe the overall pattern of growth. Instead, the data that the individual rates are based upon have to be reworked so as to yield values for the product of either *SAR* (where *P* is considered to be a minor factor) or *SARP* (where estimates of *P* are available). By evaluating the curve of *SAR* values at different times, the rate of population growth in a region can be determined. A difficulty that may likewise be encountered here, as in the case of analyzing individual variables, is the lack of a good fit between *SAR* values and standard forms of growth such as the exponential or logistic. Some effort may be required to arrive at a satisfactory characterization of patterns of growth.

Contemporaneity

We have for the most part avoided questions concerning sampling and the quality of data as they relate to the circumstances found in a given region. A methodological consideration of general importance in the use of a *SARP* approach to population estimation is the question of contemporaneity among such units as settlements or rooms.[5] This stems from the problem of having data in accumulated form in archaeological census taking. What is usually known is the number of settlements or rooms in a region with evidence for occupation during a given interval of time, which normally exceeds fifty years and can easily be on the order of several hundred years. A serious problem arises whenever such units are occupied for only a fraction of the time interval to which they are assigned. In most situations it is beyond the capacity of existing methods of chronology to determine on a regional scale the specific time or length of occupation of individual units. This means that we seldom know the exact number of settlements or rooms occupied at a given time. One way to reduce the scope of this potential problem is, of course, to keep time intervals as short as possible. Another way of dealing with the problem where a sequence of intervals is being compared is to make the working assumption (admittedly a potentially dangerous one in the context of dynamic growth situations) of proportionality between units occupied at specific times during intervals and the cumulative number of units occupied during the same intervals, which can be weighted according to their respective durations. If this treatment is accepted, estimates of relative population growth can be made readily using the *SARP* approach as indicated in the preceding examples. When it comes to estimates of actual population size, however, specific values of proportionality will have to be known or assumed, a more complicated matter. Again, it appears that population size may be more difficult to estimate than rates of growth. What would seem to be needed from a methodological point of view, if we want to use a *SARP* approach, are analytical strategies that allow us to overcome the problem of contemporaneity and arrive at solutions (even rough ones) to the proportionality question. This is obviously no small undertaking. In bringing this part of the discussion to a close, it is clear that we still have some way to go before the whole thing can be brought together.

PACKED HOUSE VOLUMES

In this section a new approach to the estimation of population growth will be presented that may help us in overcoming certain problems related to the cumulative nature of most archaeological data. It is important to emphasize at the outset that much of the following discussion is exploratory in nature. The case studies developed below—for the site of Ali Kosh in Iran and the sites in the Lower Diyala and Warka regions of Iraq—should be viewed as heuristic examples. It may be worth adding that, as is often the case, fully appropriate sets of data are often not available prior to the introduction of a new method of estimation.

The kind of question that initially directed attention toward an approach using packed house volumes was, How can we estimate the number of rooms or "houses" standing at a given time on a mound site of the type found in the Near East? Progress can perhaps be made on this question if we start looking at the world in terms of volumes. Intuitively, it is apparent that the volume of a mound is due primarily to the accumulation of collapsed houses at a site. The contribution that a particular house of pisé or mud brick makes to a mound is determined essentially by its volume, which can be archaeologically reconstructed from such things as its floor plan and the thickness of its walls. The volume of the standing house, when it has collapsed and decayed, will be called its packed house volume, or PHV. This can be viewed as the basic increment in the buildup of a mound, and particularly of early mound sites where defensive walls and large public buildings have not yet entered the picture.

Another aspect of a house to consider is its duration or life expectancy. Although relatively little attention has been paid to this question, estimates of average values and ranges of variation of "house life" should not be all that difficult to come up with if they are assigned a research priority.

If we know four quantities, we can obtain a rough idea of the average number of houses standing at one time on a mound site—the quantity N in the equation

$$N = \frac{V \cdot T}{H \cdot P},$$

where V is the volume that has accumulated at the mound over a given period of time; T is the average life expectancy of a house dating to the period; H is the average PHV; and P is the length of the period. At a given mound, it should be possible with existing archaeological methods to arrive at reasonably accurate estimates of all four quantities.

In addition, this formulation involves the following assumptions: (1) material from the mound itself is not reused in the construction of new houses; (2) erosion has not reduced the volume of the mound; (3) non-durable building materials such as wood are not included in the calculation of PHVs; and (4) volume is not contributed to the mound from sources other than houses.[6] It is worth noting that each of the first three assumptions, if found not to hold, operates in the direction of producing underestimates. Only the last assumption works in the opposite direction if not true. This means that in most cases values of N can be interpreted as "at least so many houses," which turns out to be a useful feature in the Ali Kosh case study.

Ali Kosh

There are several reasons for selecting Ali Kosh. It is one of the important early mound sites in the Near East from an economic point of view; it is also one of the few early mound sites that has been fully described in print (Hole et al. 1969). Statements have been made by the excavators about the number of people living at the site in different periods, and reservations have recently been voiced about the reliability of these population estimates (e.g., Cook 1972a). The aim of this case study is to indicate how this method of estimation works. At several points, needed information is not available and rough approximations have to be used instead in this heuristic exercise.

Our primary concern will be with the second or so-called Ali Kosh phase of occupation at the site, which is considered to have lasted from 6750 B.C. to 6000 B.C., a period of 750 years. For a concise description of this phase, we can turn to the excavators (Hole et al. 1969:349): "Ali Kosh is the only site in the Deh Luran plain which is definitely known to have been occupied during this period [the Ali Kosh phase]; the village was approximately a hectare in extent. Given the size and spacing of the Ali Kosh houses, it was probably not occupied by more than one hundred individuals. This would give us an estimated population density for the Deh

Luran plain of perhaps 0.3 persons per square kilometer." The method used in making this population estimate follows the *SAP* approach mentioned earlier, where settlement area is multiplied by a value for the number of persons per unit area of settlement.

To estimate the number of houses standing at one time during the Ali Kosh phase, information is needed on the four quantities described above. The aim here will be to draw information directly from statements by the excavators whenever possible.

Period. The length of the Ali Kosh phase will be taken as 750 years (Hole et al. 1969).

Mound Volume. The volume of the mound that accumulated during the Ali Kosh phase can be determined from the area of occupation, the depth of the deposit at various points, and the geometric solid that best approximates the form of the deposit. The extent of the settlement is considered to be approximately a hectare, or 10,000 square meters. The main trench opened near the center of the mound showed a maximum depth of deposit for the Ali Kosh phase of a little over 3 meters. There is, unfortunately, little evidence available on the thickness of the deposit near the outer edges of the Ali Kosh occupation. Given the circular shape of the mound, its volume can be expected to fall between a maximum value for a cylinder (with a base of 10,000 square meters and a height of 3 meters, or a volume of 30,000 cubic meters), and a minimum value for a cone (with the same base and height but a volume of only 10,000 cubic meters). From the contours of the mound (Hole et al. 1969: Fig. 4), the best working approximation is probably offered by a spherical segment that would yield a mound volume of 15,000 cubic meters. This estimate could definitely be improved upon by means of further archaeological work at the site. One reason for selecting the Ali Kosh phase of occupation is that by being stratified below the Mohammad Jaffar phase (6000 B.C. to 5600 B.C.) its volume has probably been less subject to long-term erosion.

PHV. The three main things needed here are (1) the floor plans of rooms or houses; (2) the thickness of walls (and perhaps also floors); and (3) the height of walls. Unfortunately, no complete plan of a room or house has been recovered in the relatively small area of the Ali Kosh phase that has been excavated. There is, however, evidence for walls in the Ali Kosh phase that suggests rooms measuring at least 3 meters on a side. In Table 5, three different average house sizes and their associated PHVs are presented. These should cover the range in which actual floor plans

TABLE 5
AVERAGE NUMBER OF ROOMS OR "HOUSES" STANDING AT ONE TIME DURING THE ALI KOSH PHASE

Floor Plan (meters)		3 × 3	4 × 4	5 × 5
Associated PHV (cubic meters)		12	16	20
House Life (years)	15	25 (225)*	18.75 (300)	15 (375)
	30	50 (450)	37.50 (600)	30 (750)
	45	75 (675)	56.25 (900)	45 (1,125)

* Numbers in parentheses indicate the total floor space at the site given by the number of standing houses and the areas of their respective floor plans.

fall; houses longer than 5 meters on a side do not seem to be common (with the exception of Cayonu) at early mound sites in the Near East. The thickness of walls ranges between about 0.30 and 1.00 meter and will be taken here to have an average value of 0.50 meter during the Ali Kosh phase, the value used in Table 5. The one quantity that may be difficult to observe directly is the height of walls, but this probably stayed within a range of 1.50 to 2.50 meters for early, single-story houses in the Near East. A working approximation of 2.00 meters is used in the calculation of the three PHVs in Table 5. Again it should be emphasized that refinements in each of the three quantities required here should be possible.

House Life. This quantity is also rather obscure at the present state of knowledge. In one of the few statements on the subject that we have come across, Braidwood and Howe (1960:159), drawing on modern informants in Iraqi Kurdistan, suggest a life expectancy of about 15 years for a pisé or *tauf* house. This is perhaps a low estimate; homes with mud brick walls may in some cases last considerably longer than this.[7] "House life" is definitely a question that deserves more research attention than it has received to date. In Table 5, three trial values for this variable have been used: 15, 30, and 45 years.

The results presented in Table 5 show that the average number of houses standing at one time varies between 15 and 75, depending upon the combination of values for PHV and house life used. This range could be narrowed somewhat if the smallest of the three floor plans (3 × 3 meters) were found to be unrealistic or a house life of 45 years is found to be too large. The number of standing houses would then fall somewhere between 15 and 50. One of the things to notice in Table 5 is that the values for standing houses are reasonably sensitive to changes in both PHV and house life. Another point of interest is that the total floor space available at the settlement tends to increase as the average house size gets larger, which can be seen by reading the numbers in parentheses across a row. It appears that one way to maximize the use of building materials and also the amount of occupation space at a site is to turn to larger structures.

Using a PHV of 20 cubic meters, population sizes have been calculated in Table 6 on the basis of different combinations of house life and values

TABLE 6
POPULATION SIZES DURING THE ALI KOSH PHASE
(PHV = 20 CUBIC METERS)

		Average Number of Persons per Room or House			
		2	3	4	5
House Life (years)	15	40	60	80	100
	30	90	120	160	200
	45	120	180	240	300

for the number of persons per house (taken only as possibly representative values). Since the PHV value used here resulted in the lowest number of standing houses in Table 5, it means that the choice of a smaller PHV value would lead to larger population sizes throughout the table. In Table 6, the range in population size is between 40 and 300 people. It is of interest that if the value for house life is of the order of 15 years the population sizes obtained are in the same basic range as the figure (i.e., not more than 100 people) put forward by the excavators. On the other hand, if the appropriate value for house life turns out to be larger, there is a good chance that population size needs to be revised upward.

One complication that has been ignored so far is that the number of standing houses being estimated is an average value. If there is even a very modest rate of population growth during the Ali Kosh phase, this average value will give us only an idea of the number of houses standing during the middle of the period. At the beginning of the period there will be fewer houses and toward the end a larger number of houses. The difference in the number of houses standing at these two times will tend to be a reflection of the size of the growth rate. If we have some idea of what the growth rate is, we can distribute the mound volume over the time period accordingly and perhaps come up with estimates of the number of houses standing during different parts of the period. Seen in these terms, it can be misleading to talk about the number of houses standing at a site during a period or the number of people living there without further qualification.

Lower Diyala and Warka Regions

Comprehensive regional surveys of mound sites have been conducted in very few parts of the Near East; notable exceptions to this are two studies carried out by Adams in Mesopotamia. A comparison of the report for the Lower Diyala region (Adams 1965) and that for the Warka region (Adams and Nissen 1972) clearly points up the considerable strides that have been made in developing this important line of research. Here we would like to use published data on mound sites in the two studies and a PHV estimation strategy to obtain growth curves and rates of growth for the two regions. Again the experimental nature of what is being attempted should be emphasized: estimates that are obtained should be regarded as crude and perhaps not even reaching the level of first approximations. In both regions, the period to be considered is roughly the same—Ubaid through Old Babylonian. This time period (c. 4000 B.C. to 1800 B.C.) represents a somewhat different cultural setting—in terms of the complexity of society, number of large public buildings, major population relocations within regions, and so forth—than an early food-producing one. It should nevertheless be possible to make use of the PHV concept in this more developed context, where the availability of historical sources may in certain cases make it possible to evaluate the reliability of the approach.

The basic ideas are again: (1) there is a relationship between the number of houses standing at a mound site and the size of its population; and (2) through the PHV concept, mound volumes reflect the number and "history" of houses that have existed at a site. We will consider two approaches to obtaining a growth curve that differ essentially in their treatment of the partitioning of mound volumes. The first approach is quite straightforward: the volume of a given mound is partitioned into different periods according to the duration of the respective periods observed at the site in proportion to the total length of occupation represented. The partitioned volumes are then summed for each period over all of the mounds in the region to yield what will be called "period volumes." The results obtained from using this approach are shown for the two regions in Figure 4. It will be noted that no allowance is made in this treatment of mound partitioning for patterns of internal growth at sites over time. There is a tendency to attribute more volume to early periods of occupation at a site than is probably warranted in many cases, and in this respect the method is likely to produce a growth curve that will provide an underestimate of the growth rate when it is evaluated.

It is worth looking at the assumptions and procedures involved in this approach in somewhat greater detail.

1. The time periods and number of sites from the respective periods used in the analysis are indicated in Table 7. For practical reasons related to the actual partitioning of mound volumes, only those mounds in the two regions without occupation after the Old Babylonian period were

FIGURE 4. Period mound volumes based on data published by Adams (1965) and Adams and Nissen (1972). Mound volumes are partitioned according to periods of occupation represented at sites (see text) and then summed for the region to yield mound volumes for the respective periods.

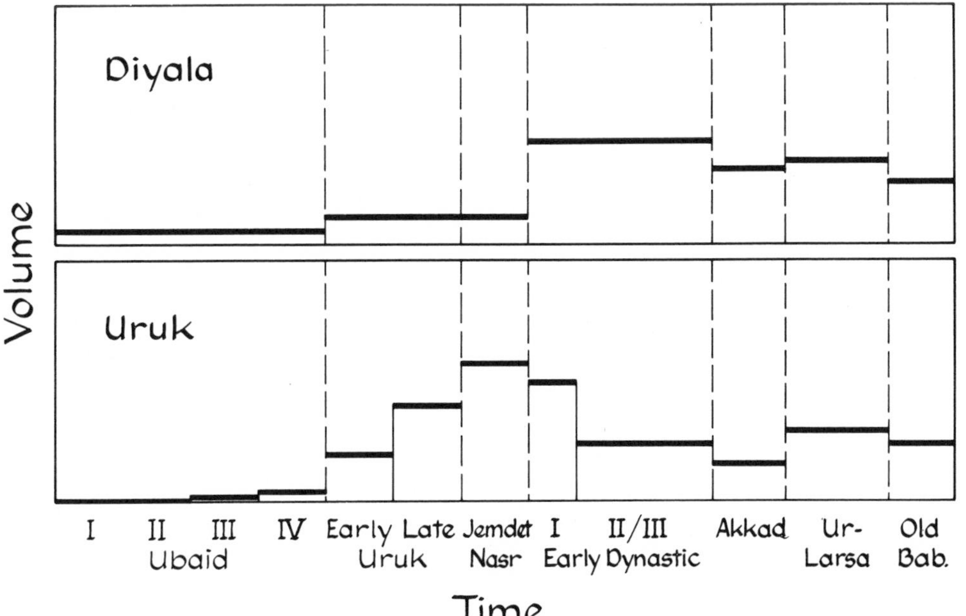

TABLE 7
NUMBER OF SITES OCCUPIED DURING THE UBAID THROUGH OLD BABYLONIAN PERIODS IN THE WARKA AND DIYALA REGIONS

Warka Region		*Diyala Region*	
Period	*No. sites*	*Period*	*No. sites*
Ubaid I	1		
Ubaid II	3		
Ubaid III	4	Ubaid	14
Ubaid IV	7		
Early Uruk	19		
Late Uruk	76	Warka-Protoliterate	27
Jemdet Nasr	80		
Early Dynastic I	48		
Early Dynastic II–III	21	Early Dynastic	56
Akkad	22	Akkad-Guti	64
Ur III-Isin-Larsa	39	Ur III-Isin-Larsa	65
Old Babylonian	18	Old Babylonian	48

included in the analysis. Mounds with subsequent occupation could also be used if detailed attention were paid to the nature and extent of later contributions.

2. The volume of a mound is generally calculated as the segment of one base of an ellipsoid, using information on the length, width, and height of mounds as published by Adams (1965) and Adams and Nissen (1972).

3. The assumption is made that the average volume of mound material generated per person per year is basically constant over time (i.e., Ubaid through Old Babylonian). This is an economic and somewhat more flexible way (where mud brick structures other than houses may be important) of stating the PHV concept. Two basic things are subsumed here: on the average, both the number of people living in a house of given PHV and house life, as described earlier, are constant over time. It is entirely possible that this assumption will need to be modified in certain cases. Fortunately, it should be well within archaeological means for assumptions along these lines to be transformed into observations that could be used to establish correction factors for various periods or classes of sites.

4. When a given mound is occupied over a certain number of periods of known duration, its total volume, V_i, is considered to have been formed during the various periods according to the relative proportion of occupation represented by the respective periods (e.g., one-quarter of the volume of a mound will be attributed to a given period lasting 200 years at a site occupied for a total of 800 years).

5. In dealing with sites that are continuously occupied over a sequence of periods, as is often the case in the two regions, it is important to realize that the initial time of occupation is not necessarily the beginning of the earliest period represented at the site. The same also applies to the last period of occupation documented at a site. As an approximation, the time interval used when these two situations arise is taken as half the length of the period under the expectation that occupation will begin and end, on the average, in approximately this manner. Here again, empirical refinements may be possible in certain cases.

6. Once the volumes of mounds have been partitioned, period volumes can be obtained by adding up the partitioned volumes for each period over all of the mounds in the region.

A clear pattern of growth is shown in Figure 4 for both regions during Ubaid through Early Dynastic times. In subsequent periods, there appears to be a leveling off of growth or even a population decline. Using the curve-fitting technique described in the appendix, one can fit a logistic curve to the Warka period volumes, which for a consistent treatment can each be attached to the end of their respective time periods. This gives a midpoint of growth, t_0, that falls in the Late Uruk period (c. 3280 B.C.) and a growth rate of 0.79 percent per year. Although the Diyala data are too sparse for the meaningful application of this curve-fitting technique, a respectable growth rate is also clearly indicated for this region. It is interesting to note the drop in period volume during Early Dynastic times in the Warka region. This is associated with a major pattern of population relocation from the countryside to the site of Uruk, which is discussed by Adams and Nissen (1972) and is also reflected in the number of occupied sites (see Table 7). The large mound of Uruk is not included among the partitioned mounds and much of the missing Early Dynastic period volume is probably to be found at Uruk. By estimating the mound volume that accumulated at Uruk during Early Dynastic times, a rough test of the PHV estimation method could be made. If information is available on the number of people living at Uruk from independent historical sources, it might be possible to calibrate the "curve" for the Warka region shown in Figure 4 in terms of actual population sizes.

The second method is similar to the first in many respects except that growth is considered to be taking place in the region in a logistic fashion and that this growth pattern is itself expressed in the buildup of individual mounds. Instead of volume being contributed to a mound at a constant rate over time as in the first method, the contribution of each year increases in a logistic manner over time. The model for logistic growth can be written as $N = (1 + \exp(-c(t - t_o)))^{-1}M$, where M is the number at saturation, c is the initial growth rate, and t_o is the midpoint of growth (i.e., the time at which $N = M/2$). For example, if a given mound has been occupied continuously from time t_1 to t_2, then its volume will be proportional to the integral of the logistic curve over that time interval, or

$$t_2 - t_1 + \frac{1}{c}\left[\log\left(\frac{1 + e^{-c(t_2 - t_o)}}{1 + e^{-c(t_1 - t_o)}}\right)\right].$$

As shown in Figure 5, the volume of a mound can be partitioned on the basis of a given logistic curve. Again, period volumes can be obtained by summing over the mounds in a region once all of the individual mounds have been partitioned. The problem is to find the best values for the parameters c and t_o in the logistic equation. One way that this can be done is by selecting trial values for the two parameters, which determine a given logistic curve, and then carrying out the partitioning of mound volumes and the calculation of period volumes according to the procedures described above. The set of *summed* period volumes (O) obtained in this way can be compared with *expected* period volumes (E) obtained by using the original logistic curve to partition the grand total of mound volume representing all of the mounds in the analysis. Comparisons can be made using the measure of discrepancy

$$\sum^{\text{periods}} (O - E)^2/E^2,$$

which minimizes the relative standard error. The trial values of c and t_o are varied so as to minimize this discrepancy. Other discrepancy measures have also been tried, for instance with E instead of E^2 in the denominator, but have indicated little difference in the resulting values.

The results obtained by employing this method are presented in Table 8. For the Warka region, a logistic treatment produces much the

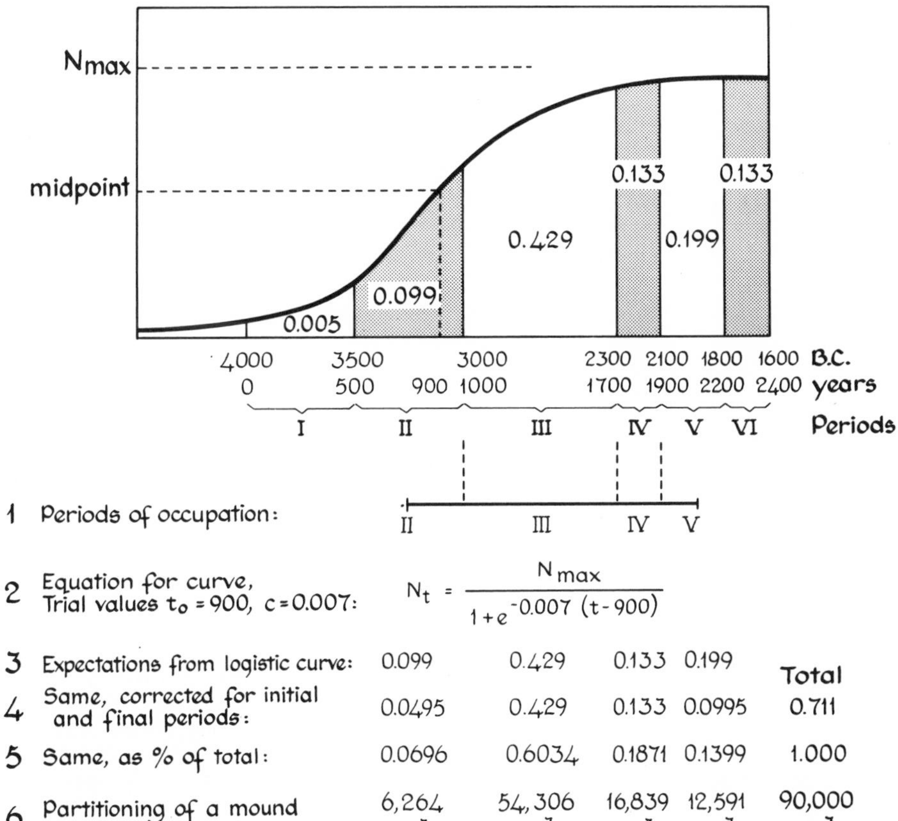

FIGURE 5. Method used in partitioning a mound's volume into its respective periods of occupation assuming a logistic model of volume accumulation. In the example shown here, the mound has a volume of 90,000 cubic meters, which is partitioned into its four periods of occupation (6) according to the trial values of the logistic equation given in 2.

same value for the midpoint of growth as the first method but, as might be expected, a somewhat higher growth rate of 0.9 percent per year. There is a strong note of agreement between the results of the two weighting methods, which both produce respectable rates of change in population size (birth and immigration minus death and emigration) between Ubaid and Early Dynastic times. In the case of the Diyala region, calculations have been carried out for a number of different combinations of periods to test how well a logistic curve fits the data. The midpoint of growth usually falls in the Early Dynastic period (i.e., a few hundred years later than is the case in the Warka region), which would agree with other sources of information on the patterns of development of

TABLE 8
LOGISTIC GROWTH CURVES FOR THE WARKA AND DIYALA REGIONS*

Periods	*No. Sites*	*Warka Region* t_o (B.C.)	*c*	*Discrepancy*
1–7	71	3,100	0.009	0.94
Periods	*No. Sites*	*Diyala Region* t_o (B.C.)	*c*	*Discrepancy*
1–6	80	2,700	0.006	0.45
1–5	37	3,000	0.007	0.37
1–4	16	3,000	0.006	0.72
2–5	29	3,800	0.011	0.84
3–6	50	2,600	0.008	0.33

* The numbers for the periods correspond to their respective positions in the lists given in Table 7 (i.e., periods 1 through 7 for the Warka region represent Ubaid I through Jemdet Nasr). The next column gives the number of sites included in the analysis. The values for the midpoint of growth, t_o, the initial rate of growth, c, and the discrepancy are given in the last three columns. The discrepancy values are relative to the total mound volume included in a given search for the "best fit" parameters of the logistic curve and for this reason cannot be directly compared between separate analyses.

these two areas. Values for the growth rate range between about 0.6 and 1.1 percent, roughly comparable with the rate obtained for the Warka region. Such values are also in broad agreement with growth rates that can be calculated from the curve of population size for the region reconstructed by Adams (1965: Table 25). There is, however, a definite suggestion in the shifts of c to t_o values for different combinations of periods that population growth in the Diyala region may not be following a simple logistic pattern. One way of trying to describe a more complex form of growth might be to calculate moving averages over time using values of c and t_o from different combinations of periods such as those presented in Table 7.

But before attempting a more refined description of growth patterns, it would seem worthwhile to indicate some of the sources of error that need to be looked at more carefully and may call for modifications in the basic estimation strategy. Space is not available to attempt such a discussion in detail but some of the potential sources of error that deserve attention are as follows: (1) systematic errors in the attribution of periods of occupation and the estimation of mound volumes may have to be taken into account; (2) rates of growth may vary substantially in different parts of a given region; (3) the volumes of defensive walls, public buildings, and other nondomestic structures may call for a more complex treatment of PHV assumptions, as mentioned earlier; and (4) the spatial framework of what is considered a "region" may have to be enlarged in order to obtain a more accurate characterization of growth patterns. Attention to factors such as these should make it possible to arrive at more refined treatments of the proportionality question and in the long run to make more reliable population estimates from archaeological evidence.

PALEODEMOGRAPHY

Skeletal remains represent another major source of potential evidence of population size and growth. This approach, which is often referred to as paleodemography, has been the subject of a fair amount of recent interest (Angel 1969; Acsadi and Nemeskeri 1970; Brothwell 1971; Weiss 1973). An extended discussion of the methods and assumptions involved in this kind of work will not be presented here for this reason. The main line of investigation is the determination of the age and sex of skeletal material. In trying to reconstruct populations in this way, the quality of results is influenced by three main factors: (1) the reliability of age and sex attributions; (2) the size of the population of skeletons from a site; and (3) mortuary practices that may affect how representative or not a given skeletal population is in terms of the population that once lived (Binford 1971). If skeletal data could provide us with basically reliable descriptions of patterns of mortality and fertility among prehistoric populations, we could use demographic theory to obtain estimates of rates of population growth. With this possibility in mind, a brief look will be taken at the present state of paleodemography with respect to these two lines of reconstruction.

Mortality

There are still few Neolithic sites in the Near East and the Balkans that have produced a sufficient number of skeletons to permit the description of patterns of mortality. Two sites for which data have been published are Çatal Hüyük and Nea Nikomedeia (Angel 1969, 1971); the results in both cases are presented in the form of the number of skeletons belonging to different age classes at death. Weiss (1973) has recently reconstructed life tables for the data and was able to avoid the problem of putatively missing infants by limiting computations to post-pubertal ages. Techniques that have been used so far in paleodemography to obtain life tables rely upon the assumption that the population is stationary (i.e., exhibits no change in size over time or has an intrinsic rate of natural increase, r, of zero). This is the approach to the construction of life tables for various sets of skeletal data used by Acsadi and Nemeskeri (1970) and by Weiss (1973), who also provides a table for correcting the age distribution of the population when r is not zero. We are confronted with something of a circular problem in trying to learn about growth rates by means of patterns of mortality, which themselves require knowledge or assumptions about rates of growth for their reconstruction. While it is likely that average rates of growth viewed in long-term perspective are low and may be on the order of 0.1 percent per year, rates of growth are probably in most cases heterogeneous over time, as mentioned earlier in this chapter. In dealing with a given skeletal population, what we need to know is not an average long-term rate, which includes both phases of active growth and those of little or no growth, but the rate applicable to the time period when the population actually lived. If the assumption that $r = 0$ is made in situations where high growth rates actually prevail, the life table obtained on the basis of this wrong assumption would be distorted. We have made some computations to evaluate the magnitude of the effect. From standard demographic theory, it is known that if age-specific fertility and mortality are constant over a few generations, by Lotka's theorem the age distribution of the population is stable and is given by $p(a) = bl(a)e^{-ra}$, where $l(a)$ is the unknown life table, b the birth rate. The number of deaths at age a is

$$D_a = \mu(a)p(a) = (a)bl(a)e^{-ra},$$

where $(a) = -dl(a)/l(a)da$ is the age-specific mortality rate.

An approximate reconstruction of the life table can be obtained by multiplying the number of deaths in each age class, D_a, by e^{ra} and then computing $l(a)$ from the thus modified distribution of ages at death. In Figure 6, we have subjected the Çatal Hüyük skeletal data to this analysis, assuming $r = 0$, 1 percent, and 2 percent. The life tables differ substan-

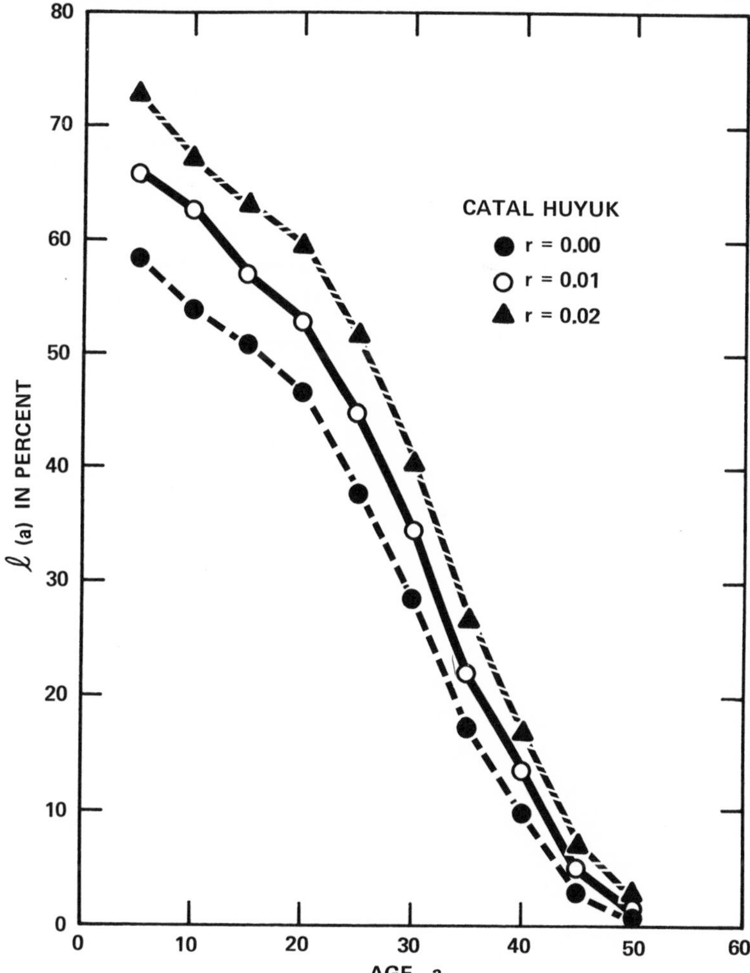

FIGURE 6. Reconstruction of life tables, $l(a)$, from age-at-death distribution of skeletons from Çatal Hüyük published by Angel (1971) and various associated values of r.

tially in the three cases: values for $l(a)$ will be underestimated, especially for early ages, if the population is growing but is assumed to be stationary ($r = 0$) as is customarily done. Thus, if independent estimates of growth rates are not available, a growing population (analyzed as a stationary one) will appear to have a worse mortality schedule than it actually has.

A difference in local growth rates is a factor that needs to be kept in mind in comparing mortality patterns from skeletal data among different sites or periods of occupation at the same site. This can perhaps be seen if a comparison is made between the sets of skeletal data from Çatal Hüyük and Nea Nikomedeia, which were both studied by Angel. When life tables are computed for both under the assumption of $r = 0$, there is a significant difference between the age-at-death distributions for the two sets of data ($X^2_{[10]} = 28.1$). Nea Nikomedeia would appear to have a higher relative mortality at the lower ages, especially in the 5- and 10-year age groups. Whether this is due to an actual difference in health factors in the two cases or to a more rapid growth rate at Nea Nikomedeia (with mortality schedules being much the same at the two sites) is difficult to determine without having access to growth estimates from other lines of evidence. In this respect, skeletal material, rather than providing a means for the estimation of growth rates, calls for a knowledge of such rates when it comes to the basic interpretation of mortality patterns.

Fertility

While there has been an increasing awareness in the more recent anthropological literature (e.g., Lee 1972; Binford in Chapter 3 of this volume) of the possible relationship between the shift from a nomadic hunter-gatherer to a more sedentary food-producing way of life and patterns of fertility and particularly changes in birth interval, relatively little attention has been paid to estimating fertility from skeletal material. One of the few attempts along these lines is the work by Angel (1969, 1971) on the skeletons from Çatal Hüyük and the Bronze Age site of Karataş. Since in many ways the methods used in determining parity among female skeletons are still open to question, the following discussion should be viewed as highly tentative. In Angel's published data, parity at a given age is the number of children to which a woman dying at that age has given birth. Mean parity is obtained by adding up the number of births of women who die at a given age and dividing by the total number of women whose death occurred at that age, whether or not they gave birth to children. Values of mean parity at various ages are plotted for Çatal Hüyük and Karataş in Figure 7. In both cases, only a fraction of the total number of skeletons identified as adult females seems to have been used to produce the original parity data.

An estimate of GRR, or the gross reproduction rate (the number of daughters born per woman who has passed through the entire childbearing span), is approximately given by half of the mean parity (the total fertility) of women who have reached the end of their childbearing span. Taking women over 40 years of age (45 years would be more appro-

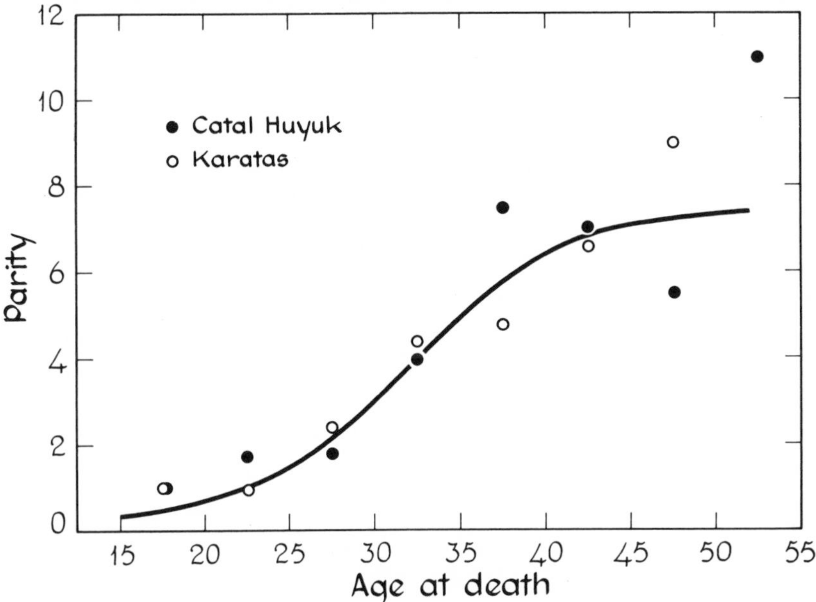

FIGURE 7. Mean parity versus age of women at death, based on skeletal data published by Angel (1969, 1971) for Çatal Hüyük and Karataş. The parity curve shown here is obtained from the combined set of data from the two sites.

priate, but it would reduce the already small sample sizes by half), GRR would turn out to be 3.58 for Çatal Hüyük (with a standard error of ± 1.17), 3.8 for Karataş (with a standard error of ± 1.28), and 3.68 for the two sets of data combined (with a standard error of ± 0.84). The magnitude of the standard errors emphasizes that larger samples are needed for the estimates of GRR to be considered statistically sound, quite apart from the question of the reliability of parity attributions. To obtain sufficient parity data on women who have passed through their reproductive span may call for several hundred skeletons from a given stratigraphic unit at a site. Changes in the design and execution of field strategies are implied if samples of this size are to be recovered.

It is suggestive and worth noting in any case that the Çatal Hüyük and Karataş parity data, if accepted as reliable, indicate higher levels of fertility than are found, for example, among contemporary groups of hunter-gatherers in Africa such as Pygmies (unpublished) and Bushmen (Harpending n.d.), where women past reproductive age would appear to have a mean total fertility of 5.20 for Pygmies (with a standard error of ± 1.08) and 4.16 for Bushmen (groups 1 through 5 pooled with an approximate standard error of ± 2.16). But fertility data alone are not enough for estimating *r*, the intrinsic growth rate of a population. The mortality schedule must also be available (Coale 1972:20) or, as a minimum, one crucial value of it, the probability of surviving to age $\bar{m}$, given by the mortality schedule, where $\bar{m}$ is the arithmetic mean of the fertility schedule. However, as we have seen earlier, the estimation of the mortality schedule from the age distribution of skeletons requires a knowledge of r. Unfortunately, it is not entirely clear how to resolve this circularity, which represents a major methodological problem in this class of work.

SUMMARY

While there has been an increasing theoretical interest in the relationships between population growth and culture change in prehistory, much less attention has been paid to the characterization of actual patterns of growth. This chapter represents an attempt to explore in some depth certain methodological aspects of the estimation of population growth in the context of Old World prehistory. As in the case of studies of growth trends in historical demography (e.g., McKeown et al. 1972), it is reasonable to expect that actual estimates may themselves play a major role in the eventual identification of the factors responsible for population growth. In the introductory section, we were concerned with such questions as the heterogeneity of rates of growth both in terms of time and space and, related to this, different levels of resolution when it comes to making estimates. We then turned to what is called the *SARP* approach and the use of settlement information for population estimates. Various aspects of this approach were discussed, including the inadequacy in most cases of trying to use a single tangible expression of growth (such as the number of settlements in a region) as a general measure of growth. In the section on packed house volumes, a new method of estimating growth was introduced which was illustrated through the use of data on settlement mounds in the Near East. The packed house volume concept may make it possible to avoid in part the fundamental problem of contemporaneity among archaeological units that arises in the analysis of settlement data. The final section of the chapter was concerned with certain aspects of the use of skeletal data in trying to make growth estimates. The exploratory nature of much of the discussion is stressed: we are still at an early stage when it comes to the development of estimation procedures in prehistoric demography and also the collection of sets of data called for by such methods.

APPENDIX

Logistic Fit Procedure

The logistic equation may be written in the form

$$N_t = \frac{N_{\max}}{1 + e^{-c(t - t_o)}},$$

where N_t is the number of sites at time t, $N_{\max}$ is the maximum number of sites, and t_o and r are parameters. Observed data, N_{t_i}, are gathered for given time values, t_i. We have, therefore, three parameters to determine: $N_{\max}$, t_o, and c. Initial estimates for the range of these parameters can be taken from a provisional graph drawn through the observed data. Note that t_o can be estimated as

$$\frac{\log\left[\frac{(N_{\max} - N_o)}{N_o}\right]}{c}.$$

These ranges are then partitioned and the expected values, $N^*_{t_i}$, are calculated for each combination of parametric values. The error for each combination of parametric values is computed as the difference between the expected N_{t_i} and observed $N^{\text{obs}}_{t_i}$ and summed for all t_i. The parameters corresponding to the minimum error are then chosen.

The chosen parameters can be characterized by one of two situations: (1) all parameters lie within the specific interval, in which case a new smaller interval is explored as above, centered around these calculated expected parametric values; or (2) one or more of the chosen parameters falls on the extremes of the expected intervals, in which case the best fit parameter probably falls outside the original estimated intervals. An overlapping interval is then specified and the process repeated.

NOTES

1. This work was supported in part by grants from the U.S.A.E.C. contract number AT(04–3)326, and the N.I.H. grant number GM 20467–01. We would also like to thank Professors Ansley J. Coale and Robert McC. Adams for their comments on a preliminary draft of the chapter.

2. The problem of the form of the growth curve may seem trivial, but it is basic

to estimating growth parameters. The two most common forms of population growth are the exponential and the logistic. In exponential growth, the rate of reproduction per individual remains constant over time and there is a continual acceleration in population numbers. Exponential growth can be represented by the formulation (Wilson and Bossert 1971)

$$\frac{dN}{dt} = rN,$$

where dN/dt is the change in population size over time, r is the rate of growth, and N is the population size. A sigmoid form of growth is seen over time in the case of logistic growth, where the increase in population numbers progressively slows down as an upper bound is approached. The formulation used to describe logistic growth is

$$\frac{dN}{dt} = rN\left(\frac{K-N}{K}\right),$$

where r is the initial growth rate and K is the maximum population size (sometimes called the carrying capacity). In some cases, more complex forms may be needed to reflect actual patterns of growth in a more accurate way.

3. One of the more promising results to date along cross-cultural lines has been the allometric relationship observed between population size and dwelling area (Naroll 1962). A more refined treatment of the two variables may, however, be called for in certain cases (Le Blanc 1971). One of the methodological questions that arises in prehistoric demography concerns the extent to which ethnographic analogies should be used. This general subject received considerable attention at a previous seminar (Longacre 1970b). While there are probably few cases where one can entirely avoid the use of such analogies in making population estimates, there is a definite latitude of choice in the kind and degree of reliance that one is prepared to accept. Much will no doubt depend on the particular archaeological context. When dealing with the more remote prehistoric past, it would seem desirable for estimates to be based as much as possible on the direct evaluation of archaeological evidence. The point here is that *estimation* tends to become a self-defeating exercise if we begin to rely too heavily on estimates drawn from the present and extrapolated back over long periods of time.

4. In considering the question of the number of persons per room or "house," it is worth noting that under normal conditions there are physical limits to the number of people that can inhabit a given amount of floor space. Conversely, there would also appear to be economic limits to the maximum amount of floor space that a family or group at a subsistence farming level is likely to create and maintain for each of its members. While neither of these limits can be more than loosely defined, they do suggest the existence of upper and lower bounds to the potential range of values of P. The trade-off between the two factors may account for much of the relationship that has been observed between floor space and population size (Naroll 1962; Cook and Heizer 1968).

5. Trigger (1965) recognizes the importance of the question of contemporaneity among sites in making population estimates and in his study of Lower Nubia tries to use cemetery data in the form of grave counts to arrive at values of proportionality for various periods. While the approach adopted by Trigger is quite promising, it is unfortunate that data in the form of extensive grave counts would not seem to be very common or easy to come by.

6. Stone foundations should be included as part of the volume of a house at sites

such as Cayonu (Braidwood et al. 1971) where they are a regular feature. In ethnoarchaeological studies at the village of Hasanabad in Iran (Watson: personal communication), stables were found to be quite common and would inflate PHVs; special account would need to be taken of stables and other related kinds of rooms in cases where they are present in the archaeological record. Pottery would not seem to make a very significant contribution to a mound's volume, unless vessels are incorporated in the deposit in unbroken form. This is evident from simple calculations of the "packed" volumes of broken pots: for example, a globular pot with a diameter of 50 cm. and walls 2 cm. thick will produce a packed pottery volume of about 0.016 cubic meter. One cubic meter would be the equivalent of some sixty such broken pots when incorporated in the deposit of the mound.

7. At the village of Hasanabad in Iran (Watson: personal communication), some *tauf* houses were found to be on the order of 30 to 50 years old, suggesting that the figure of 15 years for average house life may well be too low.

3

Nunamiut Demographic History: A Provocative Case[1]

LEWIS R. BINFORD

Department of Anthropology
University of New Mexico

W. J. CHASKO, JR.

Department of Anthropology
University of New Mexico

INTRODUCTION

Most general discussions of primitive man have been dominated by an essentially Malthusian model of demography. Malthus regarded fertility as basically a constant, a function of the "passion between the sexes." He therefore considered change in population to be a result of changing mortality rates. Anthropologists, when they have considered demographic variables, have generally taken a similar viewpoint, particularly when addressing themselves to such problems as the increase in human population that often seems to be associated with the appearance of agriculture.

The commonly held view has been that shifts to food production resulted in greater nutritional reliability, with an attendant decrease in death rates resulting in rapid and impressive population growth. In attempting to explain the shift from hunting and gathering to food production, anthropologists have generally considered demographic variables as dependent and of no explanatory consequence in understanding fundamental changes in technology and economy.

More and more anthropologists have suggested that population growth might appropriately be considered as an independent variable in discussing some aspects of culture change. Clark (1951:97) suggested that permanence of settlement and conflicts have accompanied population increase and the resultant dwindling of land resources. Carneiro (1960) argued that there was a relationship between increasing population and the level of organizational complexity achieved; Dumond (1965) argued programmatically for the consideration of demographic variables.

Ester Boserup (1965) has presented one of the more explicit challenges to the traditional Malthusian position. She states:

> Ever since economists have taken an interest in the secular trends of human societies, they have had to face the problem of the interrelationship between population growth and food production. There are two fundamentally different ways of approaching this problem. On the one hand, we may want to know how changes in agricultural conditions affect the demographic situation. And, conversely, one may inquire about the effects of population changes upon agriculture.
>
> To ask the first of these two questions is to adopt the approach of Malthus and his more or less faithful followers. Their reasoning is based upon the belief that the supply of food for the human race is inherently inelastic, and that this lack of elasticity is the main factor governing the rate of population growth. Thus, population growth is seen as the dependent variable, determined by preceding changes in agricultural productivity which, in their turn, are explained as the result of extraneous factors, such as the fortuitous factor of technical invention and imitation. In other words, for those who view the relationship between agriculture and population in this essentially Malthusian perspective there is at any given time in any given community a warranted rate of population increase with which the actual growth of population trends conforms.
>
> The approach of the present study is the opposite one. It is based throughout upon the assumption, which the author believes to be the more realistic and fruitful one—that the main line of causation is in the opposite direction: population growth is here regarded as the independent variable which in its turn is a major factor determining agricultural developments (Boserup 1965:11).

Boserup's work does not concern itself with the conditions under which we might expect population to grow but instead discusses variable technological and strategic responses in agricultural techniques that might be seen as responses to population pressure. In an initial reading, a number of apparent similarities are demonstrable between Boserup's views and a general Malthusian position. Namely, given the Malthusian argument that food is the limiting variable on population growth, it follows that selective pressure is continuously operative, favoring new means for increasing the food supply. Although specifically denying a Malthusian argument, Boserup argues that as population increases there are pressures favoring increased production of food! Admittedly, she phrases this argument in terms of "standard of living," or diminishing output from increased labor input and the like, rather than stressing food and starvation as did Malthus. In short, however, she appears to differ from a Malthusian position only in the attitude expressed. Malthus was pessimistic; Boserup is optimistic in that she sees technological responses coming "when they are needed" while Malthus saw starvation and misery coming as the population increased toward the carrying capacity. The latter analysis is shown to be incorrect in the following statement:

> Thus, the new approach to agricultural development which is signalled by the concept of frequency of cropping draws the attention to the effects upon agricultural technology which are likely to result from population changes. . . . The neo-Malthusian school has resuscitated the old idea that population growth must be regarded as a variable dependent mainly on agricultural output. I have reached the conclusion . . . that in many cases the output from a given area of land responds far more generously to an additional input of labour than assumed by neo-Malthusian authors. If this is true, *the low rates of population growth found in preindustrial communities cannot be explained as the result of insufficient food supplies due to overpopulation* (Boserup 1965:14; emphasis added).

Although Boserup does not treat the problem, she clearly acknowledges that factors other than food supply must be operative in regulating rates of population growth in preagricultural times. If we as anthropologists are going to explore the potential of demographic variability for understanding change in cultural systems, we must, if we hope to develop truly explanatory arguments, begin to understand the factors, cultural and otherwise, that may condition such variability.

In 1968 Binford explored the implication of Malthusian ideas for the development of explanatory arguments treating the history of cultural evolution. It was pointed out that, given Malthusian principles, "man would be continually seeking means for increasing his food supply" (Binford 1968:327). This view presupposes that throughout human history there have been continuous selective pressures ensuring advantage to any new technique or method for increasing the food supply. When we view the history of technological and economic development we see vast periods of time during which, as far as we can judge, there was enormous stability in the technological and organizational means employed in food getting. Under Malthusian principles we would have to seek explanations for such stability as well as for periods of accelerated change in the variable capacities of human beings for inventing or discovering new productive means. Reviewing the literature one finds that the dominant arguments have all applied to conditions that would prompt man to recognize the productive advantage of certain techniques, assuming always an advantage to increased production, or have attempted to show how the knowledge of superior techniques is transmitted from group to group. Binford has challenged this view of cultural evolution. Basic to the challenge was the argument that human populations, particularly hunters and gatherers, are regulated in their growth and size by a complex of factors resulting in the stabilization of population below the point at which its level would affect the productivity of their food supply. This point was stated as follows:

> In rejecting the assumption that hunter-gatherer populations are primarily regulated by the available supply of food, we put the problem of the development of new types of subsistence in a different light. As long as one could assume that man was continually trying to increase his food supply understanding the "origins of agriculture" simply involved pinpointing those geographic areas where the potential resources were and postulating that man would inevitably take advantage of them. With the recognition that equilibrium systems regulate population density below carrying capacity of an environment, *we are forced to look for those conditions which might bring about disequilibrium and bring about selective advantage for increased productivity* (Binford 1968:328; emphasis added).

The central issue was not the recognition that population might be seen as an independent variable nor that population increase might well provide the selective context for technological improvement—these points seem obvious. Rather Binford viewed the development of explanatory arguments as the central problem, arguments with predictive and retrodictive potential that would specify the conditions prompting population growth itself and bringing about some stress on either the available food or labor scheduling in the procurement of food. He then developed an argument having several crucial points:

1. Certain conditions obtaining during the terminal and closing phases of the Pleistocene differentially favored increased use of resources such as anadromous fish, sea mammals, waterfowl, and migratory herd mammals.

2. These being nucleated resources, there was a tendency toward reduced mobility and increased sedentism in certain areas.

3. *Population growth would be a by-product of sedentism.*

At the time that these arguments were set forth Binford was working from the empirical generalization, intuitively formulated, that sedentism and population growth were correlated. It was argued that sedentism was causal, being related to a reduction in the need for cultural means of regulating births, which were viewed as advantageous in mobile situations (Binford 1968:332).

Some critics have suggested that these basic propositions and the model on which they were built were too "limited." We recognized weaknesses in the argument but not the same ones as the critics. The weak points as we viewed them were not knowing in any concrete way either (1) the determinants of sedentism or (2) the demographic effects that sedentism might prompt. In 1968 we saw the opportunity for gaining some first-hand knowledge relevant to the second of these "weaknesses." While examining for very different reasons the literature on the Nunamiut Eskimos of north-central Alaska, Binford realized that they were one of the rare groups that had in very recent years undergone a transition from fully mobile hunting-and-gathering subsistence to sedentary hunting subsistence. This had occurred during the period of ethnographic observation and within the memory of all the people over twenty years of age in the settlement of Anaktuvuk. This fact together with other research interests led us to initiate field research there in the summer of 1969. Since then we have been involved almost continuously in fieldwork with these people and plan to continue this work for some time to come.

THE NUNAMIUT CASE

The Nunamiut are currently localized in a single community at Anaktuvuk Pass. Until 1950 they were fully mobile hunters, primarily dependent (as they remain today) on caribou for subsistence. The contemporary community is composed of two amalgamated local "bands," the Tulugakmiut and the Kilikmiut, and two attached families of the Ulumiut, a local band that broke up in 1942.

During the month of August 1969 the village of Anaktuvuk was composed of 126 permanent residents and 4 visiting Eskimos. This population was segmented into twenty-one households, seventeen of which were nuclear families (that is, composed of only a husband, wife, and their offspring). Two households were extended families; in addition to the nuclear family a widowed parent of the husband was living in the house. The remaining two households were composed of unmarried adults with their offspring in one case and adult unmarried brothers in the other. In terms of marital status there were 2 widowers, 1 widow, 19 married couples, 3 adult bachelors, 1 adult unmarried female with 3 children, and 81 unmarried children and young adults. Table 9 presents the age and sex structure of the village.

A number of interesting observations are contained in Table 9. It should be noted that the sex ratio in the village is markedly in favor of males, 70 males to 56 females. This fact should not, however, be understood as reflecting either a differential sex ratio at birth or the selective practice of female infanticide as reported for many Eskimo groups (Weyer 1962:133–37). Eleven females born to parents in the village are living elsewhere, either by virtue of having married males resident in other settlements or, in 4 cases, having been adopted out. It is interesting that no males born to parents in the village have left or been adopted out. When the emigrant females are taken into account, the ratio for the subadult dependents is 28 males to 26 females; for effective producers it is 34 males to 36 females. Among the aged there is a real difference—8 males to 3 females.

Population History

The first count of Nunamiut population was made in 1949, when 76 people were reported (Rausch 1951:154). Later, during the summer of 1957, Pospisil (1964:396) reported 85 persons in summer camp at Anaktuvuk; Gubser (1965:347) reported that during the summer of 1960 there were 96 persons. From these figures alone it is clear that the Nunamiut population has been growing. During the 1969–71 interval, intensive interviews were conducted to increase the accuracy of the demo-

TABLE 9

AGE AND SEX DISTRIBUTION OF NUNAMIUT POPULATION IN 1969

Subsistence Classification	*Age Group*	*Residents*			*Born in Village, Living Elsewhere*		
		Males	*Females*	*Total*	*Males*	*Females*	*Grand Total*
Aged Dependents	86–90 years	1	0	1	0	0	1
	81–85	0	0	0	0	0	0
	76–80	3	0	3	0	0	3
	71–75	1	1	2	0	0	2
	66–70	0	0	0	0	0	0
	61–65	0	1	1	0	0	1
	56–60	3	1	4	0	0	4
Subtotal of Aged		8	3	11	0	0	11
Effective Producers	51–55 years	0	2	2	0	2	4
	46–50	2	3	5	0	1	6
	41–45	4	4	8	0	0	8
	36–40	3	3	6	0	0	6
	31–35	6	5	11	0	1	12
	26–30	4	2	6	0	4	10
	21–25	6	3	9	0	0	9
	16–20	9	5	14	0	1	15
Subtotal of Effectives		34	27	61	0	9	70
Subadult Dependents	11–15 years	11	10	21	0	0	21
	6–10	12	11	23	0	1	24
	1– 5	5	5	10	0	1	11
Subtotal of Subadults		28	26	54	0	2	56
Grand Total		70	56	126	0	11	137

graphic picture. These data, coupled with the work of Hanson (1969), allow us to reconstruct with a great deal of accuracy the population history of the Nunamiut as far back as 1940. Relevant demographic information has been extended back as far as 1884 in some cases.

The picture of population growth is the lower half of a sigmoid curve, indicating accelerating growth until the interval between 1965 and 1970, when the curve changes abruptly. The growth of the actual population approaches a doubling time of twenty years. Put in another perspective, the growth rate advanced from something under 0.2 percent per year to over 4.0 percent per year, twice the estimated present rate of world population increase of about 2.0 percent (Krebs 1972:588). The Nunamiut case appears to be a classic situation in which rapid population growth is approaching levels referred to by demographers as "transitional" in character. According to classic demographic arguments aimed at understanding the "demographic revolution" associated with historical shifts to food production, this should be the result of depressed mortality presumably accompanying dietary and nutritional changes. Let us examine the case. Table 10 presents the data on births and deaths together with the summary data on adult numbers; Figure 8 summarizes the data on crude birth and death rates for the period 1935–70. These data show that from 1935 until 1949 the population was relatively stable with a low crude birth rate (see Nag 1962:175) and a crude death rate very close to the mean for the world population in 1947 (Dorn 1959:455). Between 1949 and 1954 the crude birth rate doubled while the death rate remained relatively unchanged. This marked increase in fertility coincides with the shift in Nunamiut ways of life to a marked sedentary community. Between 1955 and 1960 there was a slight depression in the crude death rate, while birth rates remained relatively unchanged. Between 1960 and 1964 the crude death rate dropped with an accompanying minor drop in birth rate.

This case demonstrates two major points: (1) there was a marked growth in population coincident with a shift to sedentary life; and (2) this growth was effected through a marked rise in birth rates rather than the "normal" situation in which a marked decrease in death rates is considered responsible. If this case is to be cited as relevant to understanding primitive demography and as relevant to conditions leading to stresses favoring the search for new subsistence strategies, as has been previously suggested (Binford 1968), we must attempt to understand the

TABLE 10

VITAL STATISTICS FOR THE NUNAMIUT ESKIMOS, 1935–70

Year	Live Births	Deaths	Migration In	Migration Out	Total Pop.	Mean Births/Year	Mean Deaths/Year	Mean Pop./Year	Crude Rates/1000 Births	Crude Rates/1000 Deaths
1935	1	2	—	—	66					
1936	2	2	—	—	66					
1937	1	2	—	—	65	1.4	1.2	66.4	21.1	18.1
1938	2	0	—	—	67					
1939	1	0	—	—	68					
1940	3	1	—	—	70					
1941	1	2	—	—	69					
1942	3	1	—	—	71	2.4	1.2	71.0	33.8	16.9
1943	1	1	—	—	71					
1944	4	1	—	—	74					
1945	1	1	—	—	74					
1946	1	2	—	—	73					
1947	2	1	—	—	74	2.0	1.6	74.2	26.8	21.5
1948	1	1	—	—	74					
1949	5	3	0	0	76					
1950	3	0	0	0	79					
1951	4	1	0	0	82					
1952	3	1	0	0	84	3.8	1.4	84.0	45.2	16.7
1953	5	2	0	0	87					
1954	4	3	0	0	88					

TABLE 10 CONT'D.

Year	*Live Births*	*Deaths*	*Migration* *In*	*Out*	*Total Pop.*	*Mean Births/Year*	*Mean Deaths/Year*	*Mean Pop./Year*	*Crude Rates/1000* *Births*	*Deaths*
1955	4	1	0	0	91					
1956	6	1	0	1	96					
1957	4	1	0	0	99	4.6	0.8	99·4	46.3	8.1
1958	6	1	0	0	104					
1959	3	0	0	1	107					
1960	7	0	0	2	114					
1961	3	0	0	1	117					
1962	4	0	0	1	121	4·8	0.6	121.4	39·5	4·9
1963	6	0	0	1	127					
1964	4	3	0	0	128					
1965	3	0	0	0	131					
1966	4	1	1	2	134		0.8	134·3	20.8	5·9
1967	4	2	3	2	136	2.7				
1968	0	0	3	0	136					

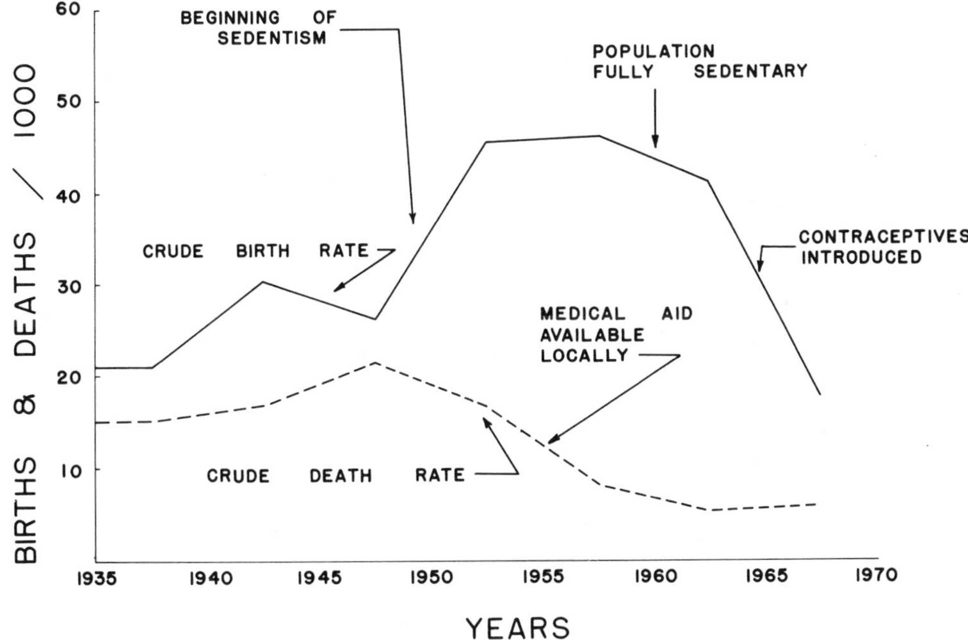

FIGURE 8. Summary of Nunamiut birth and death rates, 1935–70

mechanism that resulted in this population growth and seek to establish that this is not a unique case but an example of more general phenomena associated with hunting and gathering strategies.

At least two major features of the demographic history displayed in Figure 9 must be explained: the obvious increase in crude birth rate prior to 1960 and the decline after 1960. The latter problem is the better documented and understood and will therefore be treated before we attack the interesting problem of accounting for increases in fertility.

The Apparent Decline in Fertility Beginning in 1960

This aspect of the Nunamiut demographic situation is completely understandable in terms of three sets of conditions: (1) the inaccuracy of the crude birth rate as a measure of fertility; (2) the increased age of females at marriage after sedentism; and (3) the massive adoption of contraceptive devices by Nunamiut females beginning in 1964.

The generally used measure of fertility is the "age-specific fertility rate"; these rates for Nunamiut women in 1950 are presented in Table 11. The data summarized in Table 11 document nicely some of the changes previously discussed. The most dramatic feature is the marked reduction

TABLE 11
AGE-SPECIFIC FERTILITY RATES FOR NUNAMIUT WOMEN, 1950

	Group A Women over 35			*Group B* Women 25–34			*Group C* Women 10–24		
Age Classes	N	*Births*	*Rates*	N	*Births*	*Rates*	N	*Births*	*Rates*
15–19	40	5	125.00	30	3	99.99	55	2	36.36
20–24	40	11	275.00	30	7	233.31	55	13	236.34
25–29	39	11	282.04	25	12	490.80	52	18	346.14
30–34	34	9	264.69	30	11	366.63	48	8	166.64
35–39	33	8	242.40	30	10	333.33	42	2	47.78
40–44	29	4	137.92	30	3	99.99	5	0	0.00
45–49	22	1	45.45	30	1	33.33	0	0	0.00
Total			1,372.50			1,657.38			833.26
Expected Completed Fertility	6.86			8.28			4.16		
Mean Age of Group in 1950*	47.0 yrs.			26.4 yrs.			17.0 yrs.		
Mean Age of Group in 1964	61.0 yrs.			40.4 yrs.			31.0 yrs.		

* (1) The rates for the women with a mean age of 47.0 years in 1950 are probably high due to an absence of information regarding several women who died and two who moved at the death of their husbands. (2) Group with a mean age of 47.0 includes one sterile female. (3) Group with a mean age of 26.4 years includes one sterile female. (4) Group with a mean age of 17.0 years includes one female who produced no live births until medical aid was available to her in 1962.

in fertility between groups B and C coincident with the groups' mean ages in 1964, the year in which a family-planning program was instituted among the Nunamiut by public health personnel. Forty-two of the ninety-eight mother-years (women between 15 and 44) in 1965–70 were "sterilized" years, as the age-specific fertility rates clearly show.

The second major change illustrated by the age-specific fertility rates is the regular decrease in fertility for the 15-to-19 age group. This can be accounted for by an interesting trend through time in the mean ages of marriage for males and females. Table 12 presents the summary data.

Although the data in Table 12 are not marriage dates, they are clearly indicative of such. The trend is confirmed by informants who are well aware of the contemporary changes in marriage age and quite vocal about it. Clearly the trend is toward later marriage ages for women, and at

TABLE 12
MEAN AGE OF MALES AND FEMALES AT BIRTH OF FIRST CHILD, ARRANGED BY AGE GROUP FOR NUNAMIUT MOTHERS (1950)

	Group A *Mean Age* 47.0 *Yrs.*	*Group B* *Mean Age* 26.4 *Yrs.*	*Group C* *Mean Age* 17.0 *Yrs.*
Mean Age of Fathers at 1st Birth	27.6 yrs.	28.4 yrs.	25.6 yrs.
Mean Age of Mothers at 1st Birth	18.6 yrs.	21.2 yrs.	23.5 yrs.
Difference	9.0 yrs.	7.2 yrs.	2.1 yrs.

present there is an accompanying trend toward lower ages for males that we are certain will be amplified beyond that indicated here in the coming years. One comment we encountered over and over again regarding the age at marriage for men is that "it takes a long time for a man to learn everything he needs to know to live; he can't get married until he can take care of a family." Informants would then invariably add that the present situation in the village was certain to cause trouble. "The young men now all go away to school, they don't know anything like an Eskimo, they all think they want to get married just because they want a girl. Let them, they will see, they will all starve or freeze to death." Another informant offered the opinion that the reason he knew so much about the land of the Nunamiut was because he had lots of sisters:

> Man with lots of sisters is lucky; they marry early and then you can visit them if they leave and learn all about other places. If they catch a son-in-law for father then you have a new brother but he can take you to places your own brother don't know. A good sister catches a good husband for her brothers. Then everybody happy, brothers, father, mother, everybody.

The concern over the changing age at marriage and the effect of school on the training of young men is well demonstrated by the case of a 20-year-old girl who believed herself pregnant by a boy of 23. The girl was pressuring for marriage, but the boy was reluctant. The comments of the older people were very informative. One old woman stated that the boy was smart:

> . . . he knows school not teach him to be Eskimo and he can't feed family—besides, his father getting old, her father getting old—boy really stupid if he marry before he can feed everybody—everybody starve. Girl just as stupid—her father tell her to get married long time ago to good man who could hunt. She says no, he too old—never go to school like her. She learn now, got baby inside, wait too long, and boy stupid—can't tell difference between wolf and fox track, get lost go here to Tulugak, go out no extra mukluks. He no man, he baby, only with big penis.

Another man commented on the situation:

> Father and mother of girl to blame—before when everybody spread around, always get girls married early before anything happen. In old days the more relatives you have the better chances of catching Caribou if she leave, and if she stay you have another good hunter; now nobody care because everybody together anyway. Missionary say that Eskimo way bad, young girl with old man; missionary just Tanik and don't know what it like to chase Caribou.

Another man made a most interesting comment: "Boy and girl very different—girls get breasts, her job to fill up her stomach with babies; boy get hair, his job to fill up head with way to catch food. Girl have to marry man with head full before she fills up stomach, other way around no good, everybody starve."

The conditions suggested in the informants' comments are not unrelated to the fact that many persons adopted under very little pressure the family-planning program introduced in 1964. One woman put it this way:

> Before, kids grow up and by time father getting too old to hunt good boys are getting good. Pretty soon they marry and sometimes stay home and help old people, sometimes move away and old people if one dies can go live there and not worrry about young kids [younger siblings conceived during the mother's later years]. Now all boys go away to school and not learn to hunt, girls too and wait so long to find a husband and even then husband no good. I want to stop having babies so they won't starve if my husband dies or gets sick—school kids and boys not trying to be men are no help.

Another informant gave specific recognition to the larger families characteristic of the postsedentary period and expressed anxiety about feeding the very young children once the father is too old to hunt. Many men commented that they had too many kids to feed: "Not like old-timers with only three or four, now I have nine, too many kids." The very real fears of the older people associated with the changes in their way of life and in the training of young men, later age of girls at marriage, and increased family size were cited as the "reasons" for adopting the family-planning methods. As can be seen, their effects have been marked.

Summary: Decreases in crude birth rates since 1960. Three sets of documented conditions seem sufficient to account for the observed decreases in the crude birth rate since 1960: (1) distortion in the crude birth rate; (2) increased age of females at marriage after sedentism; and (3) massive adoption of contraceptive devices by Nunamiut females beginning in 1964. Given the fact that these conditions are understandable and clear-cut, it is good methodology to eliminate their effects on fertility before we begin our search for those variables that might be conditioning increases in fertility in a positive manner. In order to accomplish this we have calculated mother-child ratios for the period between 1935 and 1970 by eliminating from the mother-year values those unmarried females and sterile females practicing family-planning methods. These data are summarized in Table 13.

We can see that fertility, rather than declining as indicated by the crude birth rate (Table 10), would actually have accelerated after 1960, the date for full sedentism. These, then, are the figures we wish to examine in relation to measures of the other variables, those suspected of conditioning increases in fertility.

Fertility Increases prior to 1960

Nag (1962) has summarized the factors affecting fertility under three major headings: (1) factors affecting the probability of coitus; (2) those relating to the probability of conception; and (3) those relating to the growth and survival of the fetus.

Interviews with Nunamiut informants, particularly women, during the summers of 1971 and 1972 were directly aimed at attempting to isolate the factors responsible for changing patterns of fertility. Those factors upon which information was specifically sought were variations (a) in frequency of coitus, (b) in miscarriage frequencies, (c) in nutritional factors, (d) in lactation period, and (e) in such practices as abortion, contraception, and coital scheduling.

Informants insisted that abortion was not practiced during the relevant period (prior to settlement at Anaktuvuk), although they had heard of

TABLE 13
CORRECTED NUNAMIUT MOTHER-CHILD RATIOS

	1935–39	1940–44	1945–49	1950–54	1955–59	1960–64	1965–69
Number of live births	7	12	10	19	23	24	12
Number of years represented by women 15 to 44	47	57	61	73	86	85	98
Number of years represented by unmarried women	9	3	9	10	11	10	22
Number of years represented by sterilized women	0	0	0	0	0	1	42
Number of effective years for women 15 to 44	38	54	52	63	75	74	34
Effective female-child ratio per 1,000 mothers	184.17	222.12	192.30	301.50	306.59	324.24	352.92

it being done in their "grandmothers' time," particularly in cases of polygynous marriages. Three abortions have been performed in recent years, one in 1965 and two in 1970, all under modern medical supervision in cities to the south. Two cases involved the same girl, and the third case involved an older unmarried woman. All agreed that these would not have been performed in the past. "That girl would have had to get married" was the comment of the younger women; older women all agreed that such a thing couldn't have happened previously because "she would have already been married before playing around would give a baby."

Informants agreed that there was no particular scheduling of coitus in the past, with one exception: "Some men don't like women when they are bleeding." All older women stated that in their "grandmothers' time" having sex during menstruation was believed to ensure bad luck for the hunter. At best it can be judged that coitus is rare during menstruation although some men admitted to having indulged in it, particularly during illicit affairs.

Information on breast feeding was obtained from as far back as 1912 and no change is evident in practices, nor are the informants aware of any changes until after 1962. For the 26 cases documented prior to 1950, the range was from 9 to 14 months of breast feeding, with a mean of 11.3 months. After 1950 this same range is duplicated in 47 cases, with a slight increase in the mean to 12.7 months. Although slight, this change is in the wrong direction to bear on the increased fertility, since longer periods of lactation are supposed to increase birth spacing and therefore depress fertility (Lee 1972). At the urging of public health officials, some mothers began adopting bottle feeding in 1962; today all the young mothers have done so. This change is coincident with a depression in birth rate and is therefore not relevant to our understanding of fertility increases associated with sedentism.

Practices conceivably affecting the survival of the fetus and contributing to miscarriage were investigated. All those interviewed agreed that until around 1962 it was believed that a pregnant woman should "work hard" until the baby came so she would have an easy delivery. It was also believed that a woman who did not work hard would have a lazy child. There was little if any attempt to alter a woman's work load during pregnancy in the moving of camps or decisions to take extended trips. Attempts to document miscarriages revealed only minor differences before and after 1950. There were 4 known miscarriages and 29 live births for the period between 1935 and 1950, a wastage rate of 13.7 percent. After 1950 there were 5 known miscarriages and 78 live births, a wastage rate of 6.4 percent. The contrast suggests that there may be some direct link between wastage and the mobility of females, but the difference is totally insufficient to serve as an exclusive explanation of the increase in live births after 1950.

Informants cited a number of conditions they believed affected their fertility. Seasonal differences in coitus rates associated with "happiness" during periods of group festivals were mentioned by two informants: "The old-timers used to have big parties after the fall migration of Caribou and that was when most wife exchanges took place." "Until quite recently our New Year's parties were the biggest and we exchanged wives then. This got everybody excited and everybody was in bed a lot." Further questioning revealed that the "exchange" of wives at New Year's was stopped around 1956 when the "missionaries taught us to be ashamed." One woman commented that when she was first married, and they were making long hard trips to the coast during summer, coitus was less frequent because "everyone was tired."

The most commonly mentioned "causes" of reduced sexual activity were male absenteeism during hunting trips and "stopover" male visitors. Several informants agreed that visitors tended to cause a break in normal sex relations; however, it is necessary to make a distinction between three kinds of visitors. In the old days, "wife-sharing" partners were generally located at great distances from one another and tended to coincide with "trading partners." If a man made a visit to a trading partner, it was usually an extended trip during which he might be away from home for over a month. Arrival of such a visitor resulted in an increase in sexual activity for the women of the household. On the other hand, stopover visitors were parties of two to five hunters or trappers who would schedule their travels so as to "stop over" at another residential camp for a night or two during the course of their trip, usually during the winter and early spring. Informants agreed that it was not "polite" to have sex when such visitors were present because it "made them homesick." This meant that under certain settlement conditions the absence of males from their own homes had the added effect of reducing the sexual activity of other families who were not at that time separated. The third type of visiting party was the stopover of an entire family during the course of its movement of residential location or as a specific visit. Under such conditions they were normally equipped with their own tent and frequently served as a stimulus to sexual activity, "because everyone felt good having visitors." Beyond these comments, efforts to obtain historical data on coitus rates through direct questioning were completely unsuccessful.

Interviews conducted in 1971 concerning coital rates at that time among married males are summarized in Table 14. Our impression that these estimates may be slightly inflated is based on the supposition that men would not want the interviewer to think that they were not sexually active. No one reported not having intercourse at least once a week, even a man seventy-one years old! When I asked the women about the men's reports many would give no answer or simply smile, suggesting that they might have to look around for evidence of an affair if what their husbands said were true. A mean figure of around 1.5 is probably more accurate.

Conception Cycling and Settlement Subsistence Strategy

Because of the potential importance of historical data, a different line of research was undertaken. We were aware that there were marked variations in the distributions of births by season and that these variations appeared to coincide with known changes in subsistence strategy. If borne out, such variations would suggest that there was some determinant relationship between the probabilities of becoming pregnant and the character of the seasonal round of subsistence activities. Table 15 presents the frequencies and percentage occurrences of conceptions by season for the major periods during which there was general stability in settlement subsistence strategies.

We reasoned that if we could understand the conditions promoting such cycles we might well be isolating at least some of the factors responsible for the temporal trend in increasing fertility. Simply noting the totals of all conceptions, we would expect roughly 34.5 conceptions per season, assuming the random and unbiased distribution of conceptions over the year. Calculation of a chi-square value for the difference between observed and expected values under the assumption of an equal distribution yields a value of 8.202 with one degree of freedom, which exceeds the value expected at the .01 level of probability. Stated another way, the differences between the observed conception totals for the entire body of data and a uniform distribution could have arisen through chance

TABLE 14
ESTIMATES OF WEEKLY COITAL RATES FOR MARRIED NUNAMIUT MEN IN 1971

	Number of Times per Week					
Age Group	0	1	2	3	4	*Total*
15–19	—	—	—	—	—	—
20–24	—	—	—	—	—	—
25–29				1		1
30–34			2	1		3
35–39			1	1		2
40–44		1	1	1		3
45–49		1	1			2
50–54		1				1
55–59		2				2
60–64						
65–69						
70–74		1				1
Total		6	5	4		15
No. of Acts		6	10	12		28
Mean per Week = 1.86						

less than once in one hundred separate cases. Thus there is a very convincing likelihood that the overall bias in conceptions in favor of fall and winter is responsive to some causal determinant and not simply a chance phenomenon.

In order to determine whether the variability in conceptions among the different time periods, selected for their internal consistency in regard to settlement subsistence strategy, could be the result of chance fluctuations, a chi-square value was calculated for the entire matrix and found to be 28.82. With 18 degrees of freedom a value of 28.869 would be anticipated at the .05 probability level. This result reinforces the inference that factors other than chance fluctuations are operative in the data summarized in Table 15. Thus far, we can with some confidence realize that the conceptions are not uniformly distributed throughout the year. Some real conception cycling is documented, and there are meaningful changes in this cycling during the periods of time in Table 15. In order to evaluate when such changes in cycling occur, separate chi-square values were calculated for pair-by-pair comparisons between the time periods; Table 16 presents these results. These comparisons are enlightening in

TABLE 15
NUNAMIUT CONCEPTION FREQUENCIES BY SEASON

Time Period	Spring			Summer			Fall			Winter			Total
	No.	%	e	No.	%	e	No.	%	e	No.	%	e	
1882–98	1	(10.0)	1.81	3	(30.0)	2.10	1	(10.0)	2.68	5	(50.0)	3.40	10
1900–20	6	(42.0)	2.53	3	(21.4)	2.94	0	(0.0)	3.75	5	(35.7)	4.76	14
1935–39	2	(28.5)	1.26	1	(14.2)	1.47	4	(57.1)	1.87	0	(0.0)	2.38	7
1940–44	2	(15.3)	2.35	1	(7.6)	2.73	3	(23.0)	3.48	7	(53.8)	4.42	13
1945–49	2	(20.0)	1.81	1	(10.0)	2.10	5	(50.0)	2.68	2	(20.0)	3.40	10
1950–56	5	(17.2)	5.25	2	(6.9)	6.09	7	(24.1)	7.77	15	(51.7)	9.87	29
1957–70	6	(10.9)	9.96	16	(29.0)	11.55	17	(30.9)	14.74	16	(29.0)	18.73	55
Total	24	(18.1)		27	(21.0)		37	(26.8)		50	(34.0)		138

TABLE 16
PAIR-BY-PAIR COMPARISONS OF CONCEPTION CYCLING

Comparison	*Observed*	*Probability*
Rows 1 and 2	3.61	.30
Rows 1 and 2 grouped against Row 3	12.69	.01
Rows 3 and 4	5.82	.10
Rows 3 and 4 grouped against Row 5	0.86	.80
Rows 3, 4, and 5 grouped against Row 6	3.07	.30
Rows 3, 4, 5, and 6 grouped against Row 7	8.79	.05

that they demonstrate that there are essentially three periods of conception cycling. Grouped data for the three demonstrable periods are presented in Table 17.

Inspection of Table 17 reveals two trends: (1) there has been a gradual reduction in the proportion of conceptions occurring in spring throughout the data record and (2) there has been an increase in the comparability of conception frequencies among winter, fall, and summer.

As previously stated, the Nunamiut had undergone a number of documented changes in settlement subsistence strategy, including the amount of movement during an annual round, even prior to the consistent trend toward sedentary life during the 1950s. These changes may be monitored in a number of ways, the most direct being estimates of numbers of moves per season, mean distances traveled between camps, and the mean duration of stay at any one camp. The initial (and most complete) data of relevance here were collected by Charles Amsden during our first field season in 1969. Amsden interviewed five aged informants concerning the settlement history of their families, with particular emphasis on the period from 1934 to 1971. Amsden has summarized his information elsewhere (Amsden 1972), and not having the raw data available we are forced to utilize the time periods established by Amsden for summation. The data are summarized in Table 18 in seven columns: (a) the time period over which the data are summarized; (b) the actual number (*N*) of camps for which informant information is available; (c) the season of the year; (d) the mean number of weeks spent in a single camp by season; (e) the mean distance between camps for moves made during the designated season; (f) the mean number of different residential camps occupied; and (g) the mean number of air miles moved during the season.

It will be observed that the patterns of mobility and the seasonality of

TABLE 17
CONCEPTION CYCLING AMONG THE NUNAMIUT FOR THREE RECOGNIZED HISTORICAL PERIODS

	Spring		Summer		Fall		Winter		
Period	No.	%	No.	%	No.	%	No.	%	*Total*
1882–1920	7	29.1	6	25.0	1	4.1	10	41.6	24
1935–1956	11	18.6	5	8.4	19	32.2	24	40.6	59
1957–1970	6	10.9	16	29.0	17	30.9	16	29.0	55

TABLE 18

SETTLEMENT HISTORY OF FIVE NUNAMIUT FAMILIES

(*a*) Period	(*b*) N	(*c*) *Season*	(*d*) *Stay (weeks)*	(*e*) *Mean Distance between Camps (miles)*	(*f*) *Mean No. of Camps per Season*	(*g*) *Total Distance Moved by Season (miles)*
1898–1909	12	spring	5.2	40.1	2.50	100.25
	14	summer	8.3	40.2	1.56	62.71
	18	fall	2.6	48.1	5.00	240.50
	15	winter	11.9	45.4	1.09	49.48
Total					10.15	452.94
1910–1920	11	spring	3.5	17.1	3.71	63.44
	16	summer	8.3	71.4	1.56	111.38
	17	fall	2.5	62.6	5.20	325.52
	21	winter	13.4	38.1	0.97	36.96
Total					11.44	537.30
1934–1950*	31	spring	3.5	22.6	3.71	83.85
	31	summer	11.7	35.2	1.11	39.07
	33	fall	3.4	25.3	3.82	96.65
	57	winter	8.3	27.1	1.56	42.28
Total					10.20	261.85

* After 1950 many families occupied a single site on a year-round basis, and the breakdown by season becomes meaningless.

movement were essentially the same during the periods 1898–1909 and 1910–20. The only difference between the two periods is in the distances between camps and the total miles covered during an annual round. It will be recalled that we found no difference between the periodicity of conceptions for an analogous period comparison. Thus, in the seasonal pattern of movement and in the conception cycling, the period prior to 1920 is demonstrably homogeneous. It remains to ask if there is any relationship between the seasonal pattern of movement and the season cycling in conceptions. Table 19 presents the comparative data for the

TABLE 19
NUNAMIUT RESIDENTIAL CAMPS OCCUPIED AND CONCEPTIONS BY SEASON PRIOR TO 1920

	Mean No. of Camps	*% of Total*	*No. of Conceptions*	*% of Total*
Spring	2.50	28.7	7	29.1
Summer	1.56	14.4	6	25.0
Fall	5.00	47.2	1	4.2
Winter	1.09	9.5	10	41.6
Total	10.15		24	

period prior to 1920 regarding mean numbers of residential camps occupied per season and the numbers of conceptions occurring per season.

A linear regression was calculated for measuring the relationship between numbers of moves and numbers of conceptions per season. The result was a negative correlation with a correlation coefficient $r = -.93$, demonstrating a strong negative relationship between the two variables. The equation for the line summarizing the relationship is $y = 5.129 - .432(x)$, where y is the percentage of the total conceptions occurring in a given season and (x) is the percentage of the total camps occupied during that season. This relationship demonstrates that as the number of seasonal moves in residential camps increases, the number of conceptions decreases in a proportional manner. Thus, at least for this period, there is a strong pattern of interaction between the patterning in mobility and the patterning in conceptions.

A similar analysis was conducted for the subsequent period, 1934 to 1950. Table 20 presents the data on numbers of residential moves and numbers of conceptions by season.

TABLE 20
RESIDENTIAL MOVES AND CONCEPTIONS BY SEASON, 1934–50

	No. of Moves	*% of Total*	*No. of Conceptions*	*% of Total*
Spring	3.71	36.3	6	20.0
Summer	1.11	10.8	3	10.0
Fall	3.82	37.4	12	40.0
Winter	1.56	15.2	9	30.0
Total	10.20		30	

As in the previous case a linear regression was calculated for the relationship between numbers of moves and numbers of conceptions per season. The result was a moderate positive correlation with a correlation coefficient of $r = .469$. The equation for the line summarizing the relationship is $y = 1.505 + .154(x)$, where y is the percentage of the total conceptions occurring by season and (x) is the percentage of the total camps occupied during a given season.

The failure to obtain compatible results between the two periods suggests that there is some type of interaction between conception cycling and settlement subsistence strategy but that mobility per se is not the determinant. At least a third variable is at work. The periods compared are interesting in the contrasts they present concerning Nunamiut history. The period from 1898 to 1920 was one of acute subsistence insecurity for the Nunamiut. Between 1906 and 1912 subsistence security reached a low point, and these years witnessed many cases of starvation caused by a drastic decline in the caribou population in the Brooks Range. The response to the declining numbers of caribou is well documented by Burch (1972) for the Nutagmiut (or Noatakmiut), a group inhabiting the Noatauk drainage and living a life very similar to the Nunamiut.

> In northwestern Alaska, the decline of the Western Brooks Herd during the second half of the 19th century did indeed have a major impact upon all of the caribou hunting groups in the area. The experience of the Nuataqmiut is of particular interest in this respect.
>
> The home area of the Nuataqmiut was within the center of habitation of the Western Brooks Herd, and it lay directly athwart the spring and fall migration routes of the animals. During the popula-

> tion peak of the mid-19th century, the Nuataqmiut lived in a world of more or less continuous abundance, and they were generally unaffected during the early stages of the herd's decline. However, as time passed and caribou continued to decrease in numbers, the existence of the Nuataqmiut gradually became more precarious; in some winters they experienced abundance, and in others they suffered hardship and even starvation. As a result of the increasingly obvious fact that the Upper Noatuk Basin was no longer a safe place to spend the winter, the majority of Nuataqmiut decided to move to the northeast to the region of abundance which had been discovered by the exploring expedition. Other families, a much smaller number, decided instead to move to the coast, particularly to Point Hope, where they would have to switch from caribou to sea mammals as their major resource. Both groups left their homeland center of habitation of the Western Brooks Herd. However, one winter the entire population might be found around the headwaters of the Upper Utukik and Colville Rivers, and the next winter they might all be some hundreds of miles to the east in the Endicott Mountains. The third winter they might be scattered in small bands over the entire center of habitation zone, and the following winter they might all be gathered together in the Upper Noatak Basin (Burch 1972:357–58).

In this description we can see that the major responses to decreasing caribou abundance were increased residential mobility, increased dispersion over a wider territory, and increased flexibility in local group associations among families. The character of the Nunamiut response was identical judging from life-history data collected from informants who lived through this period. The expansion of the effective territory is well documented in Table 18, which shows an increase from a mean of 453 miles traveled by the average family on a seasonal round for the period 1898–1909 to a mean value of 537 miles during the period 1910–20.

If we conclude from the earlier comparisons between the two periods under consideration that a simple mechanical relationship between the frequency of moves and the probability of conception is not at work, what in the informants' descriptions of life during the two periods may provide a clue to the causation? Looking over the life-history data, two points stand out as being of possible significance. (1) All informants agreed that, during stress, residential moves were made in direct response to the state of any family with regard to the amounts of stored food or reliable resources available. We might then conclude that between 1898 and 1920 frequent residential moves were coincidental with eating less well or even in some cases poorly. This would mean that caloric intake would be negatively correlated with residential mobility and in turn directly correlated with conception probability. (2) There was agreement that, when stores were low or local resources unreliable, small parties of men traveled out from residential locations, covering many miles in search of game; if they were successful, the residence would be moved to that general area. Thus during periods of high residential mobility there would be a correlated high degree of male absenteeism from the residential camps. Conversely, during periods of stress when residential mobility was low, stores or local foods would be judged adequate and male absenteeism would be at a minimum.

Contrasting these conditions with those outlined by informants for the period 1934–50 we find an almost inverse set of relationships paralleling those noted in conception frequency and residential mobility. By 1934 the caribou herds had recovered considerably in the Brooks Range, and one can see from the data in Table 18 that there had been a concomitant contraction in the effective territory to a mean of 261 miles covered by an average family during the seasonal round. Similarly, there was an increase in the permanence of interfamilial associations such that local groups with some degree of membership stability were obvious. There are no known cases of starvation, and informants report dependability in caribou numbers and distribution. Essentially a reverse set of conditions existed regarding nutrition and male absenteeism, at a minimum during periods of high mobility. Long-term residential occupations were secure with respect to food and the men were often in the field trapping and trading with Euro-Americans. Stress periods were compensated for by importing food with the proceeds of trapping and intensified hunting. Similarly, there was no reported correlation between seasonal "hunger" and mobility during the 1934–50 period since high mobility was coincident with caribou migrations.

These contrasts coincide with those in the relationships between mobility and conceptions for the two periods under consideration. It remains for us to investigate further the possibility of male absenteeism (in the context of an extended logistical strategy of regional exploitation) and the nutritional level of the population (in the context of exploitative strategies) as possible determinants of the observed seasonal cycling in conception times. This was considered particularly important since we reasoned that if we could understand the conditions promoting the demonstrated cycles in conceptions we might well be isolating at least some of the factors that contributed to the marked changes in fertility over time.

Male Absenteeism, Nutrition, and Fertility

Quite clearly something tends to affect the probability of becoming pregnant during certain seasons. This variation would certainly affect the nature of birth spacing, which in turn could be linked to overall fertility. As stated previously, three basic sets of factors affect fertility: factors affecting the probability of coitus, those relating to probability of conception, and those relating to the growth and survival of the fetus. Many suggestions have been made relating to the effects of diet on one or all of the above; it has been argued that the nutritional state may affect sex drive, probability of fertilization, and certainly survival of the fetus. Since there seemed to be a marked relationship between changes in birth cycle and known changes in settlement subsistence characteristics, nutrition clearly merits serious consideration.

Prompted by the insistence of the informants that the absence of males and the presence of "stopover" male visitors were the major causes of reduced sexual activity, we have tried to accumulate historical data on male absenteeism as it varies with changes in the settlement subsistence history as well as nutritional information for comparable periods.

Early period: 1890–1910. Attempts to document male absenteeism through direct interviews were not entirely satisfactory. The men had definite impressions regarding the relative amounts of time that they were away from home, but obtaining estimates in absolute terms was difficult. For instance, in working with an informant we would select a year that for some reason we believed he "remembered" better than another, or one that we had knowledge of, so that questioning could be more intelligent. Knowing the camps in which the informant lived, we might ask how many nights were spent away while staying in a particular one. He would give an estimate of perhaps fifteen nights during a given month. We would then move on to another camp, and an estimate of perhaps eleven nights would be given for the next month. Later, during questioning on a different subject, the informant might tell of many packing trips made while moving the camp. We then would ask how many nights these kept him away and get a rather exact tabulation as he recalled the trips. These nights would not have been included in his original estimate because those questions had been concerned with nights away while living at the camp—and moving was not living there.

As demonstrated above, we have uncovered many of the problems in interviewing but are certain that the data to be presented are still unsatisfactory in some ways. For example, the number of nights away from camp is generally underestimated if these were accumulated during a period characterized by several overnight trips and few long ones. On the other hand, when long trips are reported the number of nights is inflated. In spite of the suspected inaccuracies and our frustrations in accumulating these data, however, they are all we have, and although certainly inaccurate in an absolute way they are probably relatively accurate and therefore informative of changes in behavior clearly recognized by the informants and well documented in their recent archaeology.

Information relevant to the "early period," during the youth of the old informants, concerns the years between 1890 and 1910. All informants agreed that the most time spent away from home was during the "fall months," explaining this in a variety of ways:

> Fall was father's big work time; he has to find Caribou for winter food, he has to build the winter house before the ground freezes up, he has to move everything there from summer camp and also go back to last year's winter camp to get everything everybody leave there. Until he does that he don't even have a sled.

> In those days Caribou pretty hard to find so our fathers could not just *sit down and wait like young people today*, they had to go out all the time looking (emphasis added).

> That was not always so easy because maybe folks in camp have little meat. Before he can go he maybe hunt sheep for many days, packing meat in so he can go look for Caribou and not worry that wife and kids not eat good.

One informant recalled an incident when he was "about seven," which would have been around 1902:

> My father, Simon's father, Tulukana's brother, Arctic Johnnie's father, and May's father have summer camp down on river by Tulugak Creek. In late summer the men hunt hard at Tiglukpuk and other salt lick up where Taniks hunt sheep in Anaktiqtauk, they go everywhere to catch sheep. Put snares all over mountain sides and

> catch 'em too. They put out snares for SicSic [ground squirrel] and women check 'em when men away, boys too. Men stay gone most of late August catching sheep for us. Then Tunganna say that people here not starve and men better go look for Caribou. All the men leave, and boys too, looking for Caribou. Pretty soon womens begins to worry, snow come and boys in camp see some Caribou go south over by Akmogulik—still men not come home. Womens begin to cry because they think maybe bear got their husbands or they fall in lake or maybe Indians get them. Every day my mother and me check for SicSic and women fish too. It really snow now and get cold and the lake freeze—nobody know what to do because men still gone. Then one day a boy is up on the side of the mountain checking trap and see 'em coming down valley from the summit with sleds. He run into camp all out of breath and everybody excited yelling, "The men coming, the men coming!"
>
> They had found the Caribou a long way away and killed 'em too, but they knew they had to build good houses near where their meat was and before freeze-up too. So they all work hard building Evrulik in a good spot with lots of good willows near the meat. By the time they finish, it was already snow, so they go to old winter camp in Okumelot to get sled and pack all winter things to new houses. By then they really homesick and they come all the way to Tulugak on sled without stopping. We have a big dance in the "happy house" and everybody happy for two-three days, then we move to new houses and men have to work hard getting everything women want to take to new house. That winter good winter, but not all like that. Sometimes men not so lucky and have to hunt hard in winter.

The informant estimated that the men were absent from their families for over six weeks at one time during that trip and more before that while hunting sheep. Many similar stories were told about the absence of the men during the fall migration and the necessary preparation of the winter camp. Most informants reported that during spring there was less male absenteeism, because "many things were cached at the old winter house and there weren't so many things to pack all over the place." They also commented that the people liked to travel in spring, when it began to warm up but before the melt.

> Men would go visiting other camps to find out what everyone was going to do during the summer. Sometimes we would have foot races then, particularly in my father's and grandfather's day when people would come from the Noatuk or camps on the Killik or Alatena but those times the women and kids would come too. Everyone move

> around a lot in spring and that way nobody miss the Caribou. Everybody going home about the time Caribou start and nobody miss 'em. Summer was the hard time; even if Caribou come they are skinny and men have to go out all the time to find fat ones. In those days mainly trade fawn skins, and in winter men only go to trap for wolf and wolverine women need for clothes. Besides, old-timers say man can't catch but four fox, wolf, or wolverine a year. If he catch more, he would get sick. Not like now, hunting wolf all the time. Then only go out a little bit in winter just for clothes. Men stay home in winter in old days if they hunt good in fall.

Although they do not provide the desired quantitative data on male absenteeism, these statements give some idea of the relative work schedule with respect to absenteeism. It is noteworthy that the informant estimates of relative absenteeism are greatest in fall, frequent in spring, common in summer, and rare in winter, corresponding exactly to the differential seasonal frequencies of conception (see Table 17 for this time period).

We were unable to gather a coherent picture of nutrition or work scheduling for the period between 1910 and 1935 since the families were distributed over the North Slope and in coastal villages.

General work scheduling, nutrition, and subsistence base: 1935–49. This is the period of the reestablishment of the three local Nunamiut groups in the mountains. One was located in the Killik River area, another in the Tulugak Lake–Anaktuvuk region, and the third in the Ulu Lake area. Initially there were no resident traders in any of these areas, the Killik and Anaktuvuk people traveling to the Kobuk River to trade. Around 1943 a trading post managed by Jim Crowder was reopened in Bettles, where the Anaktuvuk people subsequently traded. The Ulu Lake group had to go to the coast, usually to the J. W. Smith trading post at Beechy Point. Trips were also made by the Ulu Lake people to Wiseman. In all cases the distances covered in order to obtain goods were great.

The major sources of credit were prime adult wolf and fox skins, although marmot, caribou calf, and sinew were also traded. We were able to uncover only one purchase list for this period—the list of goods obtained by a member of the Ulu Lake group after a fifteen-day round trip to Beechy Point in March 1942. These represent the purchases of a single family designed to last until the next trading venture, normally the following spring.

Purchase List

5 boxes 25/25 shells
5 boxes 250/3,000 shells
5 boxes 22-special shells
2 boxes 16-gauge shotgun shells
1 lb. Granger tobacco
2 cans Western tobacco
1 carton chewing tobacco
1 pair snow glasses
1 Remington knife
1 medium-sized pocket knife
2 packs matches
61 cigarette papers
2 spools thread
1 pencil
8 yards white Indianhead cloth

Food

2 lb. coffee
2 lb. tea
3 lb. salt
25 lb. flour
10 lb. sugar
—
42 lb. total

It is clear from this list that the quantity of nonnative foods consumed annually was very limited. It was also remarked by most informants that these foods were generally consumed during late spring and early summer; by late summer no trade food was left. This was confirmed by our examination of archaeological sites of this period.

The generalization that this food list is representative, particularly for the period 1935–45, is supported by many informants, some stating that if packing were not such a problem, rice and cornmeal might have been added. The use of the foods was as follows:

1. Flour was used in thickening broth made with caribou meat and

bone juice; it was also sometimes cooked as pancakes or mixed with cornmeal to increase the "mush."

2. Coffee and tea were consumed "not all the time like now" but on special occasions such as when visitors came; occasionally the adults would drink one or the other when alone in the mornings but rarely at other times. Sugar was used with the coffee and tea.

3. Salt was put on dry meat "to make it taste good."

The Ulu Lake band broke up in the fall of 1942; during the later years of this period the Killik band continued trading on the Kobuk River and the Anaktuvuk group at Bettles. After 1946 float-plane deliveries of trade goods were made on Chandler Lake during the early summer, "after the ice was gone" (normally around June 19). The Anaktuvuk group particularly began making more frequent trading trips in the fall, generally in October.

As far as minor variations in settlement subsistence strategy during this period are concerned, the war years (1941–46) represented a brief interlude during which there was a decreasing emphasis on fur hunting and trapping in the winter months. As noted, furs were the source of credit, used primarily for shells and ammunition. Powder and shells became increasingly difficult to obtain during the war years, so there was a corresponding decrease in fur trapping and hunting. One informant stated that in 1946 he accumulated furs that brought over $1,200 when finally sold in 1947. Before that, during the war years, he could not trade them for ammunition, so he just stored them, adding to his stores whenever "I happened to see a wolf." The ammunition situation became so critical for the Nunamiut that during the summer of 1946 the "old men taught the young men to make spears and we made three kayak in the fall and drove Caribou into Chandler Lake, spearing them from kayak like the old-timers." All agree that extended winter trips and trapping came almost to a stop during these years. Other old men added that even if they could get to the places of former trade "everything was crazy and the traders were all gone" so that "we had practically nothing then, not even flour."

In 1946 contact was made by the Tulugak group with Sig Wien, who had stopped for a fishing venture on Chandler Lake. Wien was "startled" when the Eskimo approached because there had been no reports of people living in the mountains. The Tulugakmiut told him of their plight regarding their stores of skins and lack of ammunition. Wien made arrangements for the sale of the group's furs in Fairbanks, further arranging that their "order" be delivered at no charge by a military plane bringing a team of soldiers who were to "make a line to the coast." The soldiers came well supplied, giving the Nunamiut boxes of C rations and K rations. We have no exact data on the amounts of imported foods introduced between 1945 and 1949; however, the following observations were made of the archaeological remains for the sites occupied during the spring and summer of 1947 at Tulugak Lake.

Remains of Imported Foods
of Three Families of the Tulugak Band, 1947

Carnation milk cans	36
K ration hash cans	7
C ration cans	2
2 lb. coffee cans	4
#10 fruit juice cans	4
#6 soup cans	4
jam can	1
Velvet tobacco cans	2
Blazo fuel cans	2

Informants stated that Blazo cans were obtained from the soldiers in order to make a stove from the metal. The Carnation milk cans were from an order sent through Sig Wien that also included flour, sugar, tea, and dried fruit; the other goods represented gifts from the soldiers at Chandler Lake. These data confirm that after contact with Wien the imported foods were of a greater variety, but there was only a small increase in the quantity available.

Table 21 presents the data on hunting, kill counts, and days absent from the residential camp for one man of the Ulumiut band during 1941 and 1942. Although these data, obtained from his diary, represent only 59 days, they give some impression of the levels of male absenteeism, particularly when spring trading trips were undertaken.

For the 59 days recorded, 17 nights, or 28 percent of the time, were spent in the field. If such a level were maintained throughout the year, a man would spend 105 nights away from the residential location. Interviews on this subject revealed that male absenteeism was low during these

TABLE 21
HUNTING RECORD FROM THE DIARY OF ULUMIUT BAND MEMBER, 1941–42 (ABSTRACTED FOR A SINGLE FAMILY HEAD; DATA ON OTHER BAND MEMBERS EXCLUDED FROM THE TABULATION)

		Kills			Nights Spent Away		
Seasons	*Days Out Hunting*	*Caribou*	*Sheep*	*Bear*	*Hunting*	*Packing*	*Trading*
1941 Summer-Fall							
Aug. 6–31	11	10	0	1	1		
Sept. 1–19	8	4	0	0	4	1	
44-Day Total	19	14	0	1	5	1	
1942 Spring							
Apr. 2–5, 12–15 20–29	4	19*	2	0		3	8†
15-Day Total	4	19	2	0		3	8

* Ten of these were killed while on the trip to Wiseman.

† These eight days were spent on a trading trip to Wiseman between April 20 and 29. All heads of families in the band, 5 men, were on this trip.

59 days because migration apparently had not started; the move to winter camp is not mentioned in the records. Informants estimated that during the early years of the 1940s 15 nights away in spring, 35 in summer, 17 in fall, and 9 in winter were probably representative. Interviews regarding the period 1935–40 resulted in no truly internally consistent estimates. One informant estimated 50 nights in summer, another 30. Concerning the winter months, the same informants estimated 10 nights and 2 nights, respectively. However, there was general agreement on spring and fall absenteeism. Judging from the data at hand, the average head of family spent between 70 and 80 nights per year away from the residential location.

This period may be summarized as follows: 1935–40 saw the resettlement of the Nunamiut families in the interior into three local bands—the Killikmiut, the Tulugakmiut, and the Ulumiut. Trade was primarily for shells and ammunition, canvas for use with caribou skins in making tents, and some summer clothes. Very little imported food was utilized and then only seasonally, usually in late spring and early summer. Winter trapping was extensive, with trading trips largely restricted to the spring. The most male absenteeism occurred during the summer months, when local dispersed game was being taken, and the least in the fall, when hunting was conducted from the residential locations and trapping had not yet begun. During the war, furs became exceedingly difficult to sell and the needed powder, shells, and bullets could not be purchased. At this time, there was a drop in winter trapping and "men stayed home most of the time." Hand in hand with the wartime hardships went a marked reduction in the few imported foods previously available. After the war, trading and trapping were resumed and, probably as a result of increased contacts, the quantity of imported foods rose somewhat; nevertheless, they were still largely restricted to the late spring and early summer. By late summer, "all the Tanik food was gone."

Examination of the data summarized in Table 15 shows that, for these three 5-year intervals, conceptions in winter were 0.0 percent between 1935 and 1939, rising markedly to 53.8 percent during the war years (when trapping was largely suspended), and dropping again after 1945 to 20.0 percent. Conceptions during this 15-year period were consistently lowest in summer and generally low in spring, the times when imported foods were consumed. In addition, it will be noted in Figure 8 that the crude birth rate fluctuates with the change in birth cycling noted above, so that the highest rate for the 15 years was during the war, when imported foods were at their lowest but male absenteeism was reduced because of decreased trapping. These data demonstrate that at least for this period there is no direct correspondence between either crude birth rates or the periodicity of conception and fluctuations in the quantity of imported foods available. In fact, the relationship appears in inverse form. On the other hand, there appears to be a correspondence between gross fertility and estimates of male absenteeism, over the period.

Settlement subsistence strategy and fertility: 1949–56. The documentation of practically all features of Nunamiut economic life for 1949 through 1956 is excellent. This was the period during which the first moves toward sedentism were made, although the Nunamiut by no means became sedentary overnight nor can they be said to have become sedentary by the end of 1956. Forces were at work and many changes occurred, but sedentism was not completely accomplished. After word of the "inland people" spread, largely through Sig Wien and later Helge Ingstad, agencies of the larger society began intruding more and more into the mountain world of the Nunamiut. In 1949 the last of the separate bands amalgamated at the summer camp of the Tulugakmiut. The Killik people walked from the Killik River to Tulugak Lake using pack dogs, arriving in mid July and setting up their tents near those of the Tulugakmiut. This move may be explained as a response to the first of an increasing set of pressures operating on the Nunamiut to aggregate and ultimately become sedentary.

As a result of Wien's contacts with the Tulugak people, their presence was advertised, and in the summer of 1947 a teacher, a Caucasian with an Eskimo wife, was sent to the Tulugakmiut camp from Point Barrow. During the summer English classes were held for the young and old people alike, and the possibility of continued instruction was the prime motive behind the move of the Killik people to the Tulugak camp. Most of the heads of families were anxious that their children learn "to speak like Taniks," for the older men all realized that their children's futures were to be tied up with the broader "Tanik" world and wanted to see them at least have the advantage of easy communication.

Helge Ingstad arrived only two months after the Tulugakmiut and Killikmiut had amalgamated, and his book *Nunamiut* (1954) is descriptive of the first year of the bands' life in the Anaktuvuk area. The winter of 1949 marked the arrival of Pat O'Connell, who was interested in establishing a local trading business. The Nunamiut were concerned about the reliability of trading because of their past experiences and were anxious to take any steps to reduce the high freight costs of having goods delivered. Ingstad and O'Connell encouraged them to apply for a post office, arguing that if postal service were established mail order purchases as well as freight could be reliably received. O'Connell was interested because his plans for a fur-trading business with the Nunamiut would be greatly helped; the idea also appealed to Sig Wien, for he was trying to extend the scale of his growing airline company, and mail franchise was one of the major means of doing so in these years. At the urging of these men, application for a post office was subsequently made.

During the summer of 1950, school was held again in the Tulugak Lake camp, taught by a married couple named Hayden. That summer the group was visited by Dr. L. Irving and his son, Bill, who visited earlier sites with Simon Paneak, whom Dr. Irving had first met just after the war. Another visitor was Robert Rausch, now of the Arctic Laboratory in Fairbanks, who had previously visited the Nunamiut at the time of Ingstad's visit.

The pattern of movement after amalgamation was generally between

Tulugak Lake in summer and the vicinity of the present village in fall; some families then moved farther south to the "timber" for winter. These winter camps were usually extended family camps, Old Morry camping up in the Anaktiqtauk Creek area, Old Hugo at Ekokpuk, Simon Paneak, Elyjah Kakinya, and Frank Rulland at Savioyok, and Homer Mekiana at the present village site. Jessie Ahgook varied his location but generally camped with Simon and Elyjah, as did John Morry. In the summer of 1952, the mail franchise was established on a regular basis, with one mail delivery per month, increasing to two deliveries in the fall. Homer Mekiana was elected postmaster, and the post office was established at his camp at the present site of Anaktuvuk Village. The following year the regular move to the front of the mountains was not made by the entire group: Homer stayed at Anaktuvuk, Simon Paneak, Elyjah Kakinya, and Frank Rulland made the normal move to Tulugak and Jessie Ahgook, Old Hugo, and Old Morry joined Homer at Anaktuvuk, a split along old band lines that continued until 1961.

The establishment of the post office provided a fixed point around which the movements of the Nunamiut were oriented, but its location at Homer's winter camp presented certain problems. The normal movement during summer to the front of the Brooks Range was prompted by several subsistence considerations. Traditionally the exploitation of the spring caribou migration was not carried out with an eye to maintaining the local groups throughout the summer. This was primarily related to the nutritional cycle of the caribou, notoriously thin and in poor condition in the spring ("You can eat your weight in spring Caribou and starve to death"). Animals were killed and the meat dried, but this was not considered sufficient to last until the important fall migration, when the bulk of the winter subsistence was obtained. Summer therefore was thought of as the potentially "bad" season. Residential mobility was relatively low, with settlement generally adjacent to a good fishing lake where the women engaged in fishing and trapping ground squirrel while the men ranged far and wide, hunting both sheep and the scattered caribou found on the summer range and occasionally in the high mountains. With the localization of the Nunamiut, particularly the Killikmiut, around the post office, the target for their summer subsistence became the local population of Dall sheep. Table 22 presents the counts of game taken by the entire Nunamiut group during 1951 and 1952. Judging from the known food requirements of 79 people and 126 dogs, these counts

TABLE 22

GAME COUNTS FROM HOMER MEKIANA'S DIARY, 1950–51*

Year and Month	Foods						Fur Bearers				
	Caribou	*Sheep*	*Bear*	*Moose*	*Fish*†	*Ground Squirrel*	*Wolf*	*Fox*	*Wolverine*	*Marmot*	*Weasel*
1950											
June	13	—	—	—	—	—	12		17		
July‡	2	23	6		10+						
Aug.	22	8	2	1	25+	4	1				1
Sept.	54	11	1		X+						
Oct.	1	17	1		X+		3	1	21		
Nov.	84	5	1		X+		2				
Dec.	26	1					2			1	
1951											
Jan.	57	2					10	4			
Feb.	46	2					6				
Mar.	65	3					3		2		
Apr.	11						1				
May	71		1							8	
Total	452	72	12	1	150	4	40	5	40	9	1

* The game counts for 1951 are interesting in view of the fact that the caribou herds wintered in the Anaktuvuk area. This did not happen again to our knowledge until the winter of 1967–68.

† This total figure is an estimate based on an average number of fish taken by fishing parties. The diary does not report actual counts.

‡ One week missing in the records for July.

are representative of approximately 75 percent of the total caribou procured during those years. The data were obtained from the diary of Homer Mekiana and are comparable to our own game counts made in 1969 and 1972.

Men hunting in groups report their game tally, while those hunting alone normally report only if several caribou are killed. Caribou killed singly are usually not discussed, but sheep, bear, and moose are recorded regardless of numbers. Therefore, in Table 22 any inaccuracies are likely to be underestimations of caribou counts; the other counts would appear to be reliable.

As can be seen in Table 22 late summer was the time of maximum extension of the effective environment, with sheep and bear providing a major supplement to caribou (also recorded in the diary are 75 pounds of berries gathered in July and August 1950). In addition, amounts of imported food increased, as shown by the trading records of James Crowder (the manager of the trading post at Bettles during these years). Table 23 presents the data on imported foods for the period 1949–51 and represents materials for 7.5 family-years.

Although there was a substantial increase in imported goods over that reported from the previous period, the total amounts only to about 150 can-pounds per family per year, with some 90 can-pounds imported during the summer months.

The period 1950–51 was the last year families made their regular moves independently of such considerations as the location of the post office. All families were in dispersed winter camps, and the general pattern was for a group, usually of three men, to leave one residential camp, hunting and trapping the territory covered in the trip between their camp and another. At the second camp they stayed overnight as visitors, then either made the return trip or continued farther away, stopping at still another residential camp for a "night or two." Similarly, the regular moves necessitated several trips to pack belongings to be moved from the old camp to the new one. The data in Table 24, taken from Homer Mekiana's diary, are tabulations of the nights the men spent away from their families during this time, according to the tasks they performed.

Data presented in the preceding three tables are the available information for the very crucial years of the Nunamiut's initial transition to sedentism. A number of features stand out. From the perspective of wild foods, the most varied diet was clearly during the summer. From that of im-

TABLE 23
FOODS IMPORTED BY NUNAMIUT GROUP, 1949–51

Product	*Winter*	*Spring*	*Summer*	*Fall*	*Total*	*Mean Can-lb./ Family/Yr.*
Coffee	37 lb.	—	57 lb.	39 lb.	133 lb.	17.70
Tea	—	—	41 lb.	16 lb.	57 lb.	7.60
Canned Milk	48 cn.	—	36 cn.	—	84 cn.	11.20
Dry Milk	—	—	15 lb.	5 lb.	20 lb.	2.60
Sugar	75 lb.	—	205 lb.	60 lb.	340 lb.	45.30
Flour	50 lb.	—	150 lb.	50 lb.	250 lb.	33.30
Oats	10 lb.	—	100 lb.	10 lb.	120 lb.	16.00
Crackers	8 lb.	—	5 lb.	8 lb.	21 lb.	2.80
Cocoa	4 lb.	—	—	4 lb.	8 lb.	1.06
Baking Powder	1 cn.	—	—	1 cn.	2 cn.	0.26
Salt	1 lb.	—	2 lb.	1 lb.	4 lb.	0.53
Soda	1 cn.	—	3 cn.	1 cn.	5 cn.	0.66
Rice	2 lb.	10 lb.	50 lb.	—	62 lb.	8.26
Onions	—	—	2 lb.	—	2 lb.	0.26
Raisins	4 lb.	—	—	—	4 lb.	0.53
Butter	—	—	2 lb.	4 lb.	6 lb.	0.80
Cheese	—	—	5 lb.		5 lb.	0.66
Dry Beans	—	—	2 lb.		2 lb.	0.26
Total	241 (21.4%)	10 (0.88%)	675 (60.0%)	199 (17.6%)	1,125	149.78

ported foods, the greatest quantity was also consumed during the summer. On the other hand, the fewest conceptions occurred during these months. This is in line with our findings for the previous period, when higher fertility was associated with periods of least imported foods. Given the data for male absenteeism, we see that there is a very good fit between the periods of low fertility and high male absenteeism and vice versa. It could be argued that high male absenteeism, as well as high rates of imported foods, is correlated with periods of subsistence stress and concomitantly low nutritional levels. To some extent this is probably true; however, as we will see from the following data, we have some control over this factor.

Between 1952 and 1954 the early strategy of subsistence attempted in the Anaktuvuk Valley seemed to be an excellent solution to the problem of summer subsistence. Table 25 presents the data on imported foods for 1952–54, also obtained from the records of James Crowder. The purchases

TABLE 24
NIGHTS SPENT AWAY FROM CAMP BY NUNAMIUT MALES, 1950–51

Month	Caribou Hunting	Sheep Hunting	Packing	Wolf Hunting	Fishing	Other	Total for Month	Total for Season
June	5		7	70			82	
July	0	43		21			64	238
August		61	4		27		92	
Sept.			26				26	
Oct.	6	8	19	11			44	113
Nov.	31		3		9		43	
Dec.	12			9		5	26	
Jan.				42			42	88
Feb.				20			20	
March	17			10			27	
April				31			31	102
May			10	34			44	
Total	71	112	69	248	36			541*

* There were 10 married heads of households at this time, which represents 900 man-nights per season. Dividing by the 10 heads of reproductive families represented in the data, we obtain an estimate of 54.1 absent nights per man for 1950–51.

of four families are shown, representing the total for seven family-years, one family not recorded for 1952.

The total can-pound importation increased over the previous period by about 100 can-pounds per family per year. The interesting change, however, is in the season of importation. Most goods during this period were imported in winter, fewer in spring and summer, and fewest in fall. This shift confirms informants' statements that "once we learned the area well we could get sheep, bear and some Caribou all summer." An increase in local game procured during the summer months is indicated by the comparative data from the counts listed in Mekiana's diary for the summers of 1950 and 1951 and shown in Table 26.

The trends indicated in these data, although unfortunately not documented by game counts beyond 1951, are supported by informant interviews. Sheep were increasingly exploited and hunting pressure resulted in

TABLE 25
FOODS IMPORTED BY NUNAMIUT GROUP, 1952–54

Product	*Winter*	*Spring*	*Summer*	*Fall*	*Total*	*Mean Can-lb./ Family/Yr.*
Coffee	42 lb.	39 lb.	12 lb.	24 lb.	117 lb.	16.7
Tea	21 lb.	17 lb.	6 lb.	13 lb.	57 lb.	8.1
Canned Milk	138 cn.	75 cn.	66 cn.	69 cn.	348 cn.	49.7
Dry Milk	10 lb.	20 lb.	5 lb.	—	35 lb.	5.0
Sugar	214 lb.	100 lb.	118 lb.	50 lb.	482 lb.	68.8
Flour	185 lb.	100 lb.	100 lb.	105 lb.	490 lb.	70.0
Oats	10 lb.	—	—	10 lb.	20 lb.	2.9
Crackers	22 lb.	10 lb.	5 lb.	—	37 lb.	5.3
Cocoa	2 lb.	—	—	4 lb.	6 lb.	0.9
Baking Powder	—	—	1 cn.	1 cn.	2 cn.	0.3
Salt	1 lb.	2 lb.	3 lb.	—	6 lb.	0.9
Soda	2 cn.	1 cn.	—	—	3 cn.	0.4
Rice	10 lb.	10 lb.	—	—	20 lb.	2.9
Onions	—	—	—	—	0	
Butter	2 lb.	1 lb.	7 lb.	5 lb.	15 lb.	2.1
Cheese	—	—	5 lb.	—	5 lb.	0.7
Raisins	—	—	—	—	0	
Dry Beans	—	—	2 lb.	—	2 lb.	0.3
Crisco	3 lb.	3 lb.	2 lb.	—	8 lb.	1.1
Total	662 (40.0%)	378 (22.8%)	332 (20.0%)	281 (16.9%)	1,653	236.1

TABLE 26
COMPARATIVE SUMMER GAME COUNTS FROM HOMER MEKIANA'S DIARY, 1950–51

Season	*Caribou*	*Sheep*	*Bear*	*Moose*
1950				
June	13	0	0	0
July	2	23	6	0
Aug.	22	8	2	0
Total	37	31	8	0
1951				
June	26	9	1	0
July	0	21	3	0
Aug.	24	22	0	1
Total	50	52	4	1

more and more hunting trips in the summer. This happy state of affairs continued until 1955 when, in spite of the "hunters being away most of the time," few sheep were killed. In five short years the Nunamiut had depleted the local sheep population, and the numbers of bear sighted and killed diminished even before then.

In 1956 the situation was such that it was quite clear that other measures had to be taken. The response to the depletion of local sheep and bear populations was the construction of deep cellars dug into solid ice to permit the efficient storage of spring caribou meat. These were completed during the summer of 1956 and have remained in use since. With the construction of the ice cellars, the intense summer hunting stopped, and a further shift can be seen in the seasonality and quantities of imports. Table 27 presents the data on imported food purchased by four families, but as the records are incomplete for each, the totals represent only four family-years for the period from 1955 through 1957.

It will be noted that there is a return to the earlier "stress" pattern of most food being imported during the summer months. This coincides with the collapse of the effective hunting of local sheep and bear populations and the construction of ice cellars and foreshadows the shift to an increasing dependence upon imported foods in the next few years.

Unfortunately, we were unable to procure actual tabulations for the

TABLE 27
FOODS IMPORTED BY FOUR NUNAMIUT FAMILIES, 1955–57

Product	*Winter*	*Spring*	*Summer*	*Fall*	*Total*	*Mean Can-lb./ Family/Yr.*
Coffee	4 lb.	12 lb.	29 lb.	3 lb.	48 lb.	12.0
Tea	9 lb.	7 lb.	8 lb.	2 lb.	26 lb.	6.5
Canned Milk	54 cn.	45 cn.	66 cn.	12 cn.	177 cn.	44.2
Dry Milk	—	—	4 lb.	3 lb.	7 lb.	1.7
Sugar	160 lb.	14 lb.	225 lb.	75 lb.	474 lb.	118.5
Flour	25 lb.	125 lb.	230 lb.	25 lb.	405 lb.	101.2
Oats	—	—	—	—	—	—
Crackers	12 lb.	6 lb.	24 lb.	5 lb.	47 lb.	11.7
Cocoa	—	2 lb.	9 lb.	—	11 lb.	2.7
Baking Powder	—	—	—	—	—	—
Salt	1 lb.	—	1 lb.	—	2 lb.	0.5
Soda	1 cn.	—	1 cn.	—	2 cn.	0.5
Rice	—	—	25 lb.	25 lb.	50 lb.	12.5
Onions	—	—	—	—	—	—
Butter	2 lb.	—	5 lb.	—	7 lb.	1.7
Cheese	—	—	5 lb.	—	5 lb.	1.3
Raisins	—	—	—	—	—	—
Crisco	3 lb.	2 lb.	6 lb.	2 lb.	13 lb.	3.2
Dry Beans	—	—	—	—	—	—
Pepper	—	1 cn.	1 cn.	—	2 cn.	0.5
Peanut Butter	—	2 lb.	—	—	2 lb.	0.5
Jam	—	—	3 lb.	—	3 lb.	0.7
Total	271 (21.1%)	216 (26.8%)	642 (50.1%)	152 (11.8%)	1,281	319.9

variations in labor schedules for males during this period. Nevertheless, the documented archaeological sites as well as informant statements suggest a major set of changes. Prior to 1951 wolves were taken both for bounty and for skins, the Nunamiut then practicing a technique known as "wolf pupping." In spring the men would search for wolf dens, taking the litter for bounty—a pup or even a fetus bringing a bounty equal to that on adult animals. For many years this had been a supplementary strategy, the hunters preferring to take winter adults since they could both collect the bounties and sell the skins.

During the early days of settlement, largely from 1952 to 1956, the local wolf population was such that needed cash and credit could be obtained primarily through winter trapping. In addition, the then-resident trader, O'Connell, discouraged wolf pupping as his major interest was in skins. This partial suspension of wolf pupping between 1952 and 1957–58 is well documented by data collected by Robert Stephenson in conjunction with his study of wolf behavior. Stephenson worked extensively with the Nunamiut and enlisted their help in locating as many wolf dens as possible. As these were located and visited, he collected information as to the year of discovery, the years that they were active, and the names of the men who made the discoveries. Table 28 represents the data arranged chronologically for the number of new dens discovered by spring wolf-pupping expeditions.

TABLE 28
DENS DISCOVERED BY NUNAMIUT "WOLF-PUPPING" EXPEDITIONS, 1949–68

Year	*New Dens*	*Year*	*New Dens*
1949	1	1959	2
1950	1	1960	1
1951	1	1961	1
1952	1	1962	1
1953	0	1963	3
1954	0	1964	1
1955	0	1965	0
1956	0	1966	0
1957	0	1967	0
1958	3	1968	1

These data demonstrate nicely not only the suspension of wolf pupping from 1952 through 1957 but also its resumption on a large scale during the latter part of the 1950s and into the 1960s. Wolf bounty was no longer paid in Alaska after 1969.

Nine informants were consistent in their estimates of male absenteeism for the critical period 1952–54. The mean estimates were 16 nights in summer, 3 in winter, 3 in spring, and 1 in fall for a total of 26 nights, over a 50 percent reduction in one year.

Summarizing the available data, we see a number of changes representing the transition away from normal settlement subsistence strategy. Mobility patterning changed substantially in 1951 and 1952, with many families localized at Anaktuvuk Pass and others at Tulugak Lake. A change in housing began with the construction of permanent sod houses at Anaktuvuk and somewhat later at Tulugak. The nights spent away from families during which the men were engaged in packing (see Table 24) were to a great extent deleted from the work schedule, since these had been necessitated by the annual moves, particularly from summer to winter camps and back. Summer hunting expeditions over extensive territories generally decreased, and intensive local hunting of sheep, bear, and resident caribou was initiated. The earlier pattern of wolf pupping in spring was largely suspended, with winter trapping conducted close to home since there was a large local wolf population. These changes resulted in the years between 1952 and 1954 being very "fat" and a corresponding shift away from the "stress" pattern of summer food imports can be seen.

The seasonal conception data for the period 1950–56 is broken down into the three critical periods of change in Table 29. One can readily notice two features in these data. First is the doubling of births between the first and second periods with a sustained rate into the third period. This change in coincident with the establishment of the post office and the associated changes in mobility and settlement. Second, the shifts in conception time frequencies between the first and second periods are in direct correspondence with the shifts in male labor strategy. Increases in spring correspond to the deletion of packing time and a suspension of wolf pupping; the low frequency of summer conceptions corresponds to the expansion of summer hunting activities. Increases in fall relate to the suspension of major moves and the deletion of attendant packing time.

TABLE 29
NUMBER OF NUNAMIUT CONCEPTIONS PER SEASON, 1950–56

Years	*Spring*	*Summer*	*Fall*	*Winter*	*Total*
1950–51	0 (0.0%)	0 (0.0%)	0 (0.0%)	5 (100.0%)	5
1952–54	3 (25.0%)	1 (8.3%)	3 (25.0%)	5 (41.7%)	12
1955–56	2 (16.7%)	1 (8.3%)	4 (33.3%)	5 (41.7%)	12

During the first period the import of foods was largely restricted to the summer months, with the least conceptions occurring during this time. From 1952 to 1954 the most foods were imported in winter and spring respectively, and the least in fall. Although there is some correspondence between the periodicity of imported foods for this period, a reversal may be noticed between summer and fall, particularly important for the argument that general nutritional level affects conception periodicity and frequency. Summer stress was off, as shown by the shift in food imports and confirmed by informants' statements, yet we see the lowest conception rates during the summer months, corresponding to the high rate of male absenteeism associated with intensive mountain hunting. The gradual return to summer stress conditions began in 1954 with the growing depletion of local populations of sheep and bear as well as a decrease in the local wolf population. This was accompanied by a return to a "stress" import pattern, with most goods again coming in during the summer. Concurrently, deep ice cellars were constructed to preserve meat from the spring caribou migration, marking the change to the contemporary settlement subsistence strategy.

Settlement subsistence strategy and fertility: 1957–69. With the construction of the ice cellars both at Anaktuvuk and at the Tulugak Lake camp, summer hunting dropped off. Moves were very infrequent and generally only short distances away from the two settlements. The Nunamiut were now essentially dependent upon the two caribou migrations for year-round subsistence, facilitated by the cellars in summer and a strategy of caching meat in the field during winter. Winter trapping was continued, but extensive trapping trips were increasingly made by the "boys"—young unmarried men—rather than heads of families.

Obtaining sufficient cash through winter trapping became more difficult with the growing depletion of the local wolf population, and in the spring of 1957 a major effort was made to obtain wolf pups through expeditions largely revisiting known dens. During the following years increasingly extensive trips were made, interrupted for the spring caribou migration, normally around May 12–15. Parties of men would leave the village again after the meat was stored, sometimes not returning until early July. Most trips, however, were after the migration and before the melt, when streams were swollen and the tundra awash—generally by the beginning of June. In addition, there was a shift in the direction of developing other means of obtaining cash, with the development of a craft specialization—mask making—dating to this period. These years also marked the major jump in the amounts of imported food, as can be seen by the data summarized in Table 30.

For all ostensible purposes the Nunamiut can be considered fully seden-

TABLE 30
NUNAMIUT FOOD IMPORTS, 1959–60, 1963–64, AND 1970 (CAN-POUNDS/FAMILY/YEAR)

*Product**	1959–60	1963–64	1970
Coffee (lb.)	34.40	26.40	22.30
Tea (lb.)	19.80	13.50	12.30
Salt (lb.)	22.85	3.55	4.00
Flour (lb.)	284.00	415.30	510.00
Sugar (lb.)	330.00	258.00	187.00
Canned Milk (cn.)	127.00	174.00	198.00
Dry Milk (lb.)	1.00	0.00	0.00
Oats (lb.)	0.00	3.00	3.00
Rice (lb.)	18.80	37.50	110.00
Cocoa (cn.)	0.50	1.00	1.00
Crackers (lb.)	12.00	108.00	210.00
Baking Powder (cn.)	0.29	0.75	0.75
Baking Soda (cn.)	0.50	2.25	3.00
Onions (lb.)	0.21	4.70	5.30
Raisins (lb.)	0.00	0.75	0.75
Butter (lb.)	5.75	6.75	12.00
Cheese (lb.)	1.23	3.50	6.00
Dry Beans (lb.)	0.53	1.50	1.75
Crisco (lb.)	5.00	10.70	18.40
Pepper (cn.)	0.00	0.50	0.50
Peanut Butter (lb.)	2.00	6.00	10.00
Jam (lb.)	1.50	6.00	11.00
Potatoes (lb.)	4.00	10.00	12.00
Coca-Cola (cn.)	9.00	12.00	46.00
Kool-Aid (pkg.)	1.00	1.00	3.00
Ketchup (btl.)	1.00	3.00	7.00
Noodles (lb.)	2.40	4.50	6.50
Macaroni (lb.)	3.75	7.00	11.50
Eggs (dzn.)	0.00	1.00	1.80
Soup (cn.)	0.00	0.00	14.00
Apples-Oranges (lb.)	0.00	0.00	4.00
Bacon (lb.)	0.00	0.00	2.00
Total	888.51	1,122.15	1,434.85

* List arranged in order of appearance of items through time. Seasonal data not available.

tary from 1961 on. In 1960 two events occurred that reduced mobility to essentially zero: (1) the construction of a permanent airstrip at the village of Anaktuvuk; and (2) the construction of a resident school building. These events resulted in the moving into Anaktuvuk of families previously resident at Tulugak and, very important, the requirement that children be in school during the winter months eliminated even the limited moves to winter camps that had characterized the period 1956–60. The only remaining vestige of the previous pattern of high male mobility and absenteeism was the wolf-pupping expeditions in spring. Examination of Table 15 demonstrates nicely that for this period conceptions occurred with equal frequency during summer, fall, and winter. Spring—the season of wolf pupping—was the only season exhibiting depressed rates.

This period witnessed a number of other interesting features of Nunamiut settlement. With the permanent airstrip, public health visits and care of the sick increased remarkably, although some health care had been sporadically available since 1953. Beginning in 1964 the first major attempt by public health personnel to introduce a contraceptive program occurred with the adoption of "butterflies" (IUDs) by several Nunamiut women. The response was rapid, and by 1969 nine of the women in their reproductive years had such devices. The effects of this are seen in Figure 8 in the remarkable drop in crude birth rates for the 1965–70 interval.

ANALYSIS AND SUMMARY OF THE CASE

This case clearly demonstrates two interesting facts: (1) the Nunamiut population is characterized by marked seasonal variation in the frequency of conception; and (2) population growth among the Nunamiut approached "transitional" levels through a rise in birth rates rather than through a decrease in death rates.

In order to explain and understand these facts, attempts were made to control for as many "causal" variables as possible in the review of Nunamiut demographic history. It was found that there had been no changes in lactation duration over the period of relevant population growth, and no major changes had occurred in the attitudes or behaviors of mothers toward pregnancy. No regulation of fertility through such techniques as abortion, infanticide, or attempted contraception (until after the period of relevant population growth) could be demonstrated for the Nunamiut. Historical data on miscarriage rates indicated a decrease in miscarriages between the mobile and sedentary periods, but this was relatively small and certainly insufficient to account for the change in live birth rates.

Understanding Conception Cycling

Birth cycling is a phenomenon that has been observed by many investigators (Udry and Morris 1967; Katz 1972:365–69). The most frequently mentioned possibility to account for observed seasonality has been some factor affecting coital rates. Udry and Morris (1967) collected data on coital rates for a sample of fifty "white, mostly well-educated, premenopausal, married, husband present volunteers" and found that seasonality of conceptions as summarized for (1) the United States, 1963, (2) New York City whites, 1962–64, and (3) the highest socioeconomic quintile of Baltimore, 1952–56 was uncorrelated. Although there are obvious problems with the research design (data drawn from different populations used in comparison, inspectional methods only), the asserted lack of correlation has been taken as indicative of other factors seasonally conditioning conception variation. We will return to this conclusion shortly.

Conception Cycling and Illumination

Recently, Katz has cited research suggesting that the probability of conception is affected by levels of illumination. He appeals to Eskimo data as provocative in evaluating the effects of seasonal variations in illumination on conceptions:

> Of course, the question here is whether or not such light-dark rhythms are of significance in human populations and if they are, whether the development of artificial electric lighting over the last seventy years has had any effects upon natural light-dark cycles controlling fertility. To examine this hypothesis, approximately 2,000 north slope Alaskan Eskimo birth dates were plotted as a function of seasonal changes in light-dark cycles. . . . Although the results are preliminary, the data from 1920–1949 appear to indicate a significant biphasic curve of birthrate where conception took place at either the maximum period of darkness or maximum light (Katz 1972:367).

Katz goes on to point out that data from 1950 to 1968 document a reduction in the degree of seasonal cycling in conceptions, corresponding to the period during which "electric lighting, closed circuit television, and other devices interrupting the light-dark cycle were introduced."

Table 31 presents data from the U.S. Weather Bureau on the amount of solar radiation reaching the earth's surface at Fairbanks, Alaska, and

TABLE 31
CONCEPTION PERCENTAGES ACCORDING TO THE LIGHT-DARK CYCLE: COMPARISON OF DATA FROM KATZ AND THE NUNAMIUT STUDY

	Conception Percentages					
	Katz	*Nunamiut Data*				
Season	*(1972)*	*1882–1920*	*1935–1956*	*1957–1970*	*Light**	*and Dark† Data*
Spring	23.7	29.1	18.6	10.9	206.3	293.7
Summer	27.1	25.0	8.4	29.0	439.3	61.0
Fall	22.8	4.1	32.2	30.9	180.6	319.4
Winter	26.2	41.6	40.6	29.0	13.0	487.0

* Solar radiation in calories per square centimeter at Fairbanks, Alaska.
†Reciprocal of solar radiation using a value of 500.0 as a standard, i.e., 500.0 – cal./sq. cm. in light column.

compares the seasonal conception percentages found by Katz with those for the Nunamiut. The first conclusion to be drawn from the above comparisons is simply that the Nunamiut data are different from those on generalized Eskimo populations. This immediately points to factors other than illumination as primary conditioners. For instance, we might anticipate some reversals between high and low conception frequencies in summer and winter given Katz's argument; however, we would not expect to observe the absolute lows in summer shown in the 1935–56 data or the lows in spring in the 1957–70 data if the arguments presented by Katz were exclusively applicable to the case. We must therefore turn our attention to evaluating other variables believed relevant to the Nunamiut case.

Conception Cycling and Nutrition

Many researchers have pointed to strong supportive research indicating that suppression of ovulation is a response to dietary deficiencies in protein, calories, vitamin B, vitamin E, and certain minerals (Katz 1972:357; Zuckerman 1962:294–300). We might anticipate that a hunting-and-gathering strategy would produce a greater variance in the composition of daily meals and more prolonged and severe seasonal dietary deficiencies. For these reasons, data reported previously on game counts and particularly imported foods were collected in the hope of gaining some control over nutritional factors. One obvious fact is the increase during the period of demographic change in the quantities of imported foods. As it is possible that conception cycling may be responsive to seasonality in dietary differences, the periodicity of imports was monitored where possible. Table 32 presents available seasonal information on imports for three sequential periods between 1949 and 1957. Seasonality of conceptions and male absenteeism for these same periods are then summarized in Tables 33 and 34, respectively.

A linear regression was calculated for the relationship between the percentage of total cereals imported by season and the percentage of total conceptions occurring by season. The result was a negative correlation of moderate magnitude ($r = -.49$) described by the equation $y = 43.64$

TABLE 32
SEASONALITY OF NUNAMIUT FOOD IMPORTS, 1949–57

	Spring	*Summer*	*Fall*	*Winter*	*Total*
1949–51					
Dairy	0.0	7.7	1.2	6.4	15.3
Fruits and Vegetables	0.0	0.3	0.0	0.5	0.8
Cereals	1.4	40.9	9.0	9.3	60.6
Other	0.0	41.1	16.3	15.9	73.3
Total	1.4 (0.9%)	90.0 (60.0%)	26.5 (17.6%)	32.1 (21.4%)	150.0
1952–54					
Dairy	13.7	11.8	10.5	21.4	57.4
Fruits and Vegetables	0.0	0.0	0.0	0.0	0.0
Cereals	17.1	15.2	16.4	32.4	81.1
Other	23.2	20.4	13.2	40.7	97.5
Total	54.0 (22.8%)	47.4 (20.0%)	40.1 (16.9%)	94.5 (40.0%)	236.0
1955–57					
Dairy	11.2	20.0	3.7	14.0	48.9
Fruits and Vegetables	0.0	0.1	0.0	0.0	0.1
Cereals	32.7	69.7	13.7	9.2	125.3
Other	10.1	70.8	20.6	44.5	146.0
Total	54.0 (16.8%)	160.6 (50.1%)	38.0 (11.8%)	67.7 (21.1%)	320.3

TABLE 33
SEASONALITY OF NUNAMIUT CONCEPTIONS, 1949–57
(PERCENTAGES OF TOTAL)

Year	*Spring*	*Summer*	*Fall*	*Winter*	*Total*
1949–51	18.7	8.4	37.0	35.8	99.9
1952–54	25.0	8.3	25.0	41.6	99.9
1955–57	16.6	8.3	33.3	41.6	99.9

TABLE 34
SEASONALITY OF NUNAMIUT MALE ABSENTEEISM, 1949–57

	Spring		*Summer*		*Fall*		*Winter*		
Year	No.	%	No.	%	No.	%	No.	%	*Total*
1949–51	10.2	19.0	23.8	44.0	11.3	21.0	8.8	16.0	54.1
1952–54	3.0	13.0	16.0	70.0	1.0	4.0	3.0	13.0	23.0
1955–57	2.0	11.0	13.0	72.0	1.0	6.0	2.0	11.0	18.0

$- .740(x)$, where y is the percentage of imported cereals and x is the percentage of conceptions occurring by season. This relationship is in the opposite direction from that which would support the argument of a causal relationship between the periodicity in conceptions and the periodicity of imported foods. In short, as the seasonal quantity of imported cereal foods increases, conceptions decrease. This confirms the observations made while discussing the historical data, namely that imported foods are most common during periods of stress, when males tend to be away and conceptions are low. As a check on the possibility that there may be some time lag between possible effects on fecundity and the purchase dates of cereal foods, a second regression was calculated for paired values of conception percentages and cereal imports with the latter offset by one season. Conceptions in winter were paired with fall imports, conceptions in spring paired with winter imports, and so on. The result was a negative correlation of weak magnitude ($r = -.247$) summarized by the equation $y = 34.3 - .379(x)$, again with y the percentage of imported cereals and x the percentage of conceptions occurring by season.

The choice of cereals as the best candidate for possibly affecting fecundity was guided by previous studies of nutrition and fertility (see Nag 1962:116–17). To determine whether other types of imported foods were affecting conceptions, the noncereal imported consumables tabulated by season were regressed against seasonal percentages of conceptions. The result was a weak negative correlation ($r = -.295$) summarized by the formula $y = 34.36 - .38(x)$, where y is the percentage of noncereal imported foods and x the percentage of total conceptions by season. We may justifiably conclude that increased fecundity stemming from qualitative dietary change through imported foods is *not* causally related to the seasonal increases in conceptions noted among the Nunamiut. All comparisons exhibit a consistent *negative* or indirect pattern of correlation such that the greater the proportions of imported foods, the lower the rates of conception, while higher seasonal conception rates are coincident with minimal or low proportions of imported foods.

It should be noted that such a negative demonstration is not sufficient proof of the absence of a causal relationship since it is conceivable that the operation of other determinants may well be obscuring any lesser relationship, such as an anticipated increase in fertility with increased nutritional balance. Clearly, the importation of foods is associated with times of stress (that is, low caloric intake or periodic inadequacy of available food to meet the demands); therefore, the depressant effect of these conditions could well be masking any minor gains in fecundity in response to a more "balanced" diet.

Conception Cycling and Male Absenteeism

Table 35 summarizes the data on the number of nights spent away from a residential location by the average head of household for the years on which information was available. These data are then compared with the number of conceptions occurring by season for analogous time periods as reported in Tables 15 and 29 and summarized in Table 36.

Two facts are obvious from Table 35: (1) there has been a constant decrease in the number of nights spent away from residential locations over the period documented (note the total column); and (2) three recognizable patterns of seasonality are documented in the data. There is a very consistent internal pattern in 1935–51 of the most absenteeism in summer and the least in winter, with similar amounts in spring and fall. In the period 1952–54 a grossly similar pattern exists; however, there is a marked increase during summer and a reduction in fall. A shift to the greatest amount of absenteeism in spring occurred in 1959–70, with the

TABLE 35
SEASONAL CYCLING IN NUNAMIUT MALE ABSENTEEISM, 1935–69

Period	*Spring* Nights Away	*Spring* %	*Summer* Nights Away	*Summer* %	*Fall* Nights Away	*Fall* %	*Winter* Nights Away	*Winter* %	Total
1935–40	15	19.7	35	46.0	17	22.3	9	11.8	76
1949–51	10	18.5	24	44.4	11	20.3	9	16.6	54
1952–54	3	13.0	16	69.5	1	4.3	3	13.0	23
1959–60	12	70.5	1	5.8	2	11.7	2	11.7	17
1969	6	66.6	0	0.0	2	22.2	1	11.1	9

least in summer and minor amounts in both fall and winter. Table 36 displays the data grouped according to period for both male absenteeism and conceptions (expressed as percentages of the totals for each period).

Simple inspection of the data definitely reveals an indirect pattern of interaction such that as the percentage of nights away decreases the percentage of conceptions increases. The plotting of these data reveals that the relationship is well summarized by a straight line described by the equation $y = 31.263 - 3.11(x)$, where x is the percentage of the nights away and y is the percentage of conceptions occurring by season. The relationship is of moderate strength, with a correlation coefficient $r = -.443$. We may conclude from this analysis that seasonal male absenteeism is moderately related in an inverse manner with seasonal conception frequencies.

In order to evaluate the probability of a causal relationship, a theoretical argument based on Keyfitz's analysis (1971) of the effectiveness of population-control mechanisms has been prepared. Given a coital rate of 1.86 acts per week and an assumption of one fertile day per month, we may calculate the probability of becoming pregnant in any given month when males are present continuously as 0.266. Next we calculate the probability that a male would be present under differing levels of male absenteeism as follows:

$$1 - \frac{\text{number of absent days}}{91.25 \text{ (number of days in a season)}}.$$

The probability of conception in a given month with a given amount of male absenteeism is then simply obtained: the product of 0.266 and the

TABLE 36

NUNAMIUT MALE ABSENTEEISM AND CONCEPTION FREQUENCIES BY SEASON, 1935–70

Period	*Spring*		*Summer*		*Fall*		*Winter*	
	Nights Away	*Conceptions*	*Nights Away*	*Conceptions*	*Nights Away*	*Conceptions*	*Nights Away*	*Conceptions*
1935–50	19.1	20.0	45.0	10.0	21.3	40.0	14.2	30.0
1950–56	13.0	17.2	13.0	6.9	4.3	24.1	13.0	51.7
1957–70	68.5	10.9	2.9	29.0	16.9	30.9	11.4	29.0

value from the above equation. In order to evaluate the probability of becoming pregnant in a given season the following calculation is used:

$$1 - [1 - (0.266)\ (\text{probability of absenteeism})]^3.$$

A simulation was conducted for 1,000 women on the assumptions that (1) 500 were pregnant at the outset; (2) their pregnancies had been conceived equally across the seasons; and (3) upon becoming pregnant a woman was removed from the fecund population for seven seasons. Several five-year runs were made for the data in Table 35 for the 1935–40 period. Totals for each five-year run were then summed across the seasons and percentages calculated so that we would have a measure comparable to those presented in Table 36. The comparison of the observed and simulated percentages is summarized in Table 37.

TABLE 37
OBSERVED AND EXPECTED SEASONAL CONCEPTION PERCENTAGES FOR 1935–40 ABSENTEEISM DATA

Conceptions	*Spring*	*Summer*	*Fall*	*Winter*
Observed (%)	20.00	10.00	40.00	30.00
Simulated (%)	21.72	18.10	27.30	27.40
Differences	−1.72	−8.10	+12.70	+2.60

It is clear from this exercise that seasonal cycling of male absenteeism does have an effect on conception cycling; nevertheless, as observed in the regression analysis, it is insufficient to account for the magnitude of observed cycling. It should be cautioned that beginning with different assumptions regarding the pregnancy state of the population and altering the length of the runs will change the values obtained as simulated percentages. However, as the direction of the variability is relatively unchanged, we seem justified in discussing the residuals (differences between observed and expected values). In all cases the positive residuals are in fall and winter, with negative residuals in spring and summer; similarly, the greatest differences are between summer and fall. Returning now to our findings regarding the relationships between conception cycling and mobility, as well as the general historical data obtained on varying periods from informants, it will be recalled that we obtained a very high degree of correlation between mobility and conception cycling for the period between 1898 and 1920 ($r = -.93$). It was pointed out in our discussion of these years that there was a correspondence between mobility and the security of the group with respect to food stores during the period of low caribou abundance. In addition, male absenteeism was associated with residential mobility since males were frequently away in search of game and other foods, with success generally resulting in a move. In contrast, it was shown that for the period 1934–50 stress was accommodated by importation of food and intensified hunting activities resulting in increased male absenteeism. In light of these insights the distribution of residuals (Table 37) is most interesting in that negative values were obtained for spring and summer, the seasons when subsistence security was at its lowest for the Nunamiut from 1935 through 1940. Foods imported then were almost exclusively available during the late spring and summer. We suggest therefore that in addition to male absenteeism as a demonstrated factor in conceptual cycling the general nutritional state of the group as it varied seasonally also had an effect. During periods of stress (lower availability of food) probabilities of fertilization were depressed accordingly. This view is supported by those studies previously mentioned (i.e., Katz 1972; Zuckerman 1962) that demonstrate the suppression of ovulation in response to dietary deficiencies in protein, calories, vitamin B, vitamin E, and certain minerals. We might then expect a coupling of the effects of dietary deficiencies and male absenteeism in societies practicing a logistical strategy—male producers covering extensive areas but returning to a residential camp. Such coupling would tend to move away from an isomorphic or direct proportional relationship as a direct function of the degree that males are exploiting the environment for items other than consumable foods (e.g., in the Nunamiut case trapping for furs, etc., in order to participate in an exchange economy).

As a test of the probability of the above conditions, data on seasonality of food importation, male absenteeism, and seasonal variability in conceptions for the period 1949–57—the documented period during which a subsistence transition was taking place and food was being imported when possible in response to stress—were inspected for interaction by a multiple regression analysis in which conception cycling was the dependent variable. The result was an increase in the measured interaction over and above that observed for male absenteeism alone. It will be recalled that we obtained a value of $r = -.44$ for the relationship between conception cycling and male absenteeism. When seasonal data on quantities of food imports are added in a multiple regression, we obtain a multiple correlation coefficient of $r = .73$, indicating a relatively high order of interaction. The relationship is summarized by the equation $Y = 35.25 - .098(X) - 34.94(Z)$, where X equals the per family percentage of imported foods and Z the seasonal percentage of male absenteeism. Imported food is used as a measure of nutritional stress, justified by the informants' opinions regarding the motives for food importation during this period. Insofar as this equation is justified, we may conclude that the major determinants of seasonal conception cycling among the Nunamiut were (1) seasonal variability in male absenteeism and (2) seasonal variations in dietary deficiencies, particularly calories. We might suggest that the coupling of these fertility depressants would most likely occur during spring and summer and least likely occur during fall and winter. These expectations are met exactly in the overall pattern of conception cycling observed for the entire period of demographic history (see summary totals in Table 17). There were fewest conceptions during spring and summer, most during fall and winter.

Having isolated at least two conditions that appear responsible for some of the properties of the Nunamiut data, we may now return to Katz's suggestion that seasonal cycling in the north is related to illumination cycling. A multiple regression was calculated for measuring the interaction between (1) male absenteeism (Table 34), (2) seasonal nutritional stress as measured by seasonal variations in food importation (Table 32), and (3) seasonal variations in darkness (Table 31). The dependent variable was, of course, conception variability by season for the years summarized in Table 33. The result of this analysis is a correlation coefficient of $r = .92$, a very high measure of interaction among the independent variables in accounting for variability in the dependent variable. The relationships are summarized by the equation $Y = 7254.5 + .084(X) - 14.43(Z) + 6.46(W)$, where X is seasonality of imported food, Z our illumination measure, and W the seasonal percentage of male absenteeism.

Several points are of interest here. By adding data on illumination to the variables previously analyzed, we increase the value of r from .73 to .93, clearly indicating that there is some possible determinant effect on conception cycling as monitored by illumination. However, our results show a positive relationship between increased darkness and conception frequency, and no such comparable relationship, as suggested by Katz, for increased fecundity associated with periods of high light intensity. The argument presented by Katz that increased use of artificial light would tend to increase fecundity, or somehow reduce conception cycling, therefore is not supported by this analysis. It is our guess that some interaction between decreased light and increased fecundity may be operating as suggested by Katz, but other uncontrolled variables are operating to increase summer conceptions in his grouped data from the north. Without knowing something of the locations from which his data were drawn, it would be almost impossible to pinpoint the variables operative. Nevertheless, the increase in the correlation coefficient when a measure of darkness is included in a multiple correlation is supportive of the possibility that illumination may affect fecundity.

In summary, we have demonstrated impressive relationships between conception cycles and male absenteeism, an indirect measure of nutritional stress, and illumination. These three variables seem sufficient to account for the seasonal variations in conceptions noted among the Nunamiut.

Understanding Temporal Trends in Fertility

As previously suggested, it appeared reasonable to investigate those variables possibly affecting conception cycling for their possible roles in the striking temporal changes in fertility noted for the Nunamiut. Since no change could be anticipated in the illumination patterning at Anaktuvuk, we may consider this variable constant through time and therefore of no utility for understanding temporal variations. On the other hand, we might well expect changes in male absenteeism, periodicity of dietary stress, and the qualitative character of diet to be potential determinants of change.

Temporal trends of fertility and male absenteeism. It is not unreasonable to suspect that the factors contributing to marked seasonality in conceptions might equally contribute to changes in overall fertility. In order to evaluate this possibility, the summary of total nights away per year for an average household head (Table 35: total column) and fertility as measured by mother-child ratios (Table 13) are summarized together in Table 38. It should be noted that data on fertility are summarized by five-year intervals, while data on male absenteeism are available for shorter intervals or single years. Appropriate years are matched in Table 38 with relevant five-year intervals.

TABLE 38
COMPARISON OF NUNAMIUT MALE ABSENTEEISM RATES AND MOTHER-CHILD RATIOS

Period	*Mean Nights Away by Household Head/Yr.*	*Effective Mother-Child Ratio/1,000 Mothers*
1935–40	76	184.17
1949–51	54	245.40
1952–54	23	301.50
1959–60	17	315.41
1969	9	359.92

A linear regression was calculated for the paired values, with the result that a strong negative relationship ($r = -.986$) was demonstrated. The formula for the best linear fit of these data is $Y = 366.37 - 2.38(X)$. In this case Y is the effective mother-child ratio and X the mean nights away per year. This astonishingly high-order relationship strongly supports the argument that there is some determined interaction between the two variables, and it is tempting to suggest a causal relationship. Nevertheless, since a simple mechanical effect of male absenteeism on coital rates is implied, it is possible to evaluate the effectiveness of male absenteeism as a fertility depressor, assumed to have the same contraceptive effect as a random decrease in the frequency of coitus. To analyze its effectiveness as a population-control mechanism, arguments presented by Keyfitz (1971:111–13) will be used, some aspects of which will be employed in a simulation of the effects of male absenteeism on fertility.

The data employed in the study are the necessary rates computed from the vital data already presented for the Nunamiut case. From informant data, the weekly rate of copulation was obtained and converted into a probability statement for the likelihood of coitus on a given day. These probabilities were computed for zero male absenteeism (0.266) and for the greatest degree of male absenteeism (76 nights per year) indicated in the Nunamiut material (0.211). If we assume that this probability remains constant throughout the month and that a woman has a single fertile day each month, then this figure becomes the probability of conception in a given month. This probability has the following expected value (Keyfitz 1971:113), X being a random variable equal to the number of months until pregnancy, p the probability of conception in any given month:

$$E[X] = \sum_{i=1}^{400} (i)(p)(1-p)^{i-1} = 1/p.$$

The upper limit of 400 in this equation was chosen because women have approximately this many ovulations in their reproductive lifetimes. A more theoretical consideration would have run the sum from 1 to infinity.

In these data the expected time until pregnancy was 4.808 months for the group with male absenteeism (76 days per year) and 4.425 months for the group with no male absenteeism. The variance of this random variable (X and p as before) is

$$V[X] = E[X^2] - (E[X])^2$$

$$= \left[\sum_{i=1}^{400} [(i^2)(p)(1-p)^{i-1}]\right] - (1/p)^2.$$

The value for the males-absent model is $V[X] = 18.306$, for the males-not-absent model $V[X] = 15.154$.

If we allow 9 months for the gestation period and 21.2 months for the postpartum sterile period—a total of 645 days—we have the production of a child expected every 780 and 769 days with the males-absent and males-not-absent models, respectively. In other words, if we consider a cohort of 50 women over a period of 10 years in which every conception results in the birth of a child, the expected number of children produced would be 234.09 for the group with males absent and 237.35 for the group with males not absent.

As a means of approximating the variance of this figure, a computer simulation was designed employing the rates previously mentioned. At the beginning of each run, a random-number generator assigned women to a random day in the 28-day cycle, with the program checking each woman every day for 3,650 days. A woman became pregnant if her fertile day coincided with an act of intercourse. She then went through a 645-day gestation/postpartum sterile period; the child produced was added to a running total for all women. It should be borne in mind that no women were started in the gestational or postpartum sterile condition. At the end of a given run the total number of births for a cohort was printed out. Six runs were made for both the males-absent and males-not-absent models (Table 39). In spite of the differences between observed and expected values, both of the theoretical population means lay well

TABLE 39
NUMBER OF CHILDREN* PRODUCED IN A SIMULATION OF FERTILITY FOR POPULATIONS OF WOMEN WITH HUSBANDS ABSENT AND HUSBANDS NOT ABSENT

Run No.		*With Absenteeism*	*Without Absenteeism*
1		239	246
2		239	247
3		340	246
4		241	248
5		235	244
6		237	249
$\overline{X}$	=	238.50	246.70
s^2	=	23.50	14.00
s	=	4.85	3.74

* The number of births for each run exceeds the expected number in all cases as this is an artifact of the initial conditions, i.e., all women started as nonpregnant and non-lactating. This difference should not affect the variance of the sets; they should provide a reliable variance estimate.

within the first standard deviation of each other, as shown in Table 40. The observed overlapping is evidence for the lack of a statistically meaningful difference in the data from which the various vital statistics were derived.

It is difficult to assess the significance of the difference in expected values for the two groups. We would expect to observe a difference of 0.326 births per year between the two populations. If we take the difference in terms of births per 1,000 fecund women, this is a difference of 6.52 per year. An effect of this order, although possibly significant, would be swamped by random variation in a cohort of fifty women.

TABLE 40
VARIANCE IN THE POPULATIONS OF WOMEN WITH HUSBANDS ABSENT AND HUSBANDS NOT ABSENT

Population	*Theoretical Mean*	*Standard Deviation*	*Range of First Standard Deviation*
With Absenteeism	234.09	4.85	229.24–238.94
Without Absenteeism	237.35	3.74	233.61–241.09

There is both an expected "theoretical" difference and an observed difference monitoring the effects of the two observed extremes in male absenteeism. We may anticipate that in the concrete world even these minor differences may well be depressed somewhat by the relatively high variance in the observed rates. Additionally, the simulation does not take into account expected variation in the gestation or postpartum sterile periods.

Although a theoretical effect of male absenteeism on realized fertility has been demonstrated, the small practical differences observed demand that we reject the temptation to ascribe primary causal significance to the astonishingly high correlation observed between decreasing male absenteeism and increasing fertility as monitored by mother-child ratios through time. Decreasing male absenteeism would have an effect on fertility in the correct direction, but this effect is insufficient to account for the observed changes among the Nunamiut during the periods under study.

Temporal trends in the use of nonnative foods and fertility. There have been many studies reporting a relationship between nutritional factors and fertility, the most ambitious by far claiming a negative causal relationship between fertility and animal protein consumption. DeCastro (1952:63–69) has attempted to support this view through a demonstration of an inverse relationship between crude birth rate and mean daily consumption of animal protein, using data from fourteen nations that are distributed in near-perfect inverse relationships. Certainly DeCastro's data are biased, and his argument has been challenged by selecting a different sample (Nag 1962:117, 207). In the absence of controls on additional variables that might be affecting fertility, it is nearly impossible to evaluate DeCastro's claims. His arguments therefore remain a provocative case with a minimum of supporting research in which laboratory rats have shown decreases in fertility correlated with increases in animal protein in their diet (Slonaker 1928:532).

As far as the Nunamiut are concerned, a likely candidate for possible dietary deficiency is vitamin E, found mostly in leafy vegetables, cereals, vegetable oils, and wheat germ oil (Gangulee 1939:55). Some experimental work has indicated that vitamin E is essential to normal spermatogenesis (Hotchkiss 1944), and we might well anticipate such a deficiency in the Nunamiut diet. Imported foods, particularly cereal products and vegetable oil, could be expected to overcome any vitamin E deficiency and thereby contribute to increased fertility. For these reasons we have separated cereal products and vegetable oils from other imported foods and tabulated for comparison this class of imports against the others and the imported foods as a whole. These data are presented in Table 41, together with the matching mother-child ratios calculated from Table 13 for the time periods for which imported food data are available.

TABLE 41
COMPARISONS OF NUNAMIUT CEREAL AND NONCEREAL FOOD IMPORTS AND MOTHER-CHILD RATIOS

Period	*Cereal (cn.-lb.)*	*Other*	*Total*	*Mother-Child Ratio*
1949–51	60.6	89.9	150.5	246.9
1952–54	81.1	154.9	236.0	301.5
1955–57	125.3	194.7	320.0	306.6
1959–60	326.4	541.9	868.3	315.4
1963–64	589.8	532.4	1,122.2	324.2
1970	871.7	362.2	1,233.9	352.9

Linear regressions were calculated summarizing the relationships between cereal imports and mother-child ratios. A strong positive correlation was observed ($r = .819$), which is described by the equation $Y = 277.99 + .0873(X)$, where Y is the mother-child ratio and X the mean family importation of cereals per year expressed in can-pounds. It should be clear that no strong direct relationship exists between other foods (mostly sugar, coffee, and tea) and the mother-child ratio. This means that any correlation between total imports and the ratio is being carried primarily by the strong relationship demonstrated between cereal products and the fertility measure. As expected, a linear regression between imports of noncereal foods and mother-child ratios yields a moderate correlation ($r = .65$) summarized by the equation $Y = 271.578 + .116(X)$, with X and Y the same as above.

We conclude that there is a possible causal relationship between increased consumption of cereal products and vegetable oils (sources of vitamin E) and realized fertility among the Nunamiut.

Summary. Three measured interactions have been isolated that would appear to have been contributory to the observed increases in fertility. There was a decrease in the wastage rate from 13.7 percent of known conceptions prior to sedentism to 6.4 percent during the sedentary period.

This would mean that given a mean crude birth rate of 27.2/1,000 during the presedentary period and one of 45.7/1,000 after sedentism and before the effects of contraceptives, the rates would have been 31.5 and 48.4/1,000, respectively, in the absence of miscarriage. Certainly some of the increase in fertility is accounted for here, but we are unable to specify the causes of differential stillbirth or miscarriage rates. The effects of male absenteeism indicate that a difference in the mother-child ratio of 6.52 births/1,000 mothers would be expected between the maximum male absenteeism prior to sedentism and the lack of absenteeism at the end of the sedentation process. This would suggest an increase of only 1.13/1,000 in the crude birth rate given the population structure of the Nunamiut, leaving an unaccounted-for difference of 16.8/1,000. Suggestions from the analysis of conception cycling isolate seasonal variations in caloric intake as possibly affecting fecundity, and there are good indications that such seasonal variations have diminished with sedentism. Similarly, there is a demonstrable relationship between increasing carbohydrate intake in the diet and fertility.

Based on the information currently available, it would appear that miscarriages account for 6.4 percent of the difference between pre and postsedentary crude birth rates, changes in the pattern of male absenteeism account for 6.1 percent, and an overwhelming 87.5 percent of the contrast is apparently to be attributed to changes in diet (related both to reductions in seasonal variance of caloric intake and increases in the carbohydrate proportion of the diet). This generalization assumes, of course, that we have monitored all potential determinants. It must be cautioned that differences in miscarriage rates may be responding to the same determinants as fecundity; in this case a greater proportion of the difference would accrue to dietary differences.

Comparing the Two Analyses

Male absenteeism, seasonal variance in caloric intake, and some effects of seasonal variations in illumination were isolated as determinants of the marked conception cycling observed. While important in conditioning cycling in the short run, illumination must be considered constant in viewing the contrasts in Nunamiut fertility through time. As shown above, the effects of male absenteeism, while in the correct direction, are minimal in accounting for the magnitude of change observed. Similarly, miscarriage-stillbirth changes, while demonstrable, may be responding to the same determinants as fecundity. We are left with the impression that the overwhelming determinants of the change were dietary—increased carbohydrate consumption and increased stability in the yearly caloric intake.

EVALUATING THE CASE AND IMPLICATIONS BEYOND

The bearing of this case on more general problems of the relationship between sedentism and fertility is only as great as the warrant that the case is not unique. It could be reasonably argued that we are dealing with a small breeding population, in which fluctuations in birth rate can be expected to vary stochastically. Stated another way, this case may be just a coincidence, with no meaningful relationships obtaining that might be seen as components of a general set of processual relationships. We admit that this is a possibility but feel a strong case can be made that Nunamiut demographic history is not unique and as such is an example of more widespread determinant processes in operation.

Early observers of Eskimo populations almost always commented on the "low fertility of the women" (Armstrong 1857:195; Nelson 1899:29; Petroff 1884:127; Murdoch 1892:38–39; and Ray 1885:44). Such observations were commonly interpreted as racist, and later observers felt called upon to challenge the view in defense of the "Eskimo race." Weyer (1962: 124–226) and Birket-Smith (1959:45) both point out that earlier observers were not basing their estimates of fertility on actual birth statistics but rather on the number of living children per mother, which would of course be affected by the death rates. Birket-Smith cites relatively modern statistics from Greenland demonstrating a high birth rate as argument against the generalization that "Eskimo women were less fertile than other races."

Taken out of a racist context and viewed for what they were—impressions formed before the impact of Euro-American culture on Eskimo populations—earlier observers' statements would certainly be compatible with our early-period data from the Nunamiut. Low fertility associated with a heavy meat diet, high mobility, and high degree of male absenteeism in the context of a logistical strategy in which males are the primary producers of food are conditions common to most Eskimo groups. Recent data on Eskimo demography are relevant almost exclusively to sedentary

Eskimo populations participating in a broader economy, which includes imported foods. A crude birth rate approaching 50/1,000 is indicated from the village of Wainwright (Milan 1970:30); a rate of 53/1,000 is reported from the Bethel area of Alaska (Maynard 1967). These figures are only slightly higher than the maximum achieved at Anaktuvuk Village prior to the introduction of contraceptives.

Support for the contention that the Nunamiut case is not unique is also provided by regional statistics from the area around Baker Lake in Canada, where most of the once-mobile Caribou Eskimo are currently concentrated in sedentary villages. The data available refer to the region rather than any one settlement; hence for the periods reported both sedentary and mobile populations are included. Nevertheless, there has been a marked increase in the number of sedentary Eskimos over the period for which statistics are available. The birth rates for this area are: 1944–48, 29.7/1,000; 1949–53, 47.6/1,000; and 1954–58, 50.0/1,000 (Vallee 1967:13). The near doubling in birth rate between the 1944–48 and 1949–53 intervals corresponds identically to the period when there was a marked shift from a mobile to a settled way of life (Vallee 1967:17–18).

In recent years, generally since the end of World War II, it has been noted that the population in the north is growing at phenomenal rates. This is a trend documented at many locations:

> In Greenland, population is labelled the number one problem. In Canada, the Northwest Territories Council recently passed a resolution calling for an intensive program to make birth control information and appliances freely available in the Territories, and a medical study recently conducted in the East Arctic warns of the need for immediate planning to cope with the possible consequences of one of the highest rates of population growth the world has ever known (Freeman 1971:220).

In almost all cases the growth in population is associated with increased sedentism, illustrated by data for the Igloolik region of the Northwest Territories shown in Table 42.

Another interesting observation clearly supportive of the position that the Nunamiut are not unique comes from the work of a medical doctor, a longtime resident of the Arctic:

> As something of a diversion while I was in Baffin Island in the mid-1950's, I made calculations that indicated that the intervals between siblings shrank in direct relation to the mileage of the family from

TABLE 42
RECENT DEMOGRAPHIC CHANGES IN THE IGLOOLIK REGION, N.W.T.*

	1961	1968
Population size	527	735
Percentage of population living in camps	74.2	18.7
Percentage of population aged 16 years or less	34.5	55.9
Number of dependents per male aged 16 years or more	3.0	4.2

* Taken from Freeman (1971:221).

> the trading posts. The shorter the distance, the more frequently they had children. The effect of rapid development of communications and the consequent movement of former camp Eskimos into large settlements is reflected in the more than 50 percent jump in the Eskimo birth rate in the Northwest Territories alone, and the increase from less than 40 births per 1000 in the mid 1950's to an astonishing 64/1000 ten years later. In fact, it is seldom realized that in the last 20 years the Eskimo's population explosion has been as great or greater than that which has occurred in any developing nation in the world. This is due less to the reduction in infant mortality than to the jump in birth rate. It is far more intense for the urbanized Eskimo than for those who still live in the scattered hunting camps (Schaefer 1971:16).

The pattern appears clear: nonacculturated Eskimo populations are consistently reported to be characterized by low fertility and low mortality. The data presented appear to have meaning beyond the Nunamiut themselves and serve as a constructive "challenge" to commonly held generalizations regarding the demographic character of the "primitive world." Changes from the postulated demographic state of "primitive societies" are almost always viewed in the context of a "theory of demographic transition" in which societies marked by a high degree of local self-sufficiency are considered to be characterized by high death rates and correspondingly high birth rates. This is a generalized view of the preindustrial world projected onto the past. The argument goes on that "transitional conditions" are brought about by decreasing death rates in response to increasing medical aid, dietary change, and so forth. The high fertility rates, however, are not as responsive and become the driving force resulting in rapid increases in population numbers. The arguments of "transition" are essentially economic in character and based on a poorly founded set of physiological assumptions. For instance, it is generally thought that increases in population "naturally" result in sedentism or increased social aggregation and "naturally" bring about trends toward "modernity," "urbanism," and all the attendant problems of the modern social world.

It is suggested that the Nunamiut data, viewed in the context of widespread demographic changes among Eskimo populations in general, stand as a challenge to both the "theory of transition" and the accompanying simplistic notions of "primitive demography." Given the insight into possible sources of determinancy operative in modifying fertility in the Nunamiut case, we will attempt to explore briefly some provocative lines of argument that may be of interest to anthropologists. We hope that persons concerned with evaluating the role of demographic factors as determinants of culture change as well as ideas relating to more specific details of man's adaptive past will find some suggestions warranting reflection and research.

Implications

The Nunamiut case demonstrates several interesting facts: (1) population growth occurred coincidentally with sedentism, approaching "transitional" levels through a rise in the birth rate rather than the "normal" decrease in the death rate; (2) this population is characterized by marked seasonal variations in frequencies of conceptions; and (3) changes in the pattern of conception seasonality characterized the period of transition to sedentism. Taking those factors demonstrated as or suspected of being major determinants of fertility variations in the Nunamiut case and viewing them in their probable global patterning, we may gain some appreciation of the potential complexity of demographic factors as explanatory dimensions for much cultural and historical variation.

1. We have demonstrated a minor but significant effect on fertility of differential male absenteeism. Viewing the latter in global terms among hunters and gatherers, we find that male absenteeism is correlated with the degree of productive-nonproductive differentiation in the sexual division of labor. We further find that this division is patterned quite regularly geographically such that the farther one moves away from the equator the greater the probability that males are the primary producers of food (Binford n.d.). We might then expect decreasing fertility to be

similarly patterned, less in the polar regions and greater in equatorial regions, other things being equal.

2. We have demonstrated a strong relationship between seasonality of conception and an indirect measure of general nutritional state, probably seasonal variations in simple caloric intake. We can expect differences in seasonality and overall subsistence security to vary directly with the magnitude of seasonal variability in both rainfall and solar radiation. Thus depressant effects on realized fertility would vary concomitantly with the increasing magnitude of seasonal oscillations in the gross environment, other things being equal (e.g., storage potential and effectiveness). This means that, as in the previous case, fertility can be expected to be generally lower in areas more distant from the equator, other things being equal.

3. We have demonstrated an interaction between the levels of protein and carbohydrate in the diet, such that as carbohydrate consumption increases relative to protein consumption, fertility increases. The specific agents in this interaction are unknown, but vitamin E seems to be a good candidate. There are many reasons to expect a regular reduction in the carbohydrate component of the diet as one moves farther from the equator (see Lee 1968). Therefore, other things being equal, we can anticipate a depressant effect on fertility as the distance from the equator increases.

All of these predicted trends are unrelentingly in the same direction. Other things being equal, we can expect reduced fertility as a function of increase in distance from the equator. (Although a possible interaction was noted between conception cycling and illumination, we are uncomfortable with making generalizations about those relationships. If taken at face value, an increase in fertility in northern latitudes would be implied.)

Other Things Are Not Always Equal

In the Nunamiut case certain conditions suspected of having demographic effects were constant and therefore not considered in our discussion (duration of lactation, absence of infanticide, abortion, contraception, etc.). Clearly, differences in these factors are variable characteristics found in the "primitive" world. Lee (1972) has presented an elegant argument relating the work load of mothers in transporting children on their daily subsistence rounds to the advantage of having children at relatively wide birth intervals. He has pinpointed the agent responsible for widely spaced birth intervals among the Bushmen as the long period of lactation, while acknowledging the practice of infanticide as an alternative means of achieving the same end. It is acknowledged that birth spacing is another measure of fertility, high overall fertility associated with short spacing and low fertility with wide spacing. Lee noted that there would be an obvious interaction between the mobility of females on a day-to-day basis—both in terms of their subsistence activities and their overall seasonal movements from place to place—and the variability in birth spacing. Generalizing this argument: (1) as the female contribution to diet in the form of gathered foods increases among hunter-gatherer populations, we would expect increases in either duration of lactation or infanticide; and (2) as overall mobility decreases (i.e., as sedentism increases), decreasing durations of lactation and/or infanticide would occur, other things being equal, with resulting increases in fertility.

Viewing these propositions in a global and historical context, certain distributional patterns become obvious. It is demonstrable that male-female division of labor is distributed in such a way that as one moves away from the equator the female contribution to the diet decreases relative to that of males. We would therefore expect that fertility would increase geographically as a function of this patterning, with higher fertility in areas farther from the equator. Similarly, it is shown that as the distance from the equator increases, the absolute mobility as measured in numbers of residential camps occupied per year decreases. This implies an expected distribution of increasing fertility with increased distance from the equator.

It is clear, given the arguments presented thus far concerning male absenteeism, variations in caloric intake, and the proportion of the diet represented by carbohydrates, that the anticipated effects tend to depress the levels of fertility as one moves away from equatorial regions. On the other hand, the character of the relationships between female mobility and the reduction of fertility through duration of lactation and/or infanticide tends to suggest an inverse set of conditions, that is, that fertility would be depressed in equatorial settings and higher in polar areas. These patterns of opposite directionality in the effects of the variables indicate that there will always be some aspects of an equilibrium relationship in operation. Under certain conditions the factors favoring increases in fertility will be canceled out by conditions favoring the opposite results. Conversely, there are conditions under which either a positive or negative coupling could occur, and we might see drastic increases in fertility or similarly drastic decreases. We might anticipate that the varying interactions between the variables isolated thus far would have predictable geographical locations, given the arguments on anticipated geographical patterning.

Let us return now to one of our original propositions, namely, that population growth would be a by-product of sedentism. It can be argued that sedentism is one pole of a variable that might be called the relative extension of the effective exploitative space. Simply stated, the question is, How much land is used to support a given number of people? For nonindustrial, nontrading systems sedentism represents the maximum contraction of a population into a minimum of exploitative space; increases in the number of residential moves per year can generally be expected to indicate a use of a greater exploitative area. (It is recognized that this is not literally true since scheduling and nucleation of spatially differentiated resources are not being considered, and these are known to affect the number of residential moves independently of the total amount of land covered in a seasonal round.) Since we are concerned with sedentism and not the degree of mobility per se, we feel confident in arguing that trends toward increasing sedentism from whatever prior condition of mobility do in fact represent trends toward decreasing effective resource space. Thus, there is an inevitable correlation between sedentism and effective population density.

In any environment there is a direct relationship between the frequency of organisms of different body sizes and the size of the spatial unit observed. Similarly, there is an increasing differential between the amounts of biomass represented by animals and plants as one views spatial units of decreasing sizes. Therefore, as human groups make use of smaller and smaller effective exploitative areas, there will be an inevitable shift away from the exploitation of large animals in favor of smaller and smaller forms; this will be coupled with a shift to increasing use of plants, other things being equal. These expectations mean that there will be an inevitable shift in the protein/carbohydrate proportions in the diet favoring increased carbohydrate intake. As has been seen, these conditions are those that have probably caused the drastic increases in fertility among the Nunamiut, as well as among Eskimo groups all across the north. A further effect of this movement down the body-size chain of any environment and the increased use of plants would be decreased male absenteeism, a condition also favoring increased fertility.

Working in the opposite direction might be effects resulting from increased participation of females in the food-procurement process as plants and small animals play a growing role in the diet. Under these conditions, we would expect a decrease in fertility in response to increased durations of lactation or infanticide to ensure wider birth spacing as the daily mobility of females increased. Long-term trends of relatively slow rates of population increase would then occur, coupled with long-term trends in increased use of plant foods, decreased mobility, and increased innovations, such as agriculture, insuring more localized production.

In this context, another provocative suggestion made by Lee may be of importance: the duration of lactation is responsive to the roughage element of the diet. Stated another way, the softer the foods, the greater the probability that children will be fed by means other than the breast at an earlier maturational period. If true, this implies that the methods of food preparation may have an indirect effect on fertility. The most common method of homogenizing and softening food is boiling; thus, other things being equal, as boiling increases as a means of food preparation, there will be a responsive increase in fertility as a result of a decreasing duration of sustained breast feeding. Although it is recognized that boiling may be practiced in the absence of ceramics, most anthropologists would agree that the appearance of ceramics and subsequent increases in its use are probably good indicators of an increase in boiled foods in the diet. If correct, this leads us to the conclusion that as the use of ceramic containers increases, we may expect some increase in fertility through decreased periods of lactation and an accompanying decrease in birth spacing.

Ceramics is commonly added to the archaeological assemblage in the context of sedentism and is demonstrably associated with a diet characterized by small food packages and the use of stored foods. Although not well understood, the appearance of ceramics, the implied increase in the consumption of boiled foods, and trends in sedentism are commonly linked. In situations with increased consumption of boiled foods linked to increasing intensification of female labor in food procurement, the depressant effects of the latter might be prevented through increased division of labor with respect to child care. Namely, with boiled foods an elderly woman or man could feed children in the absence of their mothers, therefore obviating the disadvantages of having children closely spaced and of necessity with the mother at all times. Thus, other things being equal, we might expect increased rates of population growth in response to increased realized fertility to follow the adoption of ceramics and attendant increases in boiled foods, even with increased female participation in food-procurement activities.

Under certain conditions a shift of male labor into food procurement from plants might be anticipated. When and if this happened, a rapid increase in fertility would occur, along with a major set of density-dependent feedback relationships conditioning rapid culture change.

It may be generalized, therefore, that sedentism associated with male-intensive labor will be marked by rapid and explosive population growth, whereas that associated with female-intensive labor will produce slow and gradual population growth with long-term rates of culture change. The former conditions seem to obtain in cases of northern maritime sedentism, Upper Paleolithic sedentism as seen in some Magdelanian settlements in Europe, and at locations such as Doni Vestonecie in central Europe. Sedentism in these settings seems to be a response to the nucleation of highly productive resources coupled with a storage potential. Under such conditions there would be vast contrasts within a region among the levels of sedentism achieved and cyclical variability in both the levels of sedentism and periodicity of population growth and decline. Similar effects are achieved when men enter the argricultural labor force. However, under these conditions this would be a response to the regional packing of human populations, with a more sustained population growth and increasing problems arising from density-dependent relationships between the number of consumers and the productive means: in short, rapid and sustained culture change.

The latter situation usually occurs in arid-semiarid and forested environments. The increased intake of carbohydrates coupled with intensification of female roles in food procurement results in slower, long-term historical trends, increased use of plants, increases in regional population, and the density-dependent response of decreasingly effective resource space. This leads to sedentism and the associated techniques for ensuring sufficient food from a very limited amount of space—in short, agriculture. Such trends, as studies from a number of semiarid areas have indicated, are frequently followed by a second set of changes in which men take over agricultural tasks and we see a rapid burst of population growth.

We do not intend to expand this discussion to the provocative question of the origins of agriculture, although the reader should by now appreciate that such a discussion might be very profitable. That will come in a later treatment where the character of environmental variability is considered in some detail as it interacts with human adaptations to condition some of the global patterns of variability generalized earlier (Binford n.d.). What is being suggested, however, is that strategy changes among hunters and gatherers, in both labor organization and diet, initiated demographic changes that set up the selective conditions for favoring new productive means. Contrary to earlier arguments, it appears unlikely that agriculture occasioned a major change in carbohydrate intake; it represents instead a new means of production for already important plant materials. The demographic changes arising from fertility variability in response to increasing carbohydrates and labor changes in a density-dependent context near the close of the Pleistocene were the driving forces making new productive means of positive adaptive advantage.

Let us turn our attention for a moment to a brief consideration of mortality and a few additional suggestions regarding the effects of labor and/or technological changes on realized fertility levels. Putting the arguments made thus far in the context of the other dimension of vital analysis, mortality expectations, Dunn (1968) suggests in a provocative survey of hunter-gatherer data that mortality from both infectious and parasitic diseases will vary with the complexity and diversity of the ecosystem. Such complexity is demonstrably graded from high to low as one moves farther from the equator. Therefore, other things being equal, mortality levels will be distributed from high to low as the distance from the equator increases.

Dunn further argues that mortality from accidental conditions is variable but suggests that there may be some relationship between accidental death rates and the "constancy," or seasonal variation, of the environment (Dunn 1968:224). Thus accidental mortality would increase with the distance from the equator. Data recently reported on the Eskimo of the Baker Lake area (Vallee 1967:15) show that 23.9 percent of recorded deaths occurred from starvation, lightning, drowning, freezing, and other results of exposure. These data certainly contrast with the comments of Turnbull (1965) on the low incidence of accidental injuries and deaths among the Mbuti Pygmies. Since deaths from infectious diseases are almost always greater in any body of statistics than those from accidents, we may expect that this reversal would only depress the effects of disease-caused variations and that mortality could still be expected to pattern globally with high tropical rates and low polar rates.

The overall expectations are that tropical areas will be characterized by high fertility and high mortality levels, while low fertility and low mortality will characterize areas more distant from the equator. In the absence of medical means for reducing death rates, we can expect more variation in rates and historical patterns of population growth and decline in areas farther from the equator. This expectation is justified by pointing to the subtle responses of the birth rate to changes in diet, character of the labor organization, and perhaps technology, such as in storage capacities ensuring a more equitable seasonal supply of food. More cultural innovations would also be anticipated, occurring in direct response to increases in population in nonequatorial zones. These expectations are warranted by the observation that changes in birth rates alter the age structure of a population, while changes in death rates generally have no such effect:

> The effect of fertility . . . on the age distribution is clearest when a population continuously subject to high fertility is compared with one continuously subject to low fertility. The high-fertility population has a larger proportion of children relative to adults of parental age as a direct consequence of greater frequency of births. . . . Populations . . . can get older or younger. They get older primarily as a result of declining fertility, and younger primarily as a result of rising fertility (Coale 1956:48–52).

When the age structure of a population changes, there is a change in the relationship between the numbers of adult producers and subadult dependents such that any given producer may, in effect, have more persons dependent upon him for subsistence. This places a stress directly on him that would favor increases in his total productivity. It is in this context that technological innovations leading to increases in productive efficiency will be most advantageous and recognizable. On the other hand, changes in mortality do not have nearly the structural effects that changes in fertility have. Mortality may be distributed through all age segments of the population; an overall change in mortality figures in no way ensures a change in age structure of the population, whereas in the case of fertility all effects are in the form of added infants. Thus we may envision a population growing by reduced mortality without any marked change in the number of dependents that any one producer might have to supply. In short, changes in mortality may well result in changing relationships between components of a population without ever making direct demands for increased production on the part of a given producer. Competition and increasing specifications of restricted access of certain producers to locations of production is the more likely response to population growth resulting from decreasing mortality.

Areas experiencing exceedingly slow rates of population growth may exhibit a pattern of change in response to increasing population analogous to that suggested for changes resulting from reductions of mortality. Population could grow over long periods of time in response to a minor differential between fertility and mortality rates. If this differential remained relatively constant, no effects of age-structural changes would be felt; nevertheless, after long periods of time some pressure from increasing densities could be experienced. Under the latter conditions more competitive social means might well be selected for increasing production rather than direct technological means. Given our expectations that equatorial zones would be characterized by high fertility and high mortality, growth in population would be more likely to result from either some reduction in mortality or a minor differential between fertility and mortality, leading to long-term slow growth in population. In either case, competition and social means of adjusting population segments to resource space would be the more likely response. Technological changes would more probably arise in areas where mortality and fertility are low but the population is potentially responsive to changes in labor organization, as well as in areas with non-density-dependent stresses. To summarize, in equatorial regions competition and the appearance of social means for maintaining access to defined effective resource space would be more common responses to demographic change than technological changes or changes oriented toward increasing production per unit-producer.

In conclusion, it is suggested that the first major demographic "transition" occurring near the close of the Pleistocene was caused by changes in fertility, rather than by the "normal" condition of changes in mortality that has led to transition in modern times. Dramatic demographic changes can be related in a provocative manner to changes in fertility as conditioned by shifts in labor organization and diet. These shifts are in turn conditioned by variations in (1) the nucleation of resources, (2) the character of environmental changes in the direction of more mature ecosystems, slower rates of turnover, and therefore a decrease in secondary biomass in the form of large mammals, and/or (3) population-density thresholds, such that reduction in the effective resource space is inevitable, accompanied by increased dependence upon plant resources. Whatever the source of pressure, it seems likely that the result in many different areas of the world was increased sedentism and fertility through the causal chains that have been discussed.

NOTE

1. Research reported in this chapter was supported by grants from the Wenner-Gren Foundation for Anthropological Research and the National Science Foundation. I gratefully acknowledge this support. The authorship is primarily the work of Lewis Binford whiie the mathematical-statistical arguments presented with respect to the evaluation of the role of male absenteeism on the overall trends in Nunamiut fertility are the work of W. J. Chasko, Jr.

I would like to acknowledge the work of my students who helped gather many of the data reported here, particularly Charles J. Amsden, Peggy Schneider, and Patty Marchiando.

Finally, I would like to thank, from the bottom of my heart, the many Eskimos who gave me their time, patience, and wealth of knowledge. I must single out Johnny Rulland, Simon and Suzie Paneak, Bob Ahgook, Ellen Hugo, and Elyjah Kakinya as being particularly memorable for their warm assistance.

4
The Matrilateral Implications of Structural Cross-Cousin Marriage

EUGENE A. HAMMEL

Department of Anthropology
University of California, Berkeley

INTRODUCTION

This chapter will demonstrate that a wide variety of nonkinship biases in selection of mates have implications for the relative proportions of types of consanguineal relationships between them.[1] It is important first to clear the theoretical ground. The arguments will be presented initially uncomplicated by considerations of motivation, preference, culture, symbols, or ideology. They are not so constructed because the factors just named are thought unimportant for the study of human marriage; on the contrary, it is my intention to suggest how they build upon simpler, underlying patterns. Thus, this paper is not about what social anthropologists often call "alliance theory" nor is it part of that style of explanation termed "structuralist," although it has important implications for such analyses.

CONSTRAINTS AND HYPOTHESES

The basic argument of this paper rests on the following conditions:

1. Each mate of a pair must possess a measurable amount (r) of some attribute.
2. Mates of one sex must have on the average more of this attribute than mates of the opposite sex; that is, the mean difference between mates with respect to the attribute may not be zero.
3. The attribute must be heritable for offspring of both sexes and from the joint estate of both parents; it need not be equally heritable by sex provided that neither sex is regularly excluded from inheritance, and that any difference between the sexes is a constant proportion.

It should be noted that nothing is said here about specific modes of inheritance, lineality, locality, the locus of jural control, preference, custom, the identity of the attribute, or its direction of bias between mates. Indeed, nothing has yet been said about marriage or even about man.

The principal contention of this paper is the intuitively attractive proposition that if mating is not random with respect to a heritable attribute, it will not be random with respect to the types of consanguineal relationships existing between mates. Nonrandomness with respect to the heritable attribute can be defined as some bias in the probability of mating for two individuals, according to their position on a scale of that attribute. Particular biases in this respect will produce particular biases in patterns of consanguinity between mates.

It is first necessary to define types of consanguinity. All consanguines are either "parallel" or "cross." Later discussion will show how all relatives may be classified according to this dichotomy but for the moment we will restrict ourselves to the traditional domain of the distinction, first cousins. First cousins are the children of full siblings—that is, father's brother's child (FBC), mother's sister's child (MZC), mother's brother's child (MBC), and father's sister's child (FZC).

Parallel consanguines are typified by FBC and MZC, the individuals in the parental-sibling pair being of the same sex. It should be noted here that siblings are, by analogy, members of the same set as parallel first cousins (and other parallel consanguines), since no cross-sex consanguineal link is involved between an individual and his/her FC or MC.

Cross consanguines are typified by MBC and FZC, the individuals in the parental-sibling pair being of opposite sex. It should be noted that if a male is mated to MBD (mother's brother's daughter), his mate is coupled to FZS (father's sister's son). Viewed traditionally from the point of view of the male, this kind of coupling is referred to in the anthropological literature as matrilateral cross-cousin marriage. Conversely, if a male is coupled with FZD, she is coupled with MBS; this type of marriage is called patrilateral cross-cousin marriage. It must be stressed again that the consanguineals named are only type members of sets; the rules for the expansion of sets will be given later.

The propositions to be examined are as follows:

1. If bias in mating, with respect to the heritable attribute, is asymmetrical about the position of an individual on the scale of the attribute, the mean difference between mates will not be zero. Parallel consanguines will have the same value of the attribute as Ego, but cross consanguines will be differentiated both from parallel consanguines and from one another, according to whether they are matrilateral or patrilateral. Matrilateral cross consanguines will have a value of the attribute differing from Ego's in the same direction that Ego's mother's value differed from Ego's father's value, while patrilateral cross consanguines will have a value of the attribute in the opposite direction. The bias in mating thus distinguishes parallel from cross consanguines and subdivides the latter category without reference to the reckoning of kinship as such; in the absence of this bias there is no such differentiation.

2. If the direction of bias is consistent from one generation to the next, the proportion of matrilateral cross-cousin matings (male with MBD, female with FZS) will increase at the expense of the proportion of patrilateral cross-cousin matings (male with FZD, female with MBS).

3. If the direction of bias is inconsistent from one generation to the next, the consanguineal bias in (2) will be diminished, but if its inconsistency takes the form of a regular reversal in direction in each generation, the proportion of patrilateral cross-cousin matings will then increase at the expense of the proportion of matrilateral.

A SIMPLE CORE MODEL

To see the effect of bias between mates in a heritable attribute on the kinds of consanguineal relationships between them, consider an artificial population in which all individuals mate, but only once, and each mating produces two offspring, one of each sex. Further assume the existence of some heritable attribute, inherited equally by the children of a mating, so that the male and female offspring each acquire one-half of the joint attributes of their parents ($([r_m + r_f]/2)$) on their own mating. Define amounts of the attribute as quanta thereof, and establish the difference in amount of the attribute between mates as 2 quanta, the male having more than the female ($r_m = r_f + 2$). Figure 9 then shows the center of a network of consanguineal relationships, sufficient for the computation of the attributes of any consanguine. Ego and his sibling have a value of zero of the attribute ($r = 0$). Father has a value of +1 and mother a value of −1. It can be seen from this figure that to ascend to a male consanguine adds a quantum, as does descent from a female consanguine. These links, which add a quantum, are called credit links. Conversely, to descend from a male consanguine or to ascend to a female involves subtracting a quantum; such links are called debit links. Thus, siblings have the same value of the attribute not only because they share equally in the joint attributes of the parents but because the net change in value of the attribute, computing from Ego to FC or to MC, is zero, $[1 + (-1)]$ in the first instance and $[(-1) + 1]$ in the second. (Parallel arguments can be constructed for the case in which siblings do not inherit equally by sex but in which one sex receives a constant proportion of the share of the other—for example, in which daughters receive a half-share.)

Restricting discussion for the moment to first cousins, we see that parallel cousins must have the same value of the attribute as Ego, for the computation for FBC is the same for FC, while that for MZC is the same as for MC. Among cross cousins, however, MBC will have a value of −2 and FZC a value of +2. In this model, since male Ego's mate must have a value of −2 with respect to Ego, only MBD is eligible as a mate among first cousins.

Two points must now be observed. First, if the direction of bias is consistently reversed in each generation, the appropriate mate for Ego male is not MBD but FZD. Thus, if M has a value of −2 with respect to F, so that MBD has a value of −2 with respect to Ego while FZD has a value of +2 with respect to him, then, if the bias between mates in the filial generation is the same as in the parental, MBD is eligible as a mate. However, if the bias between mates in the filial generation is opposite to that in the parental, FZD is the eligible mate. Second, it should also be clear that even if the attribute value of M with respect to F is +2 but the bias be-

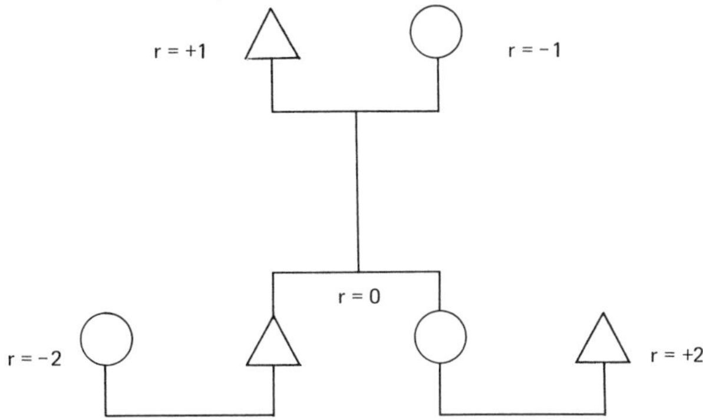

FIGURE 9. Computation of quantal attribute

tween mates is the same in adjacent generations (thus reversing all signs in Figure 9), the appropriate mate among first cousins for Ego male is still MBD, while if the bias reverses consistently in adjacent generations the appropriate mate is of course FZD again. Thus we see that, given the existence of a bias in the attribute between mates, consistency in that bias, regardless of its direction, leads to an emphasis on matrilateral cross-cousin mating. Conversely, consistent reversal in direction of bias from generation to generation leads to an emphasis on patrilateral cross-cousin mating. This pattern of consistent versus alternating bias with respect to unilineal group membership and its implications for matrilateral or patrilateral cross-cousin marriage have long been known (see, for example, Lévi-Strauss 1949).

EXTENSION OF THE CORE MODEL

It is now instructive to compute the value of the attribute for other consanguines close to Ego. In the initial attempt, let us restrict computation to consanguines in Ego's generation and the generation above (G^0, G^1). Ego and sibling(s), who can be regarded as functionally and formally equivalent except for difference in sex and thus constitute only one consanguineal type for these purposes, have a value (r) of zero.[2] M (like MB and MZ) has a value $r = -1$. F (like FB and FZ) has a value $r = +1$; FBC and MZC have $r = 0$. Unlike siblings (FC and MC), FBC and MZC cannot be merged structurally, so we must consider that we have two consanguines with $r = 0$ at this level of consanguineal remove from Ego.[3] MBC has $r = -2$, and FZC has $r = +2$. Thus we see that in Ego's generation at zero degrees of consanguineal removal there is one consanguineal type (Ego and siblings) with $r = 0$. In G^1 there are two consanguines, one with $r = -1$, the other with $r = +1$. In G^0 at the remove of first cousins there is one consanguineal type at $r = -2$, two at $r = 0$, and one at $r = +1$. The patterning of these numbers is reminiscent of a Pascal triangle (Fig. 10).

$$\begin{array}{ccccc} & & 1 & & \\ & 1 & & 1 & \\ 1 & & 2 & & 1 \end{array}$$

FIGURE 10. Pascal triangle

We may generalize from this to establish the Pascal triangle of Figure 11, valid for any two adjacent generations, for example G^0 and G^1, or G^0 and G^{-1}, where n equals the number of filial and parental links in the chain of consanguines between Ego and the designated consanguine, j the number of these that are credit links, and r the quantal value of the attribute. Note that sibling links are not counted in n, only filial and parental links, and these are not redundantly computed for siblings to establish n. Thus for Ego and siblings $n = 0$, for parents $n = 1$, for child $n = 1$, for first cousins $n = 2$ (counting one for the link from Ego to his parents and one for the link down from Ego's parent's sibling to the designated cousin), and so on. Credit links are defined as above: filial links up to a male or parental links down from a female. Because a Pascal triangle is infinitely extendible, we can say that according to these rules all consanguines in each generation can be mapped onto a Pascal triangle, regardless of their collateral distance, for any set of generations G_x, where x is a vector ranging from $-n$ to n in steps of two, for example, (G_0), (G_{-1}, G_{+1}), (G_{-2}, G_0, G_{+2}), etc.[4]

Thus the model of Figure 9 provides a way of computing the value (r) of the heritable attribute for any consanguine, and the model of Figure 11 shows how all consanguines fall with respect to Ego along a scale of r. Generalizing from the value of r for first cousins, we may define as parallel consanguines all those with a quantal value $r = 0$, as matrilateral all those with a quantal value that is negative, and as patrilateral all those with a quantal value that is positive, Ego by definition having $r = 0$ (cf. Kay

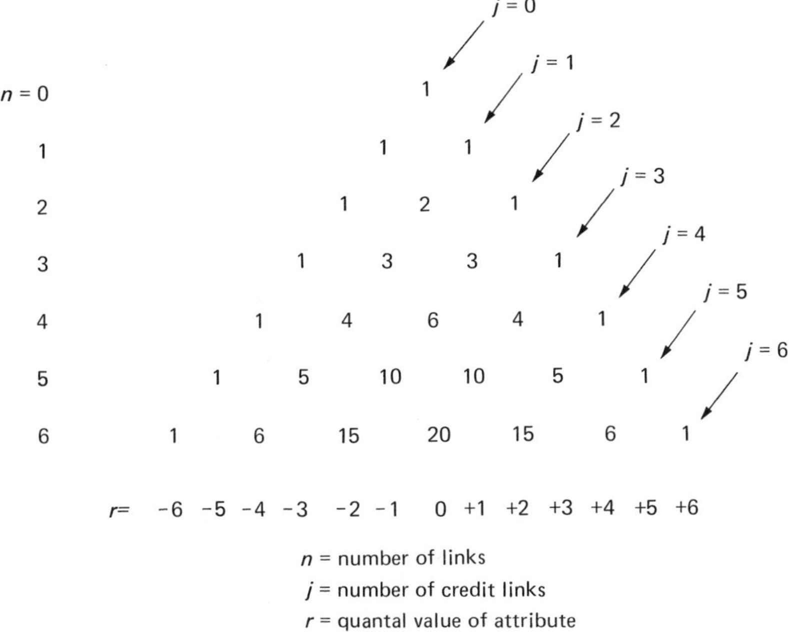

FIGURE 11. Distribution of consanguineals ($n =$ number of links; $j =$ number of credit links; $r =$ quantal value of attribute)

1965, 1966, 1967, 1968; Tyler 1966). Further it may be shown that by accepting the implications of the model (1) F = FB, (2) M = MZ, (3) MBD = W, (4) M = FW and all the derivatives therefrom, each column in the Pascal triangle (with a given value of r) can be reduced to that unique kin type that occupies the edge cell of the triangle. For example:

1. FBC reduces to
2. FC because F = FB, which reduces to
3. Ego because Ego = sibling.

---

1. MZC reduces to
2. MC because M = MZ, which reduces to
3. Ego because Ego = sibling,

thus reducing the two consanguines at $n = 2, j = 1, r = 0$ to the position of $n = 0, j = 0, r = 0$. Similarly,

1. FMBSC reduces to
2. FWBC because MBS = MBDB = WB, which reduces to
3. MBC because M = FW.

---

1. MMZSC reduces to
2. MMSC because M = MZ, which reduces to
3. MBC because MS = B.

---

1. MMBDC reduces to
2. MBWC because MMBD =MBMBD = MBW, which reduces to
3. MBC because FC = MC, that is, HC = WC.

---

1. MFBSC reduces to
2. MFSC because F = FB, which reduces to
3. MBC because FS = B.

All four consanguines at $n = 4, j = 1, r = -2$ reduce to the unique consanguine MBC at $n = 2$, $j = 0$, $r = -2$. Thus the number of consanguines at any value of r, for a triangle of given extent, is the sum of the cell values in any column, and all consanguines in any column can be reduced logically to the unique consanguine in the uppermost cell thereof.

APPLICATIONS

The commonest recognition of some of the principles described here has to do with difference in age at marriage between spouses. It is now accepted that if men on the average marry younger women, they are more likely to marry a matrilateral cross cousin than a patrilateral cross cousin or a parallel cousin. As recently as 1948 Dahlberg had assumed equiprobability of cousin matings at any given degree of relationship. Within four or five years of one another, several workers came independently to the conclusion that bias in age led to bias in type of consanguinity—Goodale in 1959, Rose in 1960 (also 1965; cf. Leach 1965), Barrai, Cavalli-Sforza, and Moroni in 1962 (also Cavalli-Sforza, Kimura, and Barrai 1966), and Hajnal in 1963. The first two drew on field data on Australian aborigines; the others provided analytical mathematical models checked against comparative data. It can be seen that since the sum of the differences from the mean age of siblings of a sibling set is by definition zero, the expected mean difference between the ages of any two randomly drawn siblings will be zero. If there is a bias in age between spouses, it will be reflected in just the same way as the bias in quantal attribute in the simple core model. All of the workers noted that their observations, although centered on close consanguines, were extendible, but only Hajnal (1963) and

Barrai, Cavalli-Sforza, and Moroni (1962) (in part) suggested a rigorous means for extension. Rose observed cryptically in 1965 that the direction of the age bias did not matter; the formal model presented here demonstrates that he was correct. Salisbury in 1956 had noted a territorial/economic gradient in marital exchange and suggested a matrilateral cross-cousin marriage rule as a potential result (cf. Leach 1957); Gilbert and I demonstrated by computer simulation in 1963 and 1966 that consistent territorial bias enhanced the probability of matrilateral cross-cousin marriage. The argument for lineage membership is common in the literature. It may be extended, theoretically, to wealth, prestige, ritual purity, stature, skin color, or any other heritable attribute that meets the criteria of the formal model.

There are of course constraints on the effects for different kinds of attributes. Any attribute that is bounded will not fit the formal model perfectly. For example, if men tend to marry women who have five hundred dollars less in net assets than they, distant matrilateral cross consanguines would be very deeply in debt and distant patrilateral ones extremely wealthy; obviously, the social system would have to be one that permitted such ranges of wealth. If men tended to marry women who were 1/*n*th of a standard deviation shorter on the scale of female stature than the men were on the scale of male stature, some distant matrilateral cross consanguines might be only a foot tall, while patrilateral ones would assume gargantuan proportions. If men tended to marry women lighter in hue, one's distant matrilateral cross consanguines would be fish-belly white and the patrilateral ones coal black. All heritable attributes save one involve boundary problems of this general kind. Only age bias is exempt, for it is perfectly reasonable to conceive of distant matrilateral cross consanguines in Ego's generation who are not yet born and of distant patrilateral ones who are deceased. However, complications arise when cross-generational matings are considered.

Other problems also arise in the application of the formal model. The formal model has no variance; the real world does. In a stochastic model, such as that used by Hajnal or Gilbert and myself, or that reported in the appendix to this chapter, there is variance. In such a model, or in the real world, the consistency of the bias in consanguineal patterning is weakened by two kinds of variance: variance in the value of the heritable attribute among siblings (within each sex if there is a standard difference in heritability by sex, otherwise for both sexes) and that in the difference in the heritable attribute between mates. Using age as an example, it is clear that if the reproductive span of females is long and/or child spacing is very great, even if males tended to mate with younger females a particular MBD might easily be older than male Ego and a particular FBD younger. Similarly, if H and W differed by greatly varying amounts in age, even though the mean difference between spouses was not zero the consistency of the model would be upset for particular spouse pairs and their descendants. Variance in the bias between spouses is, of course, less disturbing to the consistency of effect when the mean difference is relatively large. These problems can be treated in a stochastic model; the mechanical model is valuable only for its clarity of argument.

SPECULATIONS

It was observed above that if the direction of bias in the heritable attribute between spouses changes in alternate generations, the frequency of marriage with patrilateral cross consanguines will be increased. Despite the frequent cultural dissonance between generations, no social system maintaining consistent alternation seems likely (see Needham 1959). Hairstyle, for example, is not heritable in the way we have been discussing, and there are some parents who seem to inherit from their children in this regard anyway. One may speculate, however, about the effects of intersection of two cultural systems, let us say geographically, each having a value system opposite to that of the other. If one system favored marriage with younger women (or wealthier, etc.) while the other favored the opposite, any interbreeding combined with consistent rules of residence would produce increased patrilateral cross-cousin marriage at the point of intersection. Perhaps cultural dissonance or variability of some kind underlies the reported systems of patrilateral cross-cousin marriage, if any frequencies of consanguineal marriage underlie those systems.

We may also note some of the mechanisms that can ameliorate the boundary problems caused by some heritable attributes. Infinitesimal biases between spouses will of course diminish boundary problems since boundaries would be reached only in the limit, but they would also diminish any effect of the biases themselves as the mean difference between spouses would approach zero. Progressive shifts in the precise content of sets of multiple biases along a chain of consanguines would diminish boundary problems for any one attribute, since it would imperceptibly fade into another attribute that was its functional equivalent. For example, emphasis on wealth might give way to emphasis on ritual purity, and so on. Differential rates of polygyny, polyandry, and/or sex-specific celibacy or differential fertility and mortality rates might also solve some boundary problems. Closure of a chain of consanguines into a circle would solve the problem of boundary if the attribute were one of locality or of group membership. The steps of ordinalization of a nominal scale of group membership or locality and subsequent modularization into a "closed connubium" have long been recognized as attributes of unilateral alliance systems or at least of idealized models thereof, whether those of the anthropologists or of the natives. Intersection of systems based on different attributes, with patrilateral cross-cousin marriage at the intersections, as noted, might serve a similar purpose. Social mobility, in the sloughing off of consanguines upward or downward, would permit a biased system to operate (see Leach 1951), as would the analogous "trickle effect" coupled with innovation of new symbols of difference (Fallers 1954; Hammel 1964). Among all these possible concomitants of unilateral exchange of women based on biases other than age, and in systems other than those closed into a circle, one should note that there is a necessary flow of the attribute through the system of consanguines. By this I do not mean the flow of counterprestations on which Leach (1951) rightly insists but rather the regular change in value of the attribute from one generation to the next in any descent line. Given the inequity between parents and the heritability of their joint attributes, there must then be a regular inequity between parents and children proportional to the inequity between spouses. Taking wealth as an example, the flow of wealth set in motion by unilateral connubium must necessarily be one not only between local groups but also across generations, a regular schedule of impoverishment or enrichment consistent with the regularity of the connubium itself. It is not my intention to elaborate here on Leach's excellent discussion of the structural consequences of unilateral connubium (1951) but to point out that some of them may be, in a model or in real systems, consequences of other, nonkinship biases.

Most of these speculations have to do with the synchronic concomitants of biases other than that in age between mates. There are also some connected only with the age bias, which has no inherent boundary problems. Suppose that in an animal species mating occurred as soon as physiologically possible. Further suppose that females matured earlier than males. Then, necessarily, mating in that species would be biased in favor of matrilateral cross consanguines, since males would mate on the average with younger females. Animal species in which such differential maturation seems to occur are man, the apes, and the cercopiths; the same pattern is not consistently observed in the New World monkeys or the lower primates (Napier and Napier 1967). Admittedly, the data are incomplete, but they are nevertheless of interest. Other biological and social factors among the apes and cercopiths if anything intensify the pattern of differential age between mates, just as in man. Females mature osteologically at about the same time that they mature sexually, whereas male osteological maturation appears somewhat delayed beyond puberty. Granting of course some adolescent infertility in females, full physical maturation in males thus seems delayed even more than mere sexual maturation. If we add to this the social factors and training involved in the skills of bluffing and threat (or courtship), male maturation may be even later. Further, although some female primates appear to mate randomly when in estrus, even with juveniles, at the peak of estrus they seem to attach themselves to an older, dominant male. Since they are fertile at the peak of estrus but not much before, the fertile matings (which are the only ones with consequences for genealogy) are much more likely to be with an older male. Thus, among the cercopiths, apes, and man one would expect just on physiological grounds the kind of consistent bias that would increase the proportion of matrilateral cross-cousin matings among all cousin matings. It would be difficult to observe the frequency of such matings under field conditions, except for man (where it is difficult enough). However, it would be easier to observe the mean of age difference between mates in fertile pairs and the variances in that difference and in the ages of siblings. The probable frequency of matrilateral bias in matings could then be easily computed, using either an analytical model or a simulation (Hajnal 1963; Barrai, Cavalli-Sforza, and Moroni 1962; Cavalli-Sforza, Kimura, and Barrai 1966; MacCluer and Schull 1970; Hammel and Hutchinson 1972; and the appendix to this chapter).

An interesting consequence of this pattern is that, since it appears to occur only among the higher Old World primates (*Cercopithecoidea* and *Hominoidea*), it must date from the original separation of the cercopiths from the primate stem. If the pattern of differential maturation came about by a delay in the maturation of males, there would have been few interesting consequences other than that of matrilateral bias in consanguineal linkage between related mates. However, if it occurred by appearance of earlier maturation of females, the effects might have been very substantial, given that expected age at death remained the same. The average difference in most Old World primate species (other than the prosimians) between maturation of males and females is about two or three years. If this difference occurred through earlier maturation of females, the reproductive lives of females would have been lengthened by about two or three years, so that, given the expected age at death as twelve to fifteen years, reproductive capacity would have been increased by as much as 15 percent.[5] An increase in reproductive potential of that magnitude could easily have been a crucial factor in the successful expansion of the higher primates such as the dryopithecines and early hominid forms out of Africa.

But it is the cultural consequences of these patterns that arouse one's strongest interest. One point is clear: the presence of such biases in mating in a human society need not give rise to a symbolic system appropriate to that bias. The most extreme age biases known are among certain Australian tribes such as the Tiwi, yet they do not differentiate MBC from FZC terminologically, although the frequency of marriages is biased heavily toward the matrilateral cross consanguines for Ego male, certainly so for the first marriages of females. Indeed, we are faced with a paradox. Because the matrilateral bias must be common in fact, the behavioral infrastructure of asymmetric unilateral alliance systems is also common, but symbolic systems, whether of kinship terminology or phrased in some other way, are rare and located mostly in one corner of the world. Alliance theorists have of course concentrated their analyses on the symbolic systems, perhaps because they cared more for the analysis of culture than for the analysis of behavior, perhaps because their data consisted more of normative statements from informants than of actual records of marriages and alliances. Leach (1957, 1965), confronted with evidence of unilateral exchange behavior by Salisbury and Rose, stubbornly contended that that was not what he and Lévi-Strauss were talking about. He is correct. It is not what they were talking about. My suggestion is that they should have been, because the importance of symbolic unilateral alliance systems lies precisely in the fact that they are so often absent where they could easily be present.

Let us go back to the monkeys and apes, who are so useful to us because they are men without humanity. The age bias in maturation occurs among them, and as shown it is intensified by several factors. Any male monkey or ape thus has a much greater likelihood of a fertile mating with a matrilateral cross consanguine than with any other kind of consanguine. One might whimsically assume from this that if baboons could talk they would have a "Sudanese" kinship terminology. They might if there were any reason to distinguish one female in estrus from another on more than personal grounds. There would be, for example, in an endogamous troop or band within which family groupings were quite discrete over time, retaining a kind of identity and with important social relationships being adjusted between individuals in their capacity as members of such family groupings. There may be some evidence for intrafamilial recognition, but it does not appear to affect sexual behavior much, except insofar as the greater dominance of mothers blocks their being mounted by their sons and there is some sexual avoidance between siblings. It is, then, a lack of consistently coherent and important subgroups —"households," let us call them—that prevents the symbolic elaboration of an underlying biological reality.

But troops and bands are quite distinct from one another among ground-dwelling nonhuman primates. Maturing and newly mature males often live on the periphery of such groups. They may go back into their group if they can gain a place in the dominance hierarchy that permits them to remain, or they may go into another group under the same conditions. Relative age is a factor in entering a group, up to a point. Greater age, up to the decline of physical powers, means greater strength, greater skill, greater experience, greater confidence in bluffing. Thus on the average it is likely that a peripheral animal entering a new group would be more likely to go into the same one his MB went into under similar circumstances and in which his MBD now lived than into the group of FZ and FZD. That is to say that females would not generally move from one group to another but that their male siblings might, and they would be likely to move in a particular direction. Thus, ZS would follow MB. The attractions of evolutionistic fantasy aside, there is no reason to suppose that ZS would recognize MB, particularly not as such. Again, it is the absence of defined social units of regular social consequence that blocks the emergence of a symbolic system acknowledging the skewed structure of consanguineal relationships. Family units may exist, troops or bands certainly do, but regular social behavior adjusted between such units as units does not. Thus there is no symbolic system to express it. One is reminded not only of Lévi-Strauss's insistence on the formation of the family as the cornerstone of human society and culture but also of Kroeber's apposite remark that apes do not talk because they have nothing to say (cf. Wagner 1972).

Sometime in the history of man, we ceased to be dumb about kinship. But when we learned to speak of it, it must have been because the units of which we spoke had become important for other reasons—because the sexual division of labor had created enduring conjugal pairs, or because the lengthened immaturity of children had made a mother's hearth a home. And when we look at those societies in which symbolic systems are erected to describe and manipulate unilateral asymmetric exchange of women, they are societies, as Schneider (1965) has clearly said, of a particular kind. They tend to be unilineal, with firm concepts of locality and with jural authority vested in local segments of corporate descent groups. It is these other characteristics that call the code of kinship into use, as a catalyst precipitates a solution, as the application of some substance brings the latent writing of an invisible ink into manifest reality.

When some of us, in talking about social relations, use the idiom of kinship, it is for two reasons. First, in many societies kinship is emically the idiom of social relations. Second, across most societies kinship is etically the most convenient code for comparing social relations. When some of us, in talking about kinship, use the idiom of genealogy, it is for two reasons. First, in many societies genealogy is emically the idiom of kinship. Second, across most societies genealogy is etically the most convenient code for comparing kinship. Although it is clear from what has gone before that genealogy and demography are not the motor of the social universe, it is also clear that to ignore them for descriptive and analytical purposes would be unwise.

The problem I have raised here by employing an analytical demographic and genealogically oriented approach is not new at all but of ancient and distinguished lineage: it is the problem of the relationship between ideology and behavior. Of course it has been obvious, as Schneider has clearly indicated (1965), that "the matrilateral cross cousin" is more than MBD, that men whose culture prescribes marriage with MBD, or indeed "marriageable woman" however phrased, may be bedded with very different ones. What has not been clear is how very startling the contrast between behavior and ideology is in quite the opposite direction. We would not have seen this contrast if it had not been demographically and genealogically phrased in a formal way. I have shown that natural, empirically observable behavior that forms a perfect substructure for the emergence of a symbolic system is not a sufficient condition for the appearance of an ideology and occurs more often in the absence of an appropriate ideology than in its presence. The materialist underpinning is not enough, although it is quite likely, because of the apparent universality of age bias and the consequences thereof, to be a necessary condition for the ideology. Speculating on the history of man again, we would conclude that it was probably a necessary condition for the emergence of such ideologies.

If any situation shows us the mutual, interactive importance of material conditions and the selective cognition of them, it is one such as this, where an infrastructure does not automatically pass the barrier of the mind but where the mind does not create symbols without the raw material of experience. The objective realities of human existence do not exist except in man's own perception of them. Perhaps it would be sufficient to point out Marx's own conclusion that the objective existence of social domination and even of classification was not enough to create classes in his sense, or, as one of his successful students has astutely remarked, that it is always necessary to walk on two legs. We forget these simple lessons about the social creativity of man, and it leads us to misunderstand more than kinship.

NOTES

1. Preliminary versions of this paper were presented at Cambridge University in 1970, at the annual meeting of the American Anthropological Association in 1971, and to the Department of Anthropology at Berkeley in 1972. These arguments formed part of a presentation at a conference on computer microsimulation at Pennsylvania State University in 1972 and of more extended discussion of substantive problems in microsimulation at the School of American Research, Santa Fe, in 1973. The published version had to await development of a reliable microsimulation model for adequate testing; that was not achieved until late winter 1973. I am indebted to many of my listeners for their probing criticisms of what was a rather iconoclastic piece, principally J. A. Barnes, J. R. Goody, E. R. Leach, Paul Kay, William Geoghegan, and Nelson Graburn, none of whom are responsible for my errors.

2. Sex is not important except for *linking* relatives, as defined. Thus, S and D may be grouped as C; further, we assume that FC = MC.

3. FBC and MZC cannot be merged because FB = MZ.

4. The mapping of course is according to $\binom{n}{j}$. I am much indebted to Chad McDaniel for his expansion of the original applicability of the mapping which I had thought restricted only to adjacent generations.

5. I am obliged to Phyllis Dolhinow for some of these age data.

APPENDIX

A Stochastic Simulation and Numerical Test of the Deterministic Model

Eugene A. Hammel
Department of Anthropology
University of California, Berkeley

David Hutchinson
Department of Anthropology
University of California, Berkeley

Kenneth Wachter
St. Catherine's College
Oxford University

The body of this paper made reference to the rigid character of mechanical deterministic models. Such models, although they present fundamental principles with great clarity, fail to mirror the real world acceptably because they ignore variation in occurrence of events. Short of experimentation or extensive observation of naturally occurring events, one means of approaching reality is stochastic microsimulation with the aid of high-speed computers. Such simulations attempt to re-create (within limits, of course) critical events of the process under examination and to carry out replicated runs of these a sufficient number of times to give some indication of the expectable variation in results.

The authors of this appendix have been engaged in a joint endeavor to create a stochastic microsimulation computer program suitable for the examination of demographic and social processes (Hammel and Hutchinson 1972). The result is a program entitled SOCSIM, which is now sufficiently well developed to permit some simple tests.[1] In this appendix we test two of the propositions derivable from or implicit in the deterministic model, namely:

1. The *direction* of consanguineal skewing (i.e., the matrilateral skewing among cross-cousin relationships between spouses) should remain the same regardless of the *direction* of the bias in age between spouses (*i.e.*, whether men marry older or younger women). To examine this proposition we test the relationship between the *signed* value of mean age difference between husband and wife and the existence of consanguineal skewing, and also the relationship between the *absolute* value of the age difference and the existence of consanguineal skewing.

2. The deterministic model suggests nothing directly about the relationship between *strength* of age bias and *strength* of consanguineal skewing. Nevertheless, intuition suggests that if a little age bias causes some skewing, more age bias should cause more skewing, in the sense of a trade-off between the patrilateral and matrilateral varieties of cross-cousin relationships. That this result is expectable can be shown as follows: if the mean difference in age between husband and wife is very small and if there is any appreciable variance in it, the mean age of Ego's matrilateral cross cousins should differ only slightly from the mean age of his patrilateral cross cousins and the overlap in ages between matrilateral and patrilateral cross cousins would be extensive. Thus, if Ego takes a wife according to the mean age bias, he would be quite likely to select a patrilateral cross cousin, although somewhat more likely to select a matrilateral one. However, if the mean age bias were great (unless the variance increased greatly also), the age distributions of the two types of cross cousin would not overlap much, so that Ego, selecting a wife on the basis of age bias, would be very unlikely to marry a patrilateral cross cousin. Thus we would expect that the stronger the age bias, the more cleanly the consanguineal skewing would be manifested. This result is clearly suggested in the ethnographic data cited (e.g., Tiwi, Groote Eylandt) and is explicit in the analytical predictions of Hajnal's Table 27 (1963).[2]

The simulations were carried out as follows. A test population was created by first establishing an initial population and simulating its reproductive behavior and mortality for 150 years to establish a genealogy of sufficient depth. Mortality rates were taken from Coale and Demeny (1966: North, Mortality Level 2) and fertility and nuptiality rates were set to achieve near-stationarity. Marriages within the nuclear family as well as uncle-niece and aunt-nephew marriages were prohibited when not already precluded by age differences. At the end of 150 years, this population had 132 persons. The test population of 132 persons was then run 33 separate times, each time with a different starting random number to obtain an independent trial, until either it had run 400 years or the population had exceeded 400 persons or had dropped to 10 persons. For each marriage, any first-cousin or second-cousin relationship of zero removal between husband and wife was identified and tabulated. Each of the 33 runs aimed to achieve a different mean age bias between husband and wife, extending about a dozen years on both sides of zero bias.[3]

The results of the simulations are given in tabular form in Table 43,

TABLE 43
DATA FROM SIMULATION RUNS

Run No.	*Age Bias**		*Matrilateral Bias†*	*Number of Marriages*
	Mean	*Standard Deviation*		
1	−1.250	4.52	.498	1157
2	−4.420	6.50	.528	895
3	4.480	16.30	.567	854
4	4.590	13.33	.545	668
5	5.950	9.09	.500	676
6	5.970	10.85	.441	666
7	5.980	10.07	.493	739
8	−6.230	6.30	.482	634
9	−6.280	6.91	.571	679
10	−6.900	8.54	.517	624
11	7.250	6.56	.688	310
12	−8.390	8.47	.621	236
13	−8.460	5.12	.530	331
14	−8.780	8.33	.551	445
15	8.920	7.24	.534	204
16	−9.390	4.62	.741	340
17	−9.400	7.62	.732	234
18	−9.410	8.84	.571	384
19	−9.900	7.01	.519	207
20	10.060	7.54	.581	264
21	10.350	5.36	.683	792
22	−10.530	5.66	.565	38[illegible]
23	−11.300	5.66	.806	329
24	−12.110	7.23	.536	240
25	12.260	8.52	.554	408
26	12.600	7.35	.632	241
27	−12.840	7.08	.712	667
28	−13.320	6.67	.730	336
29	−13.870	6.27	.571	190
30	−14.590	6.81	.794	910
31	−14.600	6.65	.777	549
32	14.900	7.72	.695	760
33	15.270	7.59	.816	450

* (Age of husband) — (Age of wife).

† $\dfrac{\text{Number of matrilateral cross first- and second-cousin relationships between spouses}}{\text{Number of all cross first- and second-cousin relationships between spouses}}$.

which presents for each run the mean age bias, the standard deviation of the age bias, the proportion of cross-cousin marriage relationships that were matrilateral, and the number of marriages achieved in each run. Simple correlation coefficients between these variables are given in Table 44; note that both the signed and the absolute values of the age bias are included. The correlation coefficients were computed by weighting the data in the rows of Table 43 by the appropriate N, that is, the total number of marriages in each run.

TABLE 44
INTERCORRELATIONS WEIGHTED BY N*

	Mean Age Bias	*Matrilateral Bias*	*Absolute Mean Age Bias*
Mean Age Bias	1.000	−.189	−.124
Matrilateral Bias		1.000	.778
Absolute Mean Age Bias			1.000

* Weighting was achieved by counting the variables in the regression as many times as specified by N (see Table 43). Thus the values of the variables in the first row of Table 43 (Run No. 1) were counted 1,157 times. Variables in Table 44 are defined as in Table 43; note, however, the inclusion of the absolute mean age bias in Table 44.

We may now examine the relationships between these variables. Table 44 shows that the correlation between the signed value of the age bias and the proportion of matrilateral skewing is −.189, which is very likely a chance sampling deviation from a zero correlation. Contrariwise, the correlation between the absolute value of age bias and the proportion of matrilateral skewing is .778, which is clearly statistically significant.[4] The signed age biases are distributed on both sides of zero fairly evenly. Their mean is −1.48, close to zero. Thus it is not surprising that the strong correlation of absolute age bias with skewing is nullified when the signed value of age bias is used instead. These results support the predictions made. Table 44 also confirms in the same way that matrilateral skewing increases as the absolute value of the age bias increases. The linear regression coefficient is .02; that is, an increase of one year in the absolute mean age bias increases the proportion of matrilateral skewing by 2 percent (see Fig. 12).

Both the propositions derivable from the deterministic model are reflected in the simulation. We must stress here that this is not a trivial

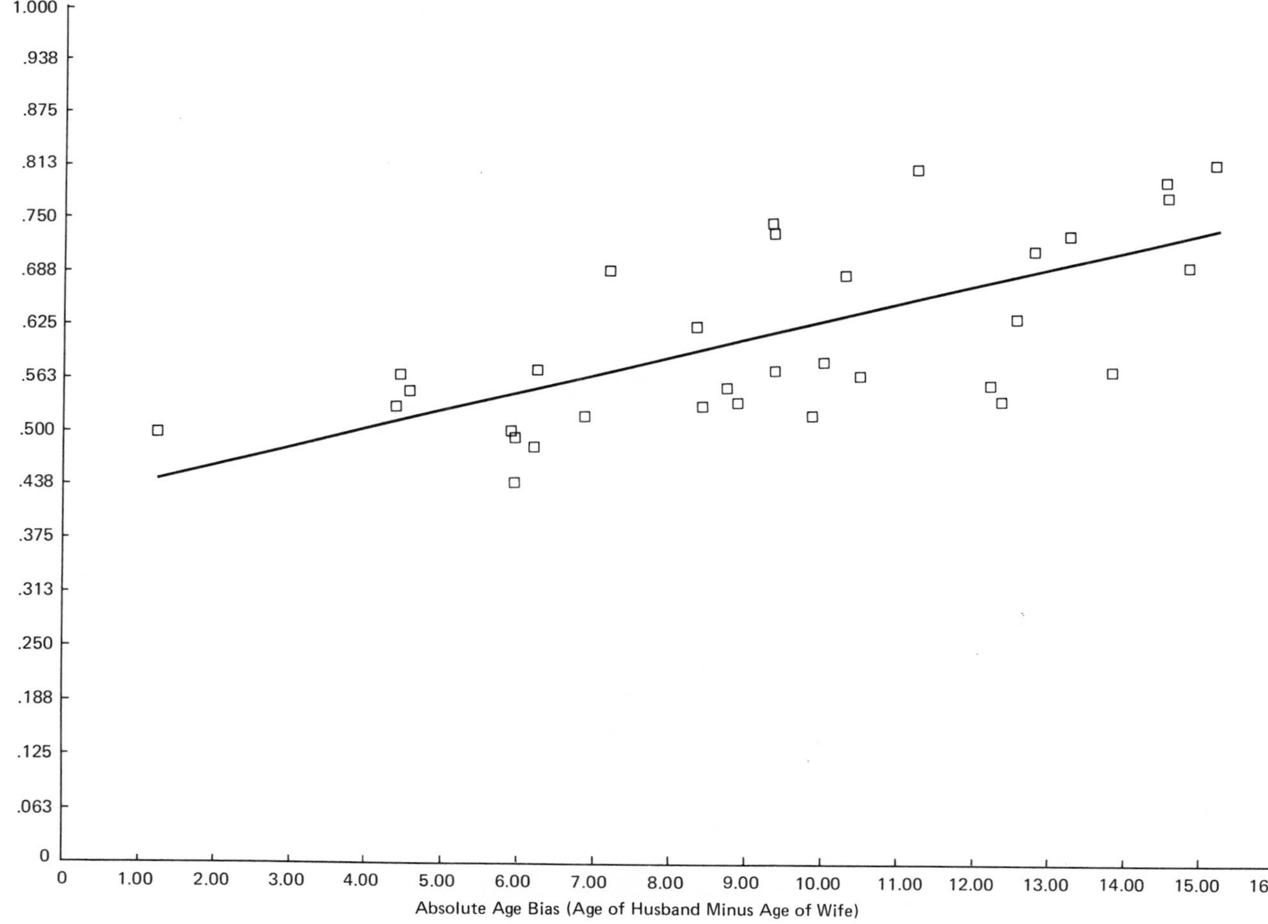

FIGURE 12. **Data plot and regression of absolute age bias and consanguineal bias**

result, as some might expect. One does not obtain from a simulation "merely what one put in." Target demographic rates are established for the simulation, but the occurrence of demographic events is subject to wide fluctuation and controlled by random processes (a two-level random-number generator). Thus the demographic output itself is never the same as the input for any given run and only approaches the input rates when the number of runs is very large. Most importantly, nothing about cousin relationships was specified in the simulation at all (except how to recognize cousins for terminal statistical counting). It must therefore be concluded that the patterning of cousin relationships between spouses results from the age biases achieved in the simulation in interaction with other demographic events, particularly since the logic of the deterministic model seems consistent and would support this interpretation.

This test is a narrow one, confined only to the age bias. It supports the ethnographic evidence, analytical models presented by Hajnal (1963), Barrai, Cavalli-Sforza, and Moroni (1962), Cavalli-Sforza, Kimura, and Barrai (1966), and an independent simulation test of Hajnal's model by MacCluer and Schull (1970), as well as the deterministic model that encompasses all of these. The deterministic model, of course, has much wider implications for other kinds of bias, as indicated. SOCSIM will be employed soon to extend simulation testing to other kinds of bias, such as that in locality—which is illustrated in some ethnographic data, e.g., Salisbury (1956), or crude simulation, e.g., Gilbert and Hammel (1963, 1966) —and biases heretofore unexplored, such as those of wealth, status, skin color, and others. Of particular importance in such extensions of testing are the boundary problems that may be expected to arise for all forms of bias other than that of age. These problems are quite difficult to assess analytically but well suited to the Monte Carlo approach achieved by simulation.

NOTES

1. Development of the simulation program was made possible by the kind cooperation of D. G. Horvitz, who provided information on a prototype program, POPSIM, developed under the auspices of the National Center for Health Statistics, and by financial support from the Institute of International Studies, Berkeley, the Social Science Research Council (Great Britain) and Cambridge Group for the History of Population and Social Structure (Great Britain), and the Computer Center of the University of California, Berkeley. Further development of SOCSIM continues under sponsorship of the National Science Foundation (GS 38293).

2. We would also expect the proportion of parallel-cousin marriages out of all cousin marriages (or out of all marriages) and the proportion of cousin marriages out of all marriages to decrease. This expectation is based on the following argument. As the age bias increases, the age distributions of matrilateral cross and patrilateral cross cousins move apart, while that of parallel cousins stays constant. At the same time, the age distribution of spouses shifts in the direction of the bias; that is, the age distribution of wives also shifts as does the age distribution of matrilateral cross cousins, while that of hubands shifts as does the age distribution of patrilateral cross cousins. Thus the overlap of the age distributions of spouses with the age distribution of parallel cousins lessens in the same way that the age distributions of parallel and cross cousins cease to overlap. Since the age bias in marriage results in a loss of consanguineous marriages with one type of cross cousin and all types of parallel cousins, gaining only in proportion of marriages with the other type of cross cousin, the proportion of cousin marriages out of all marriages should decrease. Hajnal (1963:138) also suggests a decrease in parallel first-cousin marriages in his analytical model, but his Table 28 does not bear him out. Chad McDaniel independently came upon these same arguments in his critique of an earlier draft of this paper and showed the weakening of parallel-cousin marriage at the first-cousin level from the statistics of the simulation runs. We have subsequently examined these propositions in greater detail from those same statistics. Unfortunately, the number of runs was not sufficient to achieve an unambiguous result. Furthermore, careful examination of these hypotheses would require some statistics not provided in the original runs, such as the age distributions of siblings and the various kinds of cousins. Finally, since specification of large age biases with wife older than husband (with a consequent shortening of the wife's reproductive span in consort with that of the husband) makes adjustments in birth and remarriage rates necessary to prevent population extinction, any results must be examined for the effects of such manipulations. We will pursue these issues in the near future but for the moment reserve comment on these subsidiary hypotheses, except to note our revised expectations from the earlier draft and the currently equivocal results.

3. The simulation program does not identify the fathers of children born to unmarried women, and thus cannot compute the kinship linkages between spouses when either or both are the children of unwed mothers or when any ancestor was illegitimate. Clearly, then, the presence of illegitimate children in this simulation depresses measurement of cousin marriages. We therefore kept fertility rates for unmarried women low, at 10 percent of the rates for married women. It now appears that the fertility rates for unmarried women should have been set at zero, and that the failure to do so may have markedly depressed and perturbed cousin-marriage frequencies where wives were much older than their husbands. Wives much older than their husbands could have

given birth under the unmarried fertility rates for quite some time, so that a large fraction of their children might have been illegitimate. We are pursuing this problem. It should also be noted that subsequent research by Chad McDaniel, covering a wider range of age biases and kin relationships, shows degeneration of the clear effects of the model when cross-generation marriages are frequent; such marriages should occur more frequently as the age bias becomes more extreme.

4. There are at least 32 degrees of freedom in the correlation from the 33 independent runs, but to some extent one might regard each marriage as a new, though not entirely independent, trial and assume more degrees of freedom than 32. This makes ordinary significance tests ambiguous. However, the more cônservative estimate of degrees of freedom is 32. For d.f. = 32, under usual assumptions of normality a correlation coefficient of .32 or greater would occur by chance in only 1 percent of cases. The observed coefficient, $r = .778$, is clearly much larger than that.

5

Population Dynamics at the Grasshopper Pueblo, Arizona[1]

WILLIAM A. LONGACRE
Department of Anthropology
University of Arizona

There is a long history of great interest in the study of extinct populations, sometimes referred to as prehistoric demography (e.g., Cook 1972a) or archaeological demography (e.g., Howells 1960). Lacking actual population statistics such as those provided by a census or historical documentation, the researcher is forced to estimate such basic data as population size, age and sex distribution, and the dynamics of the population. There are staggering problems in attempting estimates of this sort, some obvious and others more subtle.

It is not my purpose here to review the various attempts that have been made; Cook (1972a) presents a comprehensive review. Rather, I should like to introduce the topic by discussing some of the problems faced by a researcher interested in prehistoric demography and describe in some detail what is being done to solve these problems in one research endeavor in the American Southwest.

WILLIAM A. LONGACRE

PROBLEMS IN PREHISTORIC DEMOGRAPHY

Much of the research in prehistoric demographic studies has had a regional focus. The majority of these studies have attempted estimates of trends in regional population size over time (e.g., Colton 1936; Schwartz 1963); many have attempted explanations for the estimated trends, usually based in ecological arguments. Demographic analyses of single populations, such as in a particular community, are far less numerous. Archaeologists reporting on the excavation of a particular site usually present an estimate of the population and sometimes provide estimates of the population trends. Sometimes their analyses are documented from a number of sources and carefully argued (e.g., Hill 1970:75–77), but all too often the estimates are crude and even unexplained. Rarely does an analysis attempt any in-depth assessment of the population dynamics at a single community, providing such data as age and sex distributions over time, birth and death rates, and rates of immigration and migration. Notable exceptions would include the work at Pecos Pueblo in New Mexico (Howells 1960; Hooton 1930).

One has only to consider the sources for making estimates pertaining to population dynamics to understand the dearth of in-depth studies. These sources fall into two broad categories, cross-cultural and cultural or site specific, and form the basis for inferences about extinct population parameters.

In the former category I would include ethnographic analogy, or the use of constants that seem to correlate cross-culturally such as average floor area per person (Naroll 1962; Le Blanc 1971), numbers of hearths per family (Chang 1958), average number of persons per pueblo room (Colton 1949), and relationships between population and settlement sizes (Cook and Heizer 1965, 1968). Cross-cultural constants have been attempted as well utilizing artifactual data, sometimes in ingenious ways. For example, Turner and Lofgren (1966) determined the volume of cooking and serving vessels in southwestern Pueblo cultures by estimating family size on the basis of the ratio of cooking pot capacity to bowl size. Another interesting example is provided by Cook (1972b), who attempted to estimate population size from the volume of broken pottery found at prehistoric sites.

Site-specific information for demographic inferences would include the skeletal population, size of the site, number of structures, storage capacity, density of debris, and other such archaeological data.

Another important source for estimating critical variables is the whole realm of ecological data. To date there have been few studies employing ecological data, but they appear to hold great promise. Focusing on resources and regional carrying capacity seems to be highly useful, as demonstrated by Zubrow (1971), and I defer to him for a fuller discussion of this whole area of endeavor.

In all of these approaches, controlling chronology is critical. Rarely can we gain fine-scale temporal control, and that fact explains a great deal of the difficulty in attempting demographic studies of extinct populations. Obviously, the temporal dimension is important to an analysis of population dynamics, and the shorter the temporal duration of the population under study, the more critical chronological control becomes. Control to the nearest one hundred years may be adequate for studying gross regional trends in population growth and distribution but useless for assessing the population dynamics of a single community that existed for only a hundred years or so. This fact might explain the bias toward regional studies of this sort and the relative lack of single-community analyses.

Another source of great difficulty and often the cause of error in estimates is, of course, sampling bias. But the potential of sampling bias has caused surprisingly little concern to archaeologists until recently. This lack of concern makes frustrating many attempts to work with archaeological data. Consider, for example, that the most ready source for estimates of the vital statistics of a prehistoric population and the key for understanding population dynamics lies in the burial data, the skeletal population itself. How representative of the population of skeletons is the excavated sample of burials, and, indeed, how reflective of the living population are the dead (Underwood 1969)?

An additional dimension of importance is the social organization of the population under study. The way the society is organized and the behavioral constraints imposed by that organization are important factors to control in any attempt to describe and explain population dynamics.

GRASSHOPPER PUEBLO

Let us now turn to an example of ongoing research in the American Southwest, focusing on the ways in which we are trying to solve the problems briefly discussed above in an attempt to deal with the population dynamics at a single community. Those who anticipate a completed research report with the problems solved will be disappointed. Having spent eleven years working at the site to date, we are currently midway in the project; we anticipate another decade of research. This discussion must therefore be viewed as an in-progress statement; it should serve, however, as an indication of how we are trying to solve some of these problems and what we have learned thus far.

The research project is centered at the Grasshopper Ruin, located in east-central Arizona. A long-range program of archaeological research is being conducted at the site by the University of Arizona through the Archaeological Field School program. This program is sponsored jointly by the Department of Anthropology and the Arizona State Museum and has been supported since 1965 by the National Science Foundation.[2]

The Grasshopper Ruin (Arizona P:14:1 in the Arizona State Museum Survey) is a fourteenth-century pueblo located about ten miles west of Cibecue, Arizona, on the Fort Apache Indian Reservation. It is an example of what Rinaldo (1964) has called Late Mogollon prehistoric culture and others have termed prehistoric Western Pueblo (Reed 1948, 1950; Johnson 1965). The site consists of approximately five hundred rooms distributed into several main room clusters that are separated by a presently intermittent stream and surrounded by smaller groupings of rooms.

Our research at Grasshopper has been designed to investigate the nature of the cultural development in the Mogollon area of the prehistoric southwestern United States after A.D. 1200. Of special concern is the Late Mogollon readaptation, involving the aggregation of populations into increasingly larger settlements, and the identification of the selective pressures leading to this readaptation. We are also attempting to identify changes through time in such systemic variables as residence-unit size, nature of status differentiation, postmarital residence patterns, inheritance, and other aspects of social organization.

More specific goals of our research have been to delimit the economic basis of this extinct society, to test the hypothesis of a slight climatic shift occurring about A.D. 1300 (Schoenwetter and Dittert 1968), to determine the causes for the abandonment of Grasshopper about A.D. 1400, and to define and investigate the nature of interactions among the extinct societies in the Grasshopper area (Tuggle 1970) and among that region and those farther to the north and south. The research program for the Grasshopper region is also designed to be compatible with the goals adopted by the recently formed Southwestern Anthropological Research Group (Gumerman 1971, 1972). The details of the research strategy at Grasshopper that are pertinent to these goals are discussed by Longacre and Reid (1971).

Our primary research goals in the work at Grasshopper are to describe and analyze the extinct cultural system and its components, isolate and understand the workings of cultural processes of stability and change, and identify adaptive changes in this relatively unknown area of the Southwest during the fourteenth century. To achieve these goals we have adopted a systemic model of culture as discussed recently by Binford, Martin, and others (see Binford and Binford 1968; Martin 1971). This model seems most efficient to us as a springboard for the investigation of the nature of the processes of change and stability operative in the prehistoric past. Ignoring the arguments and completed research that led us to adopt this model and the total implications of its adoption, let us point out that it forces us to focus upon variability in archaeological sites. The structure of this variability, or the lack of it, in terms of the distribution and covariation of artifacts, features, structures, and other kinds of archaeological data leads to a rigorous description of the site and its contents; the interplay of deductive and inductive logic leads to the specific hypotheses that are being tested in our research.

We are convinced that the most powerful means for both description and the testing of multiple hypotheses lies in the various techniques of quantitative analysis developed and refined largely within the field of statistics. These quantitative techniques of description and statistical inference are based upon probability theory and rest on the assumption that an adequate and reliable sample is present in the absence of a totally excavated site.

The importance of proper sampling procedures for archaeological research involving quantitative techniques of analysis has been discussed by Vescelius (1960), Binford (1964), Cowgill (1964), Ragir (1967), Redman and Watson (1970), Cowgill (1970), Peters (1970), Rootenberg (1964), and others. James Hill, in a paper presented at the annual meeting of the Society for American Archaeology in 1967, further clarified the role of probability sampling in archaeological research. This lucid paper was aimed at a clarification of some of the misconceptions regarding sampling in archaeology, in particular the importance of the experience and expertise of the investigator in designing statistically valid sampling designs.

The following paragraphs discuss the sampling design for the excavation of the Grasshopper Ruin, given the context of method and theory discussed briefly above. The great size of the Grasshopper site precludes the possibility of total excavation (Fig. 13), presenting us with the problem of drawing a sample that will be usable in terms of our research goals. The sample must be large enough to permit quantitative analyses and so distributed as to take advantage of our experience and knowledge of sites of this sort and the Grasshopper Ruin in particular.

We are convinced that the proper sampling technique for our research is stratified sampling. Briefly, the population from which the sample is to be drawn is divided into subpopulations based upon prior knowledge, expertise, and, in some cases, observations and preliminary or exploratory research. These subpopulations or strata may then be sampled in an unbiased manner in proportion to their size relative to the total population. (In market research, for example, age, sex, economic, and neighborhood strata have been utilized in drawing samples to assess the market potential for a variety of products.) Since archaeological sites are seldom, if ever, undifferentiated, homogeneous wholes, stratified sampling seems quite appropriate. Such subpopulations as ceremonial structures or areas, habitation units, or trash concentration might be recognized in prehistoric ruins utilizing expertise. Differential densities and kinds of surface debris might also be useful. The kinds of strata that are recognized would obviously depend upon the kinds of problems being investigated.

Using the primary arguments that continuously bonded walls were built at the same time and that if walls abut one another they were either built at the same time or one wall at a later time, one can infer the relative sequence of construction of rooms and groups of rooms. Styles of masonry are useful in arguing constructional sequences as well. These arguments and their implications are more formally discussed by Wilcox (1975 and n.d.)

Fieldwork has led to the identification of a hierarchy of descriptive constructs at the site. The *construction unit* is defined as the minimal set of rooms that was built during a single building event; the *room block* is a set of three of more contiguous construction units. Wilcox (1975) recognizes an intervening category: the *aggregation unit*, the set of contiguous

FIGURE 13. The Grasshopper Ruin

rooms that was actually built as a single construction event and may be larger than a single construction unit. Identification of the aggregation unit is dependent upon excavation; in most cases it cannot be discovered from the analysis of bonded and abutted corners alone. Another key concept is the *core unit,* which is the original or earliest construction unit in each room block. The relative ordering of *contiguous* construction units with a room block is in terms of the distance from the core unit and is called the *construction phase.*

It is now also possible to argue a meaningful typology of rooms based upon size. Excavation of a number of rooms at the ruin suggested that the original function of rooms smaller than 15 square meters tended to be for storage, whereas rooms greater than 15 square meters in area were utilized for a range of domestic and habitation activities. This dichotomy is complicated by the fact that reuse of rooms, a common phenomenon at Grasshopper, often meant a change in function from the initial use. However, it does suggest two useful strata for the drawing of future samples of rooms for excavation: "large" and "small" sizes with the division at 15 square meters.

We may now describe the Grasshopper Ruin as a masonry pueblo of about 500 rooms distributed among 12 room blocks and 21 smaller groupings of rooms and construction units (Fig. 13). The main part of the site consists of 3 large room blocks located on either side of the original channel of the intermittent stream. On the east side is Room Block 1 with 93 rooms; the west unit consists of 2 room blocks, Room Block 2 on the west bank of the stream with 92 rooms plus the Great Kiva and Room Block 3 with 99 rooms. Together these room blocks bound the larger Plaza I and the smaller Plaza II. Access from the exterior was through two corridors, one to the south of Plaza I and the other to the east of Plaza II. Additional room blocks and smaller units of rooms are located adjacent to the 3 largest room blocks and on the surrounding low hills (Fig. 13). Reid and Shimada (n.d.) present a more detailed description of the ruin and especially the unique aspects of the "outliers."

Thus far we have been discussing the divisions of the community based upon the sequence of construction of rooms insofar as that can be inferred from the results of the "cornering project." A meaningful sampling design should go beyond this level, focusing on socially and behaviorally meaningful units that made up this extinct society and the changes that such units underwent during the 125 years of the community's existence.

Many of the problems we are attempting to solve at Grasshopper concern the location of such viable socioeconomic groups, their activities in the community, and their changes through time. The distribution of such units undoubtedly varied greatly over the temporal span of the community as rooms were built and abandoned, sometimes reused, sometimes not. Since most rooms at Grasshopper have more than one living surface or "floor," reflecting reuse of the rooms over time, the identification of contemporaneous utilization of floors in contiguous groups of rooms is a difficult but essential task.

I feel we should avoid a simple and mechanical application of probability sampling as a solution to the selection of rooms and areas of the site for excavation. The cornering project has given us information on the building sequence of the various parts of the ruin, but it has not provided us with the sequence of abandonment and reuse of rooms or groups or with the spatial domain of viable social units making use of such room sets. We should take advantage of the information we have from the cornering project to select initial samples of rooms to excavate; room block, construction unit, and room size might be used to partition the population of rooms into strata for sampling. The excavation of the sampled rooms should tell us how to expand the excavations to additional rooms. Thus a two-stage or "cluster-sampling" (Binford 1964) approach would seem to be most efficient. Nonroom space might be stratified on the basis of other criteria but subjected to a similar two-stage approach. For example, plazas might be stratified into space adjacent to living areas (e.g., rooms) and the more central plaza areas.

Such a two-stage sampling design takes advantage of the information we now have and plans for the expansion of the sample following the initial sampling stage. However, our sampling program for the excavation of the prehistoric burials at Grasshopper is more complicated. The skeletal population is distributed among at least seven cemeteries, as well as beneath the floors of rooms in the pueblo. Some analysis has already been carried out on the mortuary data (Clark 1969; Griffin 1967, 1969), with much additional work in progress. To date we have excavated 573 human burials, and analyses of age and sex have been completed for 471 skeletons.

Most of the cemetery areas at the site lie beneath three to five feet of modern sediment, making the excavation of burials a slow and expensive activity. We cannot define the perimeters of the burial areas nor can we discern burial densities from the modern surface. An areal approach is possible as a means for sampling, but tons of overburden would have to be removed. Thus far we have not attempted any systematic sampling scheme for the burials outside the pueblo walls; this problem remains to be solved and our sample to date, although large, is undoubtedly skewed, as the vital statistics suggest.

Walter Birkby of the Arizona State Museum, in addition to determining the age and sex of the skeletal material, has other analyses in progress. An analysis of nonmetric discontinuous traits is being carried out with the goal of elucidating aspects of social organization from biological data along lines recently described by Lane and Sublett (1972). At the least, these studies should suggest whether or not the cemetery populations were endogamous or exogamous units.

Pollen recovered from the graves indicates the use of plants in graveside mortuary ceremonies. These pollens will be compared to pollen recovered from the floors of ceremonial rooms in the pueblo in the hope of tying the use of cemeteries to specific sections of the site. Stylistic attribute analyses of the grave goods as well as variability in styles of interment and grave pits should help in this effort.

Developing a chronological sequence for the burials is a difficult task. Stratigraphic analysis of styles of grave goods, and the intrasite fossil pollen sequence are being employed. But at this point in our analysis we can only provide rough chronological control. We hope to refine the sequence through the analysis of fine-scale variation of stylistic attributes in the mortuary goods. Even with our gross control of the sequence, however, some interesting differences are suggested in mortality rates, especially of infants, as discussed below.

Our plans for sociological investigations at the community include analysis of decorative attributes on the ceramics, similar to the studies of Deetz (1965), Longacre (1970a), and Hill (1970). Many additional stylistic variables from other classes of artifactual data will be utilized as well. These analyses should permit inferences concerning inheritances, postmarital residence patterns, and other organizational and behavioral phenomena. Inferences forthcoming from these studies should be strengthened by the analysis of human burials and the interpretation of the construction sequence at the site.

With these plans for subsequent work in mind, let me briefly summarize what we do know about the community, its organization, history, and growth, and about the population there from about A.D. 1275 until its abandonment at about 1400. Let me first discuss the growth of the pueblo.

The initial construction at the site took place in the last quarter of the thirteenth century, A.D. 1275–1300, which we call the establishment period. Massive construction was carried out at the site during the period we label the expansion period, c. A.D. 1300–1330. More than half of the tree-ring dates from Grasshopper cluster during this period. Many of the central three-room blocks on either side of the stream were built by A.D. 1330. For example, the corridor south of the Plaza I was roofed in 1320, indicating that construction was under way in the southern parts of Room Blocks 1 and 2 by that time.

Dating of the building sequence after A.D. 1330 is less secure, but many of the outliers seem to have been built after this time. We have been fairly successful in controlling the time of construction and the relative time of abandonment for the seventy rooms we have excavated to date. The sequence of growth at the pueblo and the dated use of specific areas of the town provide a source of data for estimating the population at various times in the community's lifespan. At this point, it seems likely that a relatively small founding population was joined by increasing numbers of people during the earlier portion of the fourteenth century. The subsequent growth of the town is not as clear, and we do not know what proportion of the expansion was the result of natural population increase and what was caused by immigration. Fieldwork planned for the next several years may clarify this situation.

Let me now discuss the burial data themselves. We have recovered 573 burials to date at the site, but only 471 have been analyzed thus far. Of these, 289 died before reaching reproductive age and 233 of these by age 5. The average age of death for the entire group was between 15 and 16 years of age, with only 18 individuals reaching the age of 50 or greater.

Of those individuals who reached maturity, 64 were males and 115 were females, suggesting a skewing resulting from sampling bias. Interestingly, this is an opposite bias from that discovered at Pecos Pueblo (Howells 1960), where many more males were recovered than females. We hope to overcome the problem by greatly enlarging our sample size and increasing our areal coverage in the next decade of research. Although the sample appears to be biased, there are some interesting suggestions of differences in the skeletal population. For example, if individuals survived to maturity, there appears to be a slightly longer lifespan for males than for females (about 37 years for males and 34 years for females). The high infant mortality (nearly 50 percent of the burials) seems strikingly high compared with Pecos and other similar populations (Howells 1960:169–72). This may point to a sampling bias during the Pecos excavations. Most of the infant burials at Grasshopper were interred through the room floors. If excavations were not carried below room floors at Pecos beyond test pits or trenches, many of the infant burials would have been missed if a similar pattern of within-room interment was present.

Of the 246 burials that are fairly well dated as a result of the construction sequence at the site, there are some suggestions of a higher infant mortality during the late period of the occupation. This may be a factor of sampling bias, of course, but it may also point to other factors. We suspect increasing environmental stress during the later portion of the fourteenth century. If this stress, which probably led to the abandonment of the pueblo, affected the food supply, thereby decreasing nutrition, we might well expect an increase in infant mortality, abortion, and so forth. Analyses of pathologies in the skeletal material that might indicate nutritional stress are being carried out.

Another study involves a series of computer-assisted simulation models designed to model variously sized populations and pueblo growth. These analyses permit statements about the nature of population growth at Grasshopper, the initial size of the founding population, the periods and amounts of immigration, and other factors. Basic data include fluctuations in amount of construction, and, as far as I know, this represents the first time such data have been used for demographic analysis in the Puebloan Southwest.

Translating numbers of rooms into numbers of people provides great problems. I have followed Hill's arguments (1970:75–77) in estimating about 3 people per room at the Grasshopper site. In his study of the Broken K Pueblo, Hill notes an average room size of 9 square meters, suggesting on the basis of ethnographic data that about 2.8 persons per room would be a reasonable estimate. Using households rather than rooms, the estimate he arrives at is somewhat lower, 1.7 persons per room. Since the rooms at Grasshopper are much larger than those at Broken K Pueblo (the average is 16 square meters), an estimate of 2.8 persons per room seems acceptable. The important point is to hold this value constant throughout the analysis.

I have also followed Hill's argument concerning the average number of abandoned rooms in a Pueblo village at any given time (Hill 1970:75–77).

Hill uses a figure of 22 percent; I have upped his estimate slightly to 25 percent. I realize that this figure may well be too low for the final period of the abandonment process at Grasshopper, but for the purpose of this analysis it seems adequate.

Using the data from the cornering-growth project at the site, we can now estimate the size of the founding population at the Grasshopper Pueblo as approximately 100 people based upon the number of rooms in the three core construction units. This is actually a conservative estimate given the fact there are over 30 rooms in the initial construction at the site (Fig. 14). At the peak of growth there were about 500 rooms. Using the 25 percent abandonment figure this means that the maximal population must have been about 1,050 people (375 rooms, 2.8 people per room).

The population statistic that summarizes the birth and death rates of a population is the percentage of annual increase for the population. For most societies on the same level of cultural complexity as Grasshopper, the rate of annual increase is 1 percent or lower (Krzywicki 1934:271); only a few societies achieve an annual increase of greater than 3 or 4 percent and these are special cases involving particular ecological conditions in island settings. The high infant mortality evidenced in the skeletal data would argue for a low annual population growth, probably 1 percent or lower.

However, if we begin with a population of 100 individuals and increase that group by a factor of 1 percent per year, the maximal population size in 125 years (the lifespan of the Grasshopper community) would only be about 360 people. Thus, the pueblo village should only consist of approximately 125 rooms. To explain this 500-room pueblo, an annual increase of nearly 2 percent would be required, and this figure seems far too high. To account for the enormous surge of construction in the early decades of the fourteenth century at Grasshopper, the annual increase in population from A.D. 1275 to 1330 must have approached 4 percent, a figure that is also far too high.

These data suggest that the original founding population must have been joined by other groups of people who immigrated to the community in the early part of the thirteenth century. Immigration would seem to be the most reasonable explanation for the enormous amount of construction during the expansion period of the pueblo's growth. The stylistic homogeneity of the cultural materials we have recovered suggests that the im-

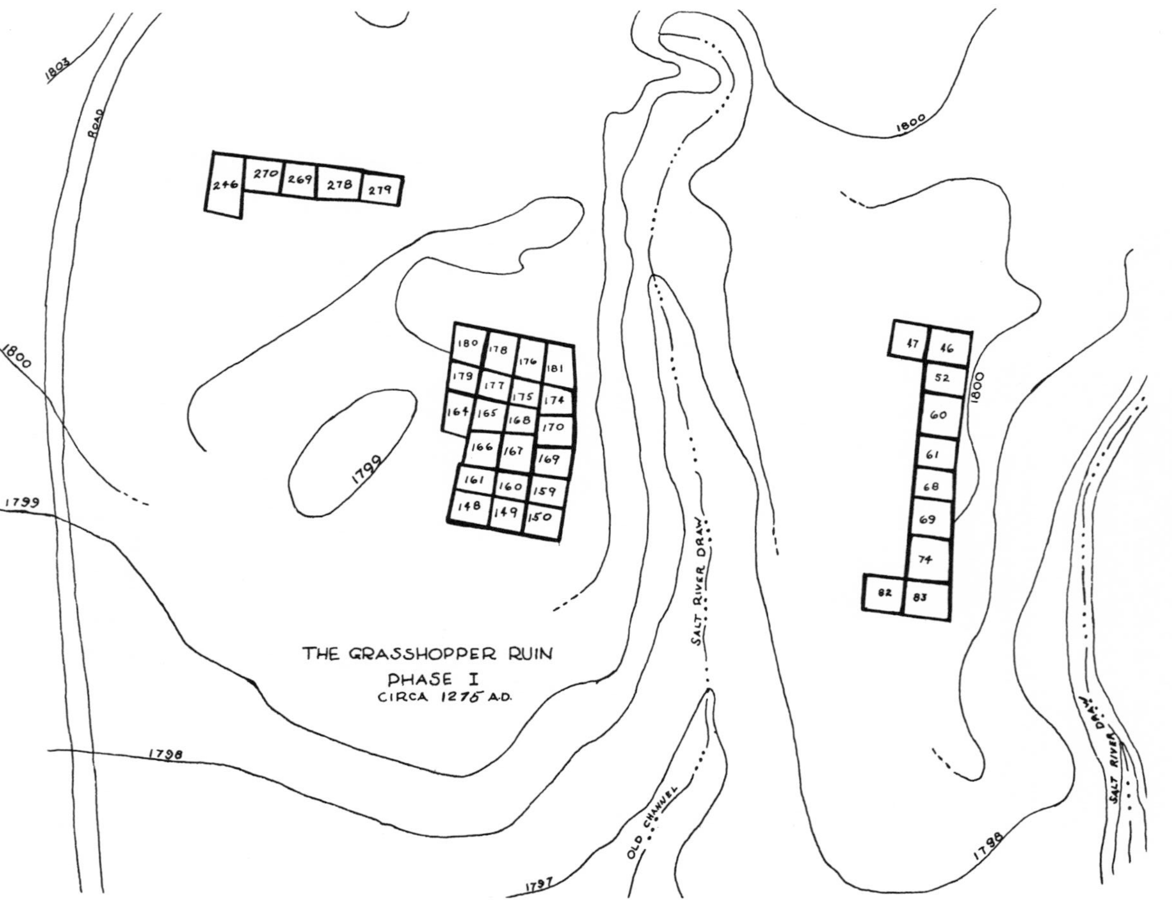

FIGURE 14. The Grasshopper Ruin, Phase I (c. A.D. 1275)

migrating populations were drawn from the local region; this is also suggested by the data from archaeological surveys carried out in the Grasshopper area (Tuggle 1970).

A Dynamo simulation program was employed to model annual population growth and immigration at Grasshopper as a means to study the population dynamics at the site. Although the rate is probably too high, I used an annual percentage of population growth of 1 percent. With a founding population of 100 people, the population would have grown to only slightly more than 150 people by A.D. 1320, when the corridor at the southern end of the western portion of the site was roofed. In order to account for the number of rooms that were constructed, I simulated an immigration of 350 people at A.D. 1315, roughly the midpoint of the expansion period.

Using the 1 percent annual increase, the population at Grasshopper by A.D. 1330 would have been 575 people, requiring just over 200 rooms. This does not seem to be out of line with what exists in the archaeological evidence. However, assuming an annual increase of 1 percent, a maximal population of about 1,050 people would not have been achieved until nearly A.D. 1400. The population must have peaked somewhat before that date. This plus the fact that much of the construction of detached room blocks, the outliers, seems to be late in the lifespan of the community leads me to suspect that additional immigration took place at Grasshopper.

An immigrating group of about 80 people at A.D. 1375 would have produced a peak population of 1,050 in 1382 with a 1 percent annual increase. That would leave only about twenty years for the population to dwindle and ultimately abandon the community. If the population did not abandon the pueblo but rather gradually died out, then the population peak must have been reached at an earlier time, and the archaeological evidence does not support this.

This initial attempt to deal with the dynamics of population at the Grasshopper Pueblo must, of course, be viewed as a crude effort at best. Nonetheless, it does show the importance of construction-sequence data as a source for permitting such analysis. Even though the study is at such a preliminary stage, it has suggested two interesting arguments. First, I have been able to argue that normal growth of the founding population cannot account for the ultimate size of this pueblo community; immigration is indicated. Second, the average annual increase in population probably was around 1 percent.

It would be interesting to model variously sized cohorts based upon age and sex for the founding population and for hypothesized groups of immigrants; one might also model small immigrant groups at a variety of times in the community's life. I have decided to defer such simulation until additional excavations have been carried out that could provide some insight into the nature of the founding population, such as its age and sex composition. Subsequent archaeological work might shed light as well on the nature of immigration at Grasshopper. Simulation of population dynamics at that point could be a powerful tool rather than an interesting exercise.

NOTES

1. I acknowledge and thank the following persons for their generous help over the past several years in developing the ideas expressed in this paper. R. H. Thompson, institutional director of the Archaeological Field School, has been a constant source of encouragement and support. The assistant directors of the Field School since 1965 have been particularly helpful in all stages of the research: James E. Ayres, P. B. Griffin, Jr., H. David Tuggle, R. Gwinn Vivian, and J. Jefferson Reid. My heartfelt thanks are also due the other members of the professional staff of the Field School, especially the more than two hundred students who have participated in the research and training at Grasshopper. Special thanks go to the directors of the "Cornering Project": David R. Wilcox, Michael Collins, J. Jefferson Reid, and Izumi Shimada. I have benefited from discussions with a number of nonarchaeologists, especially R. R. Laxton, Department of Mathematics, University of Nottingham; Perry Gluckman, statistician on the staff of the Center for Advanced Study in the Behavioral Sciences, Stanford, California; Professor Alan Stuart, Department of Statistics, University of London; and Professor L. L. Cavalli-Sforza, Department of Genetics, Stanford University. In addition, special thanks are due Walter Birkby, Dr. H. K. Bliebtreu, and Dr. Jane Underwood, physical anthropologists at the University of Arizona. I also thank Dr. Robert F. Heizer and Dr. Alan Swedlund for helpful comments and suggestions.

I am grateful to all the above persons for their beneficial suggestions and discussions. I alone, of course, am responsible for the shortcomings in this statement, particularly where their advice has not been followed.

Preparation of this paper was completed during my fellowship year at the Center for Advanced Study in the Behavioral Sciences, Stanford, California.

2. Support of the research and student training at Grasshopper has been provided by the National Science Foundation over the past ten years. Aid from the Division of Graduate Education, Advanced Science Program of the National Science Foundation, came in a number of grants awarded to the University of Arizona (GE-7781; GZ-22; GZ-397; GZ-745; GZ-1113; GZ-1493; GZ-1924). In addition, research grants were awarded to the University of Arizona for the prehistoric investigations at Grasshopper by the National Science Foundation (GS-2566 and GS-33436).

6

The Maximum Opportunity for Natural Selection in Some Human Populations

JAMES N. SPUHLER

Department of Anthropology
University of New Mexico

NATURAL SELECTION AND BIOLOGICAL FITNESS

Natural selection includes all those complex ways in which gene frequencies are changed between generations through the action of differential fertility and mortality. "Fertility" here is used in the demographic sense of reproductive performance rather than in the medical sense of reproductive capacity; we will use "fecundity" to cover the latter topic. If we let the mortality and fertility of one class of individuals, phenotypes, genotypes, or genes be used as a standard of comparison, we can find out if other classes show the same, a higher, or a lower mortality and fertility.

We say natural selection takes place when some kinds of individuals, phenotypes, or genes have more or less descendants than the other kinds. Genes that, on the average, increase the probability of survival to the reproductive age, or increase the probability of higher fertility, or both will increase in number in later generations.

The notion of "fitness" is used to talk about natural selection. Two classes of individuals or genes have the same fitness if they are observed to have the same relative fertility and mortality. Genetic fitness, sometimes called "Darwinian fitness," refers only to facts about, or theoretical statements about, differential mortality and fertility. "Fitness" defined in this way is, of course, quite different from other kinds of "fitness" where the criteria may involve social or cultural rather than reproductive performance.

The purpose of this paper is to review the literature on the application of Crow's index of the opportunity for selection and its components due to mortality and fertility in human populations. New calculations of the indices for a number of human populations selected for the anthropological interest are included. Where data are available, the standard errors of the index and its components are presented.

The potential intensity of natural selection due to mortality before the reproductive period may be assessed by the ratio of the number of individuals or gametes eliminated to those selected. We will call this ratio z. Haldane (1932) showed that the value of z varies greatly in natural populations of different species of plants and animals. When prereproductive mortality is as low as 4 percent, as in some human populations, z is only $4/96 = 0.04$. If the selection is as intense as among pollen grains of the giant redwood tree, *Sequoia gigantea* (of which, during a period of several hundred years, only one pollen grain fertilizes a seed that grows into an adult giant tree), then z would be very large, perhaps larger than 10^{12}. Values of z from 100 to 10,000 are common in nature.

Total selection intensity due to mortality is low in human populations compared with that found in species with higher reproductive rates, for example field mice, robins, and *Drosophila*. Yet many contemporary human populations, and especially many of those traditionally of "anthropological interest," produce five or more children per family—a reproductive rate allowing maintenance of the population number with the death of 60 percent or more offspring before completion of the reproductive period.

Index of Opportunity for Selection

Consider a population with k genotypes g_i, in proportions p_i, and fitness w_i (Crow 1958):

$$\begin{array}{lll} \text{Genotypes, } g: & g_1, g_2, \ldots, g_i; & \\ \text{Proportions, } p: & p_1, p_2, \ldots, p_i; & (\Sigma p_i = 1) \\ \text{Fitness, } w: & w_1, w_2, \ldots, w_i. & \end{array}$$

Here "fitness" is the expected number of progeny counted at birth.

In the initial generation g, the mean fitness $\overline{w}$ and variance in fitness V_w are

$$\begin{aligned} \overline{w} &= \sum_{i=1}^{k} p_i w_i / p_i \\ &= \sum p_i\, w_i, \end{aligned}$$

and

$$\begin{aligned} V_w &= \sum_{i=1}^{k} p_i (w_i - \overline{w})^2 \\ &= \sum p_i w_i^2 - \overline{w}^2. \end{aligned}$$

If we assume that fitness of each genotype is constant between generations, after selection the new proportions p' in the offspring generation $g + 1$ are

$$\begin{array}{ll} \text{Proportions, } p': & p_1 w_1, p_2 w_2, \ldots, p_i w_i; \\ \text{Fitness, } w: & w_1, w_2, \ldots, w_i. \end{array}$$

The relative frequency of the *i*th genotype in generation $g + 1$ is

$$p'_i = p_i w_i / \overline{w},$$

and the new mean fitness, $\overline{w}^1$, is

$$\begin{aligned} \overline{w}' &= \sum_{i=1}^{k} p_i w_i \\ &= \sum (p_i w_i) w_i / \overline{w} \\ &= \sum p_i w_i^2 / \overline{w}. \end{aligned}$$

Thus, the change in mean fitness due to selection between generations g and $g + 1$ is

$$\begin{aligned} \Delta \overline{w} &= \overline{w}' - \overline{w} \\ &= (\sum p_i w_i^2 / \overline{w}) - \overline{w} \\ &= (\sum p_i w_i^2 - \overline{w}) / \overline{w}, \end{aligned}$$

and the relative increment in fitness in one generation is

$$\frac{\Delta\overline{w}}{\overline{w}} = \frac{\sum p_i w_i^2 - \overline{w}^2}{\overline{w}^2}.$$

Now, if we define I, Crow's index of the maximum opportunity for selection, as $I = \Delta\overline{w}/\overline{w}$, then

$$I = \frac{V_w}{\overline{w}^2}.$$

If we set $\overline{w} = 1$, as the standard is arbitrary, the expression

$$\Delta\overline{w} = V_w^2 \,/\, \overline{w}$$

is identical with R. A. Fisher's Fundamental Theorem of Natural Selection, which is that "the rate of increase in fitness of any organism at any time is equal to its genetic variance in fitness at that time" (Fisher 1958: 37). This theorem holds in general for single loci, but it is inexact for some models of interacting loci.

Mortality and Fertility Components of Selection

Natural selection operates by differential mortality or fertility. The index of opportunity for selection may be separated into two components associated with differential mortality and fertility (Crow 1958; Jacquard 1970; Cavalli-Sforza and Bodmer 1971).

The interval between successive human generations g and g + 1 may be partitioned into (1) prereproductive and (2) reproductive periods. The prereproductive period goes from birth to puberty, or, by the convention adopted by most demographers, from 0 to 15 years of age. The female reproductive period goes from menarche to menopause, or, by convention, from 15 to 40 (sometimes 45) years of age.

Assume that a proportion of p_d of persons counted at birth dies before the reproductive age and a proportion $p_s = (1 - p_d)$ survives to the reproductive period and has varying numbers of offspring. Let $p_0, p_1, p_2, \ldots, p_n$ represent the proportion of women who survive to 15 years and who give birth to X_i offspring $(X = 0, 1, \ldots, n)$.

Let

$\overline{X}$ = overall mean number of female births, and
$\overline{X}_s$ = mean number of female births per surviving women.

Then

$$p_s = \sum_{i=0}^{n} X_i,$$
$$\overline{X}_s = \sum_{i=0}^{m} x_i p_i \,/\, \sum_{x=0}^{n} p_i,$$

and

$$p_s = \overline{X} \,/\, X_s,$$
$$\overline{X}_s = \overline{X} \,/\, p_s.$$

Remembering that the zeros are averaged in to obtain $\overline{X}$ and $\overline{X}_s$ and that the nonsurvivors are counted as having zero children, the mean $\overline{X}$ and the variance V_x of the numbers of children born alive are

$$\overline{X} = \sum_{x=0}^{n} X_i p_i$$

and

$$V_x = p_d(0-\overline{X})^2 + \sum_{i=0}^{w} p_i(X_i - \overline{X})^2.$$

Now *I* can be written

$$I = V/\overline{X}^2 = \frac{1}{\overline{X}^2}\,[p_d(0 - \overline{X})^2 + \sum_{s} p_i(X_i - \overline{X})^2] \tag{1}$$

or, by adding and subtracting $p_s(\overline{X}_s - \overline{X})^2$ from the right side of equation (1),

$$I = \frac{1}{\overline{X}^2}\,[p_d(0 - \overline{X})^2 + p_s(\overline{X}_s - \overline{X})^2 + \sum_{s} p_i(X_i - \overline{X})^2$$
$$-p_s(\overline{X}_s - \overline{X})^2]. \tag{2}$$

Now let V_m be the variance due to differential mortality and V_f be that due to differential fertility, so that

$$V_m = p_d \overline{X}^2 + p_s(\overline{X}_s - \overline{X})^2$$
$$= \overline{X}^2 \, p_d/p_s \tag{3}$$

from the relation $p_s = \overline{X}/\overline{X}_s$, and

$$V_f = (1/p_s) \sum_s p_i \, (X_i - \overline{X}_s)^2$$
$$= (1/p_s) \, [\sum_s p_i \, (X_i - \overline{X})^2 - p_s(\overline{X}_s - \overline{X})^2]. \tag{4}$$

Thus, from equations (2), (3), and (4)

$$I = V_m/\overline{X}^2 + p_s(V_f/\overline{X}^2)$$
$$= (V_m/\overline{X}^2) + (1/p_s) \, (V_f/\overline{X}_s^2)$$
$$= I_m + (1/p_s) \, I_f. \tag{5}$$

Since $\overline{X}_s = \overline{X}/p_s$, we can rewrite the components so that Crow's index of the opportunity, due to differential mortality, is

$$I_m = \frac{p_d\overline{X}^2 + p_s(\overline{X}_s - \overline{X})^2}{\overline{X}^2}$$
$$= p_d + p_s \left(\frac{1}{p_s} - 1\right)^2$$
$$= [p_d p_s + (1 - p_s)^2]/p_s$$
$$= p_d/p_s. \tag{6}$$

DATA ON CROW'S INDEX

Data on Crow's index and its components in 53 populations are given in Table 45. Additional details about each population sample, including the references, are given in the notes to the table in the appendix to this chapter. Except for a few cases included for comparison, data on the index and its components for large state and national populations are not presented here(data are given on 20 such populations in Spuhler 1962, 1963).

The columns of Table 45, reading from left to right, give the number of the population (which also serves as a key to the notes); the name of the population; the period when the data apply; the size of the population (usually the number of persons in the local population, for instance, a village or tribe); N_f, the number of females sampled who have completed the reproductive period (usually taken as 40 or 45 years); $\bar{x}_8$, the number of live-born children to women at the end of the reproductive period; V_f, the variance in number of live-born children; p_d, the probability of dying before reaching reproductive age; I_m, the component of the maximum opportunity for selection due to mortality before the beginning of the reproductive period (usually taken as 15 years), with its standard deviation; I_f, the component due to fertility with its sigma; and I_t, the total index and its standard deviation.

The rows of Table 45 are listed in order of increase in I_t.

The variances (V) of I_t, I_m, and I_f, obtained by Barrai and Fraccaro (1965) and based on the method outlined in Kendall and Stuart (1958: 233), are

$$V_{I_f} = \frac{I_f^2}{n}\left(\frac{4 - V_f^2}{V_f^2} + \frac{4V_f}{\bar{x}_8^2} - \frac{4_3}{V_f\bar{x}_8}\right),$$

where n is the sample size and μ_3 and μ_4 are the third and fourth moments about the mean.

The standard deviation of I_f is

$$\sigma_{I_t} = \sqrt{V}_{I_t}.$$

The standard deviation of I_m is

$$I_m = p_d/p_8^2 = [p_d(1 - p_d)/n]/p_8^2.$$

The standard deviation of I_t is computed as σI_f, but the n is increased by adding the expected number of women who die before reproductive age to those entered in the fertility distribution as having zero live-born children.

The means and ranges of the populations in Table 45 plus the latest cohort of the five populations in Table 46 are

	$\bar{x}_8$	V_f	I_m
Means	5.200 ± 2.098	8.440 ± 4.622	0.555 ± 0.464
Ranges	1.32–9.92	1.81–23.52	0.030–2.267

	I_f	I_t
Means	0.416 ± 0.334	1.176 ± 0.781
Ranges	0.071–1.681	0.229–3.689

TABLE 45

DATA ON CROW'S INDEX OF THE MAXIMUM OPPORTUNITY FOR SELECTION (ARRANGED BY INCREASING VALUES OF THE TOTAL INDEX, I_t)

Population	*Period*	*Size*	N_f	$\bar{x}_s$	V_f	p_d	I_m	I_f	I_t
1. Hutterites	1950	8,542	340	8.97	13.43	.051	0.053 ± .013	0.167 ± .016	0.229 ± 0.023
2. Azapa, Chile	1966	314	18	6.40	8.40	.117	0.132	0.232	0.364
3. Deerfield, Mass., 1	1810	1,700	41	6.63	—	.209	0.264	0.136	0.436
4. Yanomama	1967	400	33	3.79	2.77	.180	0.219 ± .090	0.193 ± .054	0.455 ± 0.126
5. "Replacement Man"	—	—	—	2.10	—	.050	0.050	0.410	0.460
6. San Juan, N.M.	1925–36	504	24	9.92	6.99	.294	0.417 ± .157	0.071 ± .025	0.517 ± 0.172
7. Molinos, Chile	1965–66	105	16	7.20	11.91	.196	0.243	0.229	0.527
8. Tallensi	1943	3,000	40	5.98	3.12	.414	0.425 ± .123	0.088 ± .025	0.550 ± 0.138
9. Deerfield, Mass., 2	1810	1,700	—	6.22	—	.260	0.351	0.155	0.560
10. Chapiquiña, Chile	1965–66	200	27	8.50	—	.249	0.331	0.232	0.563
11. Yao	1946–47	762	78	4.86	8.86	.160	0.167 ± .050	0.375 ± .062	0.605 ± 0.100
12. Terena	1955–60	5,000	81	5.51	8.60	.210	0.272 ± .065	0.284 ± .043	0.632 ± 0.100
13. Belen, Chile	1965–66	177	47	5.82	6.95	.263	0.360	0.205	0.638
14. Khanna, Punjab	1959	10,692	459	7.48	8.01	.306	0.440 ± .037	0.143 ± .012	0.646 ± 0.046
15. Arica, Chile	1965–66	5,266	—	4.34	8.53	.128	0.146	0.453	0.665
16. Yako	1935–39	20,000	42	2.95	1.81	.274	0.381 ± .112	0.207 ± .042	0.667 ± 0.147
17. S. Pahira II	1963	c. 450	50	5.70	4.45	.326	0.484	0.137	0.687
18. S. Pahira I	1963	c. 450	50	5.44	4.05	.346	0.529	0.137	0.738
19. Xavanti	1964	796	35	5.66	5.37	.330	0.493 ± .145	0.168 ± .037	0.743 ± 0.178
20. New South Wales	1900	1 × 10[6]	10,272	6.19	15.26	.202	0.253 ± .006	0.399 ± .006	0.753 ± 0.011
21. !Kung, Farms	1969	2,000	91	4.11	6.65	.211	0.264 ± .060	0.394 ± .061	0.761 ± 0.114
22. Bengali Villages	1957	4,000	80	6.96	10.76	.313	0.450 ± .090	0.222 ± .040	0.722 ± 0.123
23. Nayasaland	1957	1,419	150	5.76	11.89	.242	0.320 ± .053	0.358 ± .044	0.793 ± 0.093
24. Karluk Eskimo	1962–64	148	12	8.75	23.52	.294	0.417 ± .222	0.307 ± .089	0.852 ± 0.316
25. Hottentot-Boer	1908	2,500	44	7.70	14.84	.309	0.545 ± .138	0.250 ± .060	0.932 ± 0.196
26. U.S. Whites	1964	191 × 10[6]	—	2.20	—	.030	0.030	0.920	0.950

TABLE 45 CONT'D.

Population	Period	Size	N_f	$\bar{x}_s$	V_f	p_d	I_m	I_f	I_t
27. Ngbaka	1957	375	64	5.48	11.78	.296	0.422 ± .097	0.392 ± .091	0.979 ± 0.186
28. Hirado, Japan	1965	40,881	—	5.10	—	.220	0.280	0.760	1.040
29. Lesu	1929–30	222	295	2.63	2.58	.346	0.529 ± .052	0.374 ± .038	1.100 ± 0.092
30. Northern Pahira	1963	c. 450	39	4.97	4.33	.449	0.815	0.175	1.133
31. !Kung, Ngamiland	1969	1,000	109	4.14	5.24	.395	0.651 ± .099	0.306 ± .051	1.157 ± 0.154
32. Ashanti	1945	81,894	1,017	3.89	10.41	.219	0.280 ± .019	0.687 ± .031	1.159 ± 0.051
33. Black Carib	1954–55	6,154	391	5.42	11.51	.365	0.575 ± .048	0.392 ± .027	1.192 ± 0.079
34. San Carlos Apache	1905	2,148	37	6.97	7.81	.479	0.919 ± .218	0.161 ± .036	1.227 ± 0.263
35. Tsumje, Nepal	1952–53	218	21	4.00	4.86	.417	0.714 ± .242	0.304 ± .090	1.234 ± 0.351
36. Caingang	1958	1,658	217	6.12	14.34	.410	0.696 ± .074	0.383 ± .040	1.345 ± 0.122
37. Rungus-Dasun	1956	192	34	3.79	6.75	.393	0.647 ± .177	0.469 ± .119	1.420 ± 0.326
38. Oglala Sioux	1897–1908	6,690	80	7.66	9.27	.540	1.112 ± .171	0.158 ± .034	1.446 ± 0.211
39. U.S. Nonwhites	1964	22 × 10⁶	—	2.70	—	.050	0.050	1.410	1.460
40. Thule Eskimo	1951	302	70	3.46	2.62	.511	1.043 ± .174	0.219 ± .036	1.491 ± 0.225
41. Cocos Island	1947	1,802	150	8.08	10.13	.551	1.227 ± .135	0.155 ± .025	1.572 ± 0.166
42. Huallatire, Chile	1966	218	27	7.30	9.89	.541	1.178	0.185	1.581
43. Pima	1905	3,900	35	7.03	11.80	.540	1.171 ± .270	0.239 ± .072	1.690 ± 0.369
44. Sioux-Ojibwa, mixed	1890	—	141	7.87	15.38	.540	1.177 ± .135	0.247 ± .034	1.716 ± 0.184
45. Nonoai	1958	507	162	2.37	3.63	.417	0.716 ± .087	0.646 ± .076	1.824 ± 0.193
46. Guarita	1958	515	185	2.39	4.94	.410	0.697 ± .080	0.866 ± .092	2.166 ± 0.216
47. Basoga	c. 1900–1905	500,000	36	7.03	6.97	.640	1.778 ± .370	0.141 ± .038	2.170 ± 0.436
48. Sioux-Ojibwa	1890	53,000	577	5.92	16.45	.540	1.173 ± .066	0.469 ± .030	2.193 ± 0.118
49. Ligeiro	1958	178	90	1.56	2.89	.439	0.744 ± .120	1.195 ± .184	2.829 ± 0.415
50. Cacique Doble	1958	132	57	1.74	5.07	.327	0.491 ± .113	1.681 ± .548	2.998 ± 0.871
51. Banyoro	c. 1900–1905	110,000	27	3.74	7.16	.634	1.741 ± .420	0.511 ± .162	3.142 ± 0.775
52. Australian Aborigines	1935	746	141	1.32	2.26	.450	0.816 ± .102	1.299 ± .180	3.173 ± 0.403
53. Peri	1928–29	210	15	4.27	7.93	.532	2.267 ± .702	0.436 ± .152	3.689 ± 1.125
Population	*Period*	*Size*	N_f	$\bar{x}_s$	V_f	p_d	I_m	I_f	I_t

The Australian aborigines have the lowest value of $\bar{x}_s$ (1.32) and San Juan Pueblo the highest (9.92). The variance in fertility, V_f, ranges from a low of 1.81 among the Yako to a high of 23.52 among the Karluk Eskimo (who are represented by a sample of only 12 women). The mortality component, I_m, is lowest in U.S. whites (0.030) and highest in the Peri (2.267); that of fertility, I_f, is lowest in the highly fertile San Juan Pueblo (0.071) and largest in the Cacique Doble (1.681). The total index, I_t, ranges from 0.229 in the Hutterites to 3.689 in the Peri.

The mortality component is greater than the fertility component in 35 of the 57 populations (61.4 percent), omitting the estimates for the hypothetical "Replacement Man" from the count.

The results of ten regression ($Y = a + bX$) and product-moment correlation analyses on the components of Crow's index are shown in Table 46.

TABLE 46
REGRESSION AND CORRELATION AMONG THE COMPONENTS OF CROW'S INDEX FOR 57 POPULATIONS

Y	X	a	$b \pm \sigma$	t	$s_{y \cdot x}$	r	r^2
I_t	I_f	0.650	+1.272 ± 0.262	4.846***	0.661	+0.544***	0.2960
I_t	I_m	0.461	+1.287 ± 0.145	8.885***	0.507	+0.765***	0.5850
I_t	V_f	1.448	−0.026 ± 0.025	1.046	0.807	−0.148	0.0220
I_t	$\bar{x}_s$	1.883	−0.136 ± 0.046	2.938***	0.733	−0.366**	0.1330
I_f	I_m	0.455	−0.074 ± 0.096	0.771	0.335	−0.102	0.0100
I_f	V_f	0.500	−0.013 ± 0.009	1.377	0.476	−0.023	0.0005
I_f	$\bar{x}_s$	0.981	−0.109 ± 0.015	7.066***	0.245	−0.687***	0.4710
I_m	V_f	0.625	−0.002 ± 0.015	0.160	0.476	−0.023	0.0005
I_m	$\bar{x}_s$	0.432	+0.029 ± 0.029	0.804	0.465	+0.107	0.0110
V_f	$\bar{x}_s$	0.822	+1.449 ± 0.245	5.912***	3.566	+0.645***	0.4160

** Significant at the 0.01 level.
*** Significant at the 0.001 level.
Unmarked values are not significant at the 0.05 level.

The columns of the table from left to right are as follows: Y = dependent variable; X = independent variable; a = Y intercept; $b \pm \sigma$ = regression coefficient with its standard error; $t = t$ value of the regression; $s_{y \cdot x} =$ standard error of estimate; $r =$ product-moment correlation coefficient; and $r^2 =$ the coefficient of determination expressing the proportion of the variance of Y given by X.

The total index, I_t, is more strongly determined by I_m than by I_f in the populations sampled, is not significantly determined by variation in V_f, and shows a significant negative regression on and negative correlation with $\bar{x}_s$.

Variation in the component due to mortality, I_m, is not significantly related to variation in V_f or $\bar{x}_s$.

About 42 percent of the variation of the variance in fertility, V_f, is determined by variation in the mean number of live-born children, $\bar{x}_s$.

These results support the conclusion of Neel and his associates (e.g., Salzano, Neel, and Maybury-Lewis 1967; Neel and Schull 1972) that known hunters and gatherers have relatively low fertility and mortality, lower than many agricultural peoples. The Australian aborigines (no. 52), the most primitive economically of the 57 peoples sampled here, have the lowest fertility, intermediate mortality, but variances sufficiently high to place the next to the highest in the total opportunity for selection. The other economically and technologically primitive groups, the !Kung hunters (no. 31), Thule Eskimo (no. 40), Yanomama (no. 4), and Xavanti (no. 19), are relatively low in fertility and mortality and intermediate in I_t, although only 3 of the 57 groups have a lower I_t than the Yanomama.

The mean total index for races is highest in the native Australians, followed in descending order by the Melanesian-Papuans, Africans, American Indians, Asians, Europeans, and Lapps. The range of the total index among races is greatest in the Amerindians (who make up nearly 40 percent of the groups sampled), followed in descending order by the Africans, Melanesian-Papuans, Asians, Europeans, and Lapps.

The two hybrid populations (nos. 25 and 44) are not remarkably distinguished in either fertility or mortality, but the mixed Sioux-Ojibwa-Europeans are more fertile than their unmixed Indian relatives.

Although the maximum opportunity for selection is lower in most modern industrial populations than in most developing nations and tribal groups, it is significantly greater than zero in all known human populations.

PRE AND POSTNATAL MORTALITY COMPONENTS

Crow (1973) extended the index and its components by considering separately mortality during the prenatal period and the period from birth to reproductive maturity.

If we let p_b designate the proportion of embryos (counted at conception or some early embryonic stage) that survive to live birth and let p_s represent the proportion of live born that survive to reproductive maturity, then $p_e p_s$ is the proportion of early embryos that survive to adulthood.

Setting

$\overline{X}_e$ = mean number of offspring per embryo (when counted during early embryonic stages),

$\overline{X}_b$ = mean number of offspring per newborn (when counted at birth), and

$\overline{X}_s$ = mean number of offspring per surviving adult, then

$$\overline{X}_e = p_b \overline{X}_b = p_b p_s \overline{X}_s.$$

The variance for embryonic mortality, V_{me}, is

$$\begin{aligned} V_{me} &= (1 - p_b)\ (0 - \overline{X}_e)^2 + p_b\ (\overline{X}_b - \overline{X}_e)^2 \\ &= \overline{X}_e^2\ [(1 - p_b)/p_b]. \end{aligned}$$

The variance of mortality from the embryonic to the reproductive period, V_m, is

$$\begin{aligned} V_m &= (1 - p_b p_s)\ (0 - \overline{X}_e)^2 + p_b p_s (\overline{X}_s - \overline{X}_e)^2 \\ &= \overline{X}_e^2\ [(1 - p_b p_s)/p_b p_s]. \end{aligned}$$

The variance of childhood mortality from birth to maturity, V_{mc}, is

$$\begin{aligned} V_{mc} &= V_m - V_{me} \\ &= [(1 - p_b p_s)/p_b p_s] - [(1 - p_b)/p_b]\overline{X}_e^2 \\ &= (1 - p_b)[(1 - p_s)/p_s]\overline{X}_e^2. \end{aligned}$$

The component of the total selective opportunity due to embryonic mortality, I_{me}, is the ratio of deaths to survivors counting from the early embryonic stages,

$$I_{me} = (1 - p_b)/p_b,$$

and the three components of the index, I, are

$$\begin{aligned} I &= V_{me}/\overline{X}_e^2 + V_{mc}/\overline{X}_e^2 + (p_b p_s)\ (V_f/\overline{X}_e^2) \\ &= (1 - p_b)/p_b + (1/p_b)\ [(1 - p_s)/p_s] + (1/p_b p_s)\ (V_f/\overline{X}_e^2) \\ &= I_{me} + (1/p_b) I_{mc} + (1/p_b p_s) I_f. \end{aligned}$$

The multiplicative nature of the three components of the total index is shown by rewriting in the form (Crow 1973)

$$1 + I = (1 + I_{me})\ (1 + I_{mc})\ (1 + I_f).$$

Johnson and Kensinger (1971) report a wastage rate of 0.208 in 158 pregnancies of Cashinahua women, giving the following indices calculated from the early embryonic stage: I_{me}, 0.263; I_{mc}, 0.786; I_f, 0.109; and I_t, 1.500. Their estimated pregnancy loss is central to that of 14.7 ± 0.4 in a study at the Montreal Children's Hospital of 6,835 conceptions (Warburton and Fraser 1964) and about 25 percent in the Kauai Pregnancy Study, Hawaii, on 3,082 conceptions (French and Bierman 1962).

CORRECTIONS TO THE INDICES FOR MATERNAL MORTALITY DURING THE FERTILE PERIOD

Kobayashi (1969) modified Crow's formulas for the variance in mortality and fertility to include the distribution of live births to women who die after puberty but before menopause as follows:

$$\begin{aligned} V_m &= p_d\,(0 - \bar{x})^2 + \sum_j p_j\,(\bar{x}_j - \bar{x})^2 \\ &= \sum_j p_j \bar{x}_j^2 - \bar{x}^2, \end{aligned}$$

where p_j denotes parents dying at age j during the childbearing period and $\bar{x}_j$ denotes mean number of births per parent dying at age j.

$$\begin{aligned} V_f &= \frac{1}{p_s} \sum_j \sum_i p_{ij}\,(x_i - \bar{x}_j)^2 \\ &= \frac{1}{p_s} (\sum_j \sum_i p_{ij}\, x_i^2 - \sum_j p_j\, x_j^2), \end{aligned}$$

where p_{ij} denotes parents having i births and dying at age j and p_s denotes $\sum p_j$.

Tomisaki is a fishing community, today a part of Tateyama City, on the southern coast of Boso Peninsula, Chiba Prefecture, Honshu, Japan. The official *koseki* records as well as temple records were used to obtain data on date of birth, date and place of each childbirth, and date of death for each individual in these birth cohorts. Since *koseki* records movements in and out of the district, it was possible to obtain the required information on females in the cohort who had moved away from Tomisaki. The distribution of births in two Tomisaki female birth cohorts is presented in Table 47.

Table 48 shows the effect of Kobayashi's correction on the indices and their components.

Neel and his associates (Neel and Chagnon 1968 and later papers) suggest that Crow's index and its components would be more realistic biologically if data on births to women dying during the reproductive period were included in the calculations. They indicate that omission of such data may be a considerable source of error, especially in agrarian populations. Their inclusion would lower the mean number of live-born children, increase the variance in fertility, and increase the value of I_f.

CRITICISM OF CROW'S INDICES

The most stringent criticism of the index of opportunity for selection was made by Morton (1970:255):

> The opportunity for selection through mortality is higher in primitive populations than in modern ones, but surprisingly the opportunity for selection through fertility is still relatively high. What can we conclude from these results? In particular, do they tell us more than infant mortality, mean family size, or other demographic indices? The answer is negative. Neither mortality nor fertility is entirely heritable, and estimates of heritability are notoriously unreliable. Do accidental deaths in primitive populations reduce heritability more than contraception in modern populations? To phrase this question is to realize the hopelessness of answering it. And if we could randomize the environment to obtain a valid estimate of heritability, what then? It would apply to all causes of morbidity and to no particular genetic system. Estimated from family resemblance it would reflect additive variation, but heterosis is largely non-additive.

TABLE 47
NUMBER OF CHILDREN EVER BORN AND AGE OF MOTHERS AT DEATH IN TWO TOMISAKI, JAPAN, FEMALE BIRTH COHORTS

Number of Children Ever Born	*Age at Death of Mothers*									*Total*
	0–14	15–19	20–24	25–29	30–34	35–39	40–44	45–49	50+	
					Cohort Born in 1896–1900					
0	38	8	7	6	—	1	—	1	23	84
1	—	1	2	1	1	1	1	2	6	15
2	—	—	—	—	—	1	—	—	7	8
3	—	—	—	1	3	—	1	1	9	15
4	—	—	—	—	1	1	—	—	13	15
5	—	—	—	—	—	—	—	—	10	10
6	—	—	—	—	—	—	—	1	10	11
7	—	—	—	—	—	—	—	—	13	13
8	—	—	—	—	—	—	1	—	6	7
9	—	—	—	—	—	—	—	—	5	5
10	—	—	—	—	—	—	—	—	3	3
11	—	—	—	—	—	—	—	—	2	2
12	—	—	—	—	—	—	—	—	2	2
Total	38	9	9	8	5	4	3	5	109	190
					Cohort Born in 1916–1920					
0	53	12	5	1	2	—	—	20		93
1	—	—	4	2	—	—	—	17		23
2	—	—	—	2	—	1	1	11		15
3	—	—	—	—	—	—	2	26		28
4	—	—	—	—	—	—	—	13		13
5	—	—	—	—	—	—	—	15		15
6	—	—	—	—	—	—	—	6		6
7	—	—	—	—	—	—	—	2		2
8	—	—	—	—	—	—	—	—		—
9	—	—	—	—	—	—	—	1		1
Total	53	12	9	5	2	1	3	111		196

Crow's theory is to this generation what the twin method was to our predecessors: it may be applied but not defended.

Several other investigators have pointed out difficulties in the use and interpretation of Crow's *I* (see, for example, the discussions by Bourgeois-Pichat, Hajnal, Lerner, Mather, Morton, and Neel in Spuhler 1962). The index is based on total mortality from birth to sexual maturity and on variation in fertility during the reproductive period. Thus it does not include prenatal deaths or loss of individuals from the breeding population from death or emigration during the reproductive period, nor does it distinguish sterile from fecund survivors. As defined by Crow, it does not distinguish populations using or not using modern contraceptive methods. Even in countries with relatively good vital records, statistics on the variance in the number of live-born children per mother are among the least precise data in the demographic literature (Bourgeois-Pichat in Spuhler 1962:251). In the cases where information is collected by interview, the mortality data are equally untrustworthy. Fertility and mortality are not fully heritable and heritability cannot be accurately estimated in human populations. The index does not distinguish deaths that are fully determined by genes (e.g., cystic fibrosis) from those that are not genetic at all (e.g., deaths in railway or airplane accidents). Nor does it distinguish sterility with high genetic determination (e.g., hereditary intersexuality) from that with a low genetic determination (e.g., gonorrhea). But, in general, all of these difficulties were anticipated by Crow in his original paper. We now consider methods for dealing with two difficulties: mortality during the reproductive period and the distinct contributions to variance in fertility due to sterility and fecundity during the reproductive period.

ADJUSTMENTS FOR INCOMPLETE FERTILITY

Jacquard (1970) used a method devised by Henry (1953) to adjust French and United States data from incompleted families. Henry's method involves the formula

$$(\text{Number of } n\text{th births in year Y}) = \sum_{t=1}^{\infty} x_t b_t^{\,n-1}$$

where b_t^{n-1} is the number of $(n-1)$th births t years before y, and x_t is a factor derived from data collected on a national scale in Czechoslovakia, relating to the frequency of birth of children by birth order in the family.

The "probabilités d'agrandissement" (in percentages) of two French cohorts are

TABLE 48
KOBAYASHI'S CORRECTION OF CROW'S INDICES

	Cohort 1896–1900		*Cohort 1916–1920*	
Item	*Crow*	*Kobayashi*	*Crow*	*Kobayashi*
N_f	114	213	111	213
$\overline{X}$	3.16	2.44	1.85	1.66
$\bar{x}_s$	4.21	—	2.73	—
p_d	0.25	0.18	0.32	0.25
I_m	0.33	0.96	0.48	0.65
I_f/p_s	0.80	1.01	0.80	0.74
I	1.13	1.97	1.27	1.39

Cohort	a_0	a_1	a_2	a_3	a_4	a_5	a_6	a_7	a_8	a_9
1830	886	836	744	725	712	714	694	681	657	647
1900	814	690	590	580	600	630	630	630	630	630

From the above figures Jacquard obtained the distribution of completed family size among 1,000 women who had reached the reproductive age, based on the experience of the 1830 cohort. Of the 1,000, 886 had at least one child, so 1,000 − 886 = 114 had none; 886 (836/1,000) = 741 had at least two, so that 886 — 741 = 145 had one child, and so on. The distribution of family size for the 1,000 women is shown in Table 49.

In several cases I have used the method of Wilson and Hilferty (1935), based on the experience of native white mothers of New York State, exclusive of New York City, from 1920 to 1933 to estimate completed family size. They estimate, at any birth i, the number of future births to be expected by simply dividing the number of births of order higher than i by the number of births of order i.

SECULAR CHANGE IN SELECTION INTENSITIES

The patterns of survival and reproduction have changed markedly in the United States and most other industrialized nations during the past century (Kirk 1968). The mortality component of selection has been

TABLE 49
DISTRIBUTION OF FAMILY SIZE OF TWO FRENCH COHORTS

Cohort 1830		*Cohort 1900*	
Size	*No. Women*	*Size*	*No. Women*
0	114	0	186
1	145	1	255
2	190	2	232
3	152	3	137
4	115	4	77
5	82	5	41
6	62	6	27
7	45	7	20
8	33	8	9
9	22	9	6
10	14	10	3
11	13	11	3
12	10	12	1

dramatically reduced; the percentage of females surviving to fifteen years in the United States was 66.4 in 1840, 73.1 in 1880, 89.9 in 1920, and 97.5 in 1960. About 85 percent of each U.S. white female cohort now lives to reproductive age, marries, and has one or more children. After the long decline in U.S. fertility ending in the 1930s, $\bar{x}_s$ has risen slightly, but the variance in fertility is much reduced in the last two decades. However, in the United States the possible selective intensity of the natality component did not decline with the long secular decline in average number of children per couple: women born between 1871 and 1875 averaged 3.5 children and had an I_f of 0.710; those born in 1909 averaged 2.3 children (the lowest number for any U.S. cohort) and had an I_f of 0.881 (Kirk 1968). Crow (1973) reports a steady increase in I_f in U.S. women aged 45 to 49 years, with I_f reaching a maximum of 1.04 in 1955 and declining to 0.74 by 1969.

The patterns of mortality and reproduction through time in five other populations are given in Table 50. All cohorts are of women with completed fertility.

The opportunities for selection in five cohorts of Ramah Navajo women born from 1844 to 1924 in west-central New Mexico are given in Table 50, population 54. The increase with time in I_t is highly significant and

TABLE 50

SECULAR CHANGES IN THE COMPONENTS OF CROW'S INDEX OF MAXIMUM OPPORTUNITY FOR SELECTION IN FIVE POPULATIONS

Population	*Period*	*Size*	N_f	x_s	V_f	p_d	I_m	I_f	I_t
54. Ramah Navajo	1844–1879	71	29	7.69	15.52	.030	0.034 ± .035	0.262 ± .082	0.306 ± .096
	1880–1894	102	28	5.25	11.04	.200	0.250 ± .106	0.401 ± .123	0.751 ± .213
	1895–1904	183	36	5.39	15.24	.120	0.139 ± .066	0.525 ± .140	0.736 ± .189
	1905–1914	243	42	4.67	13.65	.140	0.167 ± .068	0.627 ± .149	0.898 ± .206
	1915–1924	327	70	5.37	16.60	.230	0.300 ± .075	.0576 ± .103	1.048 ± .178
55. Lapps, settled	1791–1840	3,442	253	5.93	13.70	.055	0.058 ± .016	0.390 ± .040	0.470 ± .048
	1841–1890	8,991	693	5.98	12.64	.072	0.077 ± .011	0.354 ± .022	0.459 ± .028
56. Lapps, nomadic	1791–1840	2,046	334	5.21	12.41	.116	0.131 ± .021	0.457 ± .041	0.648 ± .055
	1841–1890	2,177	305	4.83	10.35	.097	0.107 ± .020	0.443 ± .039	0.598 ± .052
		(× 1,000)							
57. Great Britain	1846–1862	24,525	9,775	5.55	12.22	.214	0.273 ± .006	0.397 ± .006	0.778 ± .011
	1870–1872	27,431	35,313	4.85	10.59	.078	0.084 ± .002	0.450 ± .004	0.572 ± .004
	1880–1882	31,015	69,255	3.96	8.38	.067	0.071 ± .001	0.536 ± .003	0.646 ± .004
	1890–1892	34,264	100,786	3.11	6.26	.064	0.068 ± .001	0.648 ± .003	0.760 ± .004
	1900–1902	38,237	82,971	2.49	4.93	.058	0.061 ± .001	0.703 ± .004	0.808 ± .004
58. Tomisaki, Japan	1896–1900	—	114	4.21	10.66	.250	0.333 ± .062	0.601 ± .091	1.135 ± .158
	1916–1920	4,000	111	2.73	4.02	.323	0.478 ± .080	0.539 ± .084	1.274 ± .174

that in I_f is significant at the 0.02 level. The low value of I_m for the 1844–79 cohort is not reliable. The tendency toward increased mortality in the last three cohorts is not statistically significant, having a probability of $0.2 > P > 0.1$, under the null hypothesis of no change.

Among the Swedish Lapps (populations 55 and 56), the opportunity for differential selection in fertility tends to decrease with time, but the decline is not significant statistically in either the nomadic or settled group. The decrease in maximum selection between the groups is stronger, approaching significance in the later period. Mortality rates before sexual maturity are significantly lower in the settled group and I_m shows a decrease with time in the nomadic and a slight increase in the settled Lapps.

The time trends in the opportunity for selection in women of Great Britain born from about 1846 to 1902 based on the 1946 survey is of special interest because data for high birth orders are not lumped and the samples are large. The values of $\bar{x}_s$, V_f, I_m decrease steadily and significantly while those of I_f and I_t (excepting the 1870–72 cohort) increase steadily and significantly. As expected, the secular changes in Great Britain correspond to those in the United States and most other industrial nations.

The secular changes in the large Japanese village of Tomisaki (population 58) resemble those of the Navajo more than those of Japan as a whole (see p. 198), Great Britain, and the United States. Although $\bar{x}_s$, V_f, and I_f appear to decline, and I_m and I_t to increase, the differences between cohorts do not reach statistical significance.

FAMILY PLANNING AND THE OPPORTUNITY FOR SELECTION

Birth control in some populations, or population segments, has so greatly reduced the variance in number of live children per women that it is approaching zero. Thus in some population segments the force of natural selection is greatly reduced—though not, of course, eliminated. But such segments are rare in the total population of the world.

"Family planning means to have children in a desired number, each child at a desired time" (Matsunaga 1966). The genetic aspect of family planning may be studied at a number of levels in a specified population: individual, phenotypical, genotypical, and genic. Here we are concerned with some possible effects of family planning at the level of the individual, that is, with those effects that may be measured by means of standard demographic variables.

To date no fully adequate study in this field has been made. Potter (1969) gives some of the difficulties in this area of study:

> Given the paramount importance of potential fertility and typical lengths of usage of a contraceptive together with their widely varying combinations of value, one can only anticipate that the new contraceptives like the IUD and the pills will exhibit widely varying levels of average impact and age differentiation from one family planning program to another. Hence, it is very unlikely that any universal rule of thumb—such as one birth averted per first segment of IUD—will find empirical support. For a serious evaluation of the demographic effectiveness of a specified contraceptive in a given population, there is no choice but to work for suitable information concerning the two most critical aspects. For this purpose we need, first, follow-up data on the acceptors to ascertain lengths of successful usage and to verify that low rates of accidental pregnancy obtain, and second, data regarding the acceptors' potential fertility and the selectivity of that fertility relative to the rest of the population.

History of Family Planning

Deliberate control of family size by infanticide probably dates from Paleolithic times. Family planning by contraception is about as old as recorded history. Use of medicated vaginal contraceptive tampons by ancient Egyptians (with lactic acid from fermented acacia as the spermatocidal agent) is recorded in the Ebers Papyrus, dating about 1150 B.C. (Himes 1936).

Prior to about the middle of the seventeenth century, that is, before "the" demographic transition (earlier "transitions" obtained when man changed from a mainly vegetarian to a carnivorous-omnivorous diet and when he started food production by agriculture), family size was controlled largely by balance between high fertility and high mortality, at least in the densely populated European peasant communities, a demographic situation not typical for preindustrial agriculturalists in most of the world. Nonetheless, some "planned" forms of fertility and mortality control have long been universal in human societies. Abortion and infanticide are fully effective methods of family planning. Both are old in human affairs. Abortion is still the most widespread, effective means of family planning, even in the developed countries (Hawthorn 1970).

It is convenient to label family-planning methods "primitive," "traditional," and "modern." Traditional methods were in use effectively from about 1650 to 1960 and included the condom, diaphragm, jellies, creams, and foam tablets; the term "modern" is restricted to oral and intrauterine contraceptives (Tietze 1967).

Natural Fertility Rates

Estimates of natural fertility rates provide a possible baseline for remarks on the genetic consequences of family planning. Henry (1961) found that the mean number of children per completed family of women married at age 20 in 13 population samples that did not practice deliberate birth control ranged from 10.9 in the Hutterites (marriages from 1921 to 1930) to 6.2 in Guinea villages (marriages from 1954 to 1955); the mean of the 13 samples is 8.42.

Bourgeois-Pichat (1965, 1967) calculated the probable rate of live births per year of marriage by age for a population of women married between the ages of 20 and 24 who do not practice deliberate birth control, whose coital frequency is eight per cycle, who experience a conception delay of 1.90 cycles, whose pregnancy and postpartum infecundity is 24 cycles, and whose delay from fetal deaths is 5.90 cycles:

Age:	15–19	25–29	30–34	35–39	40–44	45–49	50–54
Rate:	.471	.463	.441	.420	.392	.371	.350

Bourgeois-Pichat estimates the annual natural fertility rate as 0.474 births per woman.

A number of social, cultural, and biological factors lie between the hypothetical fecundity rate and the natural fertility rate experiences in different populations lacking deliberate birth control. Bourgeois-Pichat (1965) distinguished 280 logically possible types of natural fertility by identifying 8 types of fertility, 7 types of sterility, and 5 types of marriage pattern.

The eight types of fertility are differentiated by three criteria: coital frequency of 8 or 12 per cycle; all or one-fourth ovulations fecund; and short 1 cycle or long 14 cycles temporary sterility after birth.

Table 51 gives his calculations of annual natural fertility rates for women married between the ages of 20 and 24.

TABLE 51
BOURGEOIS-PICHAT'S CALCULATIONS OF ANNUAL NATURAL FERTILITY RATES FOR WOMEN 20–24

	Fecund Ovulations			
	All		*¼*	
	Temporary Sterility			
Coital Frequency per Cycle	*Long*	*Short*	*Long*	*Short*
8	.474	.902	.395	.654
12	.485	.941	.426	.743

The two types of fertility assuming all ovulations fecund and a postpartum infecundity of one cycle, giving a natural fertility of 0.9 births per woman married between ages 20 and 24 per year, do not appear to have existed in natural populations. Bourgeois-Pichat found acceptably close fits in existing populations for the other six types illustrated above.

The seven types of degrees of permanent sterility range from the low of 2.5 percent estimated for early eighteenth-century French Canadians to the high of 38.2 percent recorded from the Caribbean.

The five types of marriage range from a low marriage age with a large portion married (Type 1 = 60 percent at ages 15 to 19 and 95 percent at ages 25 to 29) to a relatively high marriage age with a low portion married (Type 5 = 5 percent at ages 15 to 19 and 80 percent at ages 30 to 34).

Despite the probabilities of misuse, there is some interest in getting one figure for expected completed family size under natural fertility. Ignoring the distribution of permanent sterility and the different types of marriage and assuming a coital frequency of eight per cycle in women 20 to 24, all ovulations fecund, and postpartum temporary sterility of 14 cycles, Bourgeois-Pichat's mean yearly natural fertility of 0.443 gives an expected completed family size of 13.248.

Some Comparative Data on Family Planning

Among Western European populations, birth control seems first to have been widely established, if only within one stratum of society, in France by the middle of the seventeenth century. Henry and Levy (1960) studied 59 families of dukes and peers of the realm during the period 1655–1799. In those families where the wife married before age 20 and the marriage lasted until she was between 45 and 50, the number of children was 6.15 for marriages between 1650 and 1699, 2.79 for 1700–49, and 2.00 for the period 1750–99.

The fullest historical information on *early* and *directly reported* practice of birth control from Europe comes from Great Britain. Hawthorn (1970) summarizes the available cohort data as shown in Table 52.

TABLE 52
COHORT DATA ON THE PRACTICE OF BIRTH CONTROL IN GREAT BRITAIN

	Percentage of Women Reporting Use of Birth Control at Some Point in Marriage
Birth Cohort 1835–45	19.5
Marriage Cohort	
Before 1900	15.0
1910–19	40.0
1920–24	58.0
1925–29	61.0
1930–34	63.0
1935–39	66.0
1930–39	65.5
1940–47	55.0
1940–49	72.7
1950–59	70.1

Westoff et al. (1961) reported that 96 percent of 1,165 fecund white couples interviewed in 1957 in the survey of the growth of American families had used or expected to use some form of birth control during their marriage.

It is perhaps too early to have a reliable estimate of the demographic effectiveness of the use of the Pill in the United States. Ryder and Westoff (1967) suggest that there may be a causal relation between fertility decline in the United States since 1960 and the use of the Pill but conclude that a causal link cannot be established on the available evidence.

Bumpass and Westoff (1970), using data from the 1965 National Fertility Study in the United States, report that one-third of the married couples who did not intend to have any more children already had at least one unwanted child. In the period 1960–65, nearly 20 percent of all live births were reported as unwanted by their parents. About 5 percent of first births and nearly 50 percent of sixth or higher births were unwanted. Only one-fourth of all parents claimed to have been completely successful in preventing both unwanted and unplanned pregnancies.

The mean number of children considered ideal by non-Catholic women in the United States differs surprisingly little by education and income. These survey data, compiled by Blake (1969), are presented in Table 53.

Berelson (1967) gives the following rough picture of the general situation in the developing countries with regard to attitudes toward family planning:

	In percentages
Practice family planning now	5–20, say 10
Have some detailed information about reproduction and contraception	10–40, say 20
Want no more children, of those with three or more	40–60, say 50
Interested in learning about family planning	50–70, say 60
Approve of birth control	65–80, say 75

TABLE 53
MEAN NUMBER OF CHILDREN CONSIDERED IDEAL BY NON-CATHOLIC U.S. WOMEN

Year	*Age*	*Sample N*	*Mean*
1943	20–34	1,893	2.7
1952	21+	723	3.3
1955*	18–39	1,905	3.3
1955†	18–39	1,905	3.4
1957	21+	448	3.3
1959	21+	472	3.5
1960*	18–39	1,728	3.2
1960†	18–39	1,728	3.4
1963	21+	483	3.4
1966	21+	378	3.3
1967	21+	488	3.3
1968	21+	539	3.3

* Minimal ideal number.

† Maximal ideal number.

Berelson concludes that "contrary to the usual belief, sufficient motivation exists to make a demographic difference if it could be implemented. To be sure, the actual practice of family planning is scarce in the typical developing country, and knowledge about contraception and reproductive physiology is not much better" (see Berelson 1969 for a reaffirmation).

Table 54 presents data from South Korea and Taiwan, where family-planning programs are strongly supported by the local governments, and gives personal characteristics of various groups and their acceptance of family planning by IUD (Berelson 1969).

Davis (1967) estimates the maximum impact on (nuclear) family size of all family planning in Taiwan in recent years by considering the difference between the number of children women have been having and the number they want to have. The number of children wanted by women aged 15 to 29 varies from 3.75 for women in urban Taipei (the largest city on the island) to 5.03 in rural farming villages. Davis estimates that (as of about 1960) if Taiwanese women used contraceptives that were 100 percent effective and had the number of children that they desired they would have 4.5 children each. In the past, Taiwanese women who married and lived through their reproductive period (some using primitive contraceptive methods) had an average of about 6.5 children. By 1960 the impact of family planning on Taiwanese women who survive their reproductive period seemed to be some 2 children.

The demographic effectiveness of the IUD in a given population depends on the number of users, the length of successful retention, and the fertility foregone during retention of the device. Lee and Isbister (1966) investigated the demographic effect of the IUD family-planning program in South Korea. Using an empirical distribution of ages at the time of insertion averaging 33 years, they calculated that 1.5 births are averted on the average per first period of IUD retention. When they used a hypothetical age distribution averaging 29.5 years, their estimate was increased to 1.9 births averted per first segment of IUD.

In a study of the Taiwan IUD program, Potter (1969), using a medium estimate of the average duration per birth that might have been required had the IUD not been adopted, arrived at the following estimates by age of births averted per first segment of IUD:

20–24	25–29	30–34	35–39	All ages
.54	.68	.72	.54	.64

TABLE 54
ACCEPTANCE OF IUD IN SOUTH KOREA AND TAIWAN

Characteristics of Group	*Percentage of Each Group Accepting IUD*	
	South Korea	*Taiwan*
Number of Living Children		
0 or 1	2	4
2	7	16
3	18	26
4	29	24
5 or more	37	21
Age of Mother		
Under 25	3	8
25–29	14	20
30–34	29	28
35–39	29	23
40–44	23	12
Date of Latest Birth		
Over 30 Months	8	11
Within 30 Months	43	24

Family Planning in Japan

Japan is unique among industrial nations in both the pace and the path of its demographic transition. Matras (1965) outlined four strategies of family formation important in demographic revolution:

		Fertility	
		Uncontrolled	*Controlled*
Marriage	Early	A	B
	Late	C	D .

Most contemporary societies are still using strategy A, where "uncontrolled" fertility means not using modern methods. In the sixteenth century, populations of northwestern Europe started moving from A to C. The white colonial societies tended to move from A to B. Japan, uniquely, moved from A to D in a rapid transition that started in the 1920s and was completed after 1945 (Taeuber 1958). The Japanese transition was multiphasic and complex in causation (Davis 1963).

Standardized birth rates per 1,000 population and means and variances of maternal age based on data from the Institute of Population Problems, Tokyo (Matsunaga 1966), are presented in Table 55.

TABLE 55
STANDARDIZED BIRTH RATES AND MEANS AND VARIANCES OF MATERNAL AGE IN JAPAN

Year	Standardized Birth Rate	Maternal Age, Years	
		Mean	Variance
1925	35.3	28.4	45.48
1930	32.4	28.6	42.50
1940	27.7	29.3	37.29
1947	30.7	29.1	36.36
1950	25.3	28.2	33.45
1954	17.4	27.8	27.04
1960	14.6	27.1	19.93

Some additional features of population trends in Japan (with comparisons of relevant data from 1947 with those from 1953 and 1960, based on vital statistics of the Ministry of Health and Welfare, Tokyo) assembled by Matsunaga (1966, 1967), together with some data for 1967 from the U.N. *Demographic Yearbook*, 1969, are given below:

1. Live birth rate per 1,000 population:

1947	34.3
1953	21.5
1960	17.2
1967	19.4

2. Infant death rate per 1,000 live births:

1947	76.7
1953	48.9
1960	30.7
1967	14.9

3. Total number of live births:

1947	2,678,792
1953	1,868,040
1960	1,606,041
1967	1,935,647

4. Total number of reported induced abortions:

1947	—
1953	1,068,066
1960	1,063,256
1967	878,748

5. Total number of reported sterilizations:

1947	—
1953	32,552
1960	38,722

6. Percentage of live births by birth order:

	Order 1 to 3	Order 4 or more
1947	64.1	35.9
1953	75.1	25.0
1960	90.3	9.7
1967	96.9	3.1

7. Percentage of live births by age of mother:

	Under 19	20–29	30–34	Over 35
1947	2.3	53.9	24.1	19.8
1953	1.7	64.3	21.9	12.1
1960	1.2	74.2	18.7	5.8

8. Mean age of women at first marriage:

1947	22.9
1953	23.4
1960	24.2

Matsunaga (1966, 1967) provides some additional information from Japan important to the interpretation of the genetic consequences of the demographic transition:

9. Secular change in the mean inbreeding coefficient among 3,427 couples in Ohdate City (wife's age ranged from 30 to 40 years; the mean ages of wives at marriage were 21.7 for unrelated and 19.8 for related couples):

Year of marriage	Before 1945	1946–1949	1950–1953	1954–1957	1958–1961
Percent inbred	9.01	6.32	3.42	1.29	1.08
F coefficient	.0033	.0021	.0010	.0003	.0003

10. Percentage of "present contraceptors" (excluding induced abortions):

1950	19.5
1952	26.3
1955	33.6
1957	39.2
1959	42.5

Secular Changes in I *due to Fertility Differences in Japan*

The genetic implication of variation in the value of I_f may be quite different in populations using no contraception, those using primitive methods of birth control, and those employing modern methods. In Japan family-planning practice resulted in a drop in the mean number of live-born children from 2.878 in 1950 to 1,784 in 1963 and a drop in the variance of live-birth orders of all live-born children from 3.847 in 1950 to 0.999 in 1963. The corresponding values of I were 0.465 in 1950 and 0.314 in 1963 (Matsunaga 1966).

In a study of the possible consequences of family planning in Japan, Matsunaga (1966) separated the fertility component of I into I_i, the intensity of the opportunity for selection due to infertility, and I'_f, the intensity due to variations in the number of children of women with at least one live-born child:

$$I_i = p_o/1 - p_o$$

$$I'_f = V'_f/\bar{x}'^2_s$$

$$I_f = I_i + (1/1 - p_o)\, I'_f,$$

where p_o is the proportion of married women who have completed the reproductive period having no live-born children and x'_s and V'_f are, respectively, the mean and variance of the number of live births per fertile women.

Table 56 shows the secular change based on the 1960 census report in married Japanese women 40 or more years of age (Matsunaga 1966). The proportions of infertile married women decreased slowly from about 10 percent for those aged over 60 years in 1960 to less than 8 percent for those aged 40 to 49 years. The component due to infertility dropped from a high of 0.122 in women aged 75 to 79 to below 0.084 in those aged 40 to

TABLE 56

SECULAR CHANGES IN SELECTION INTENSITY DUE TO FERTILITY DIFFERENCES IN JAPANESE MARRIED WOMEN*

Age	$\overline{X}_s$	X'_s	V_f	V'_f	P_o	I_t	I'_f	I_f
80–	4.670	5.159	8.462	6.798	0.096	0.106	0.255	0.388
75–79	4.574	5.132	8.661	6.842	.109	.122	.260	.414
70–74	4.683	5.261	8.992	7.152	.108	.121	.258	.410
65–69	4.680	5.209	8.717	7.000	.100	.111	.258	.398
60–64	4.688	5.191	8.791	7.093	.098	.108	.263	.400
55–59	4.675	5.130	8.458	6.966	.088	.096	.265	.387
50–54	4.466	4.846	7.320	6.054	.080	.087	.258	.367
45–49	3.919	4.249	5.455	4.514	.076	.082	.250	.353
40–44	3.286	3.563	3.682	3.021	0.077	0.083	0.238	0.341

* Data are based on the 1960 census report in Japan.

49; the subcomponent, I'_f, due to variation in the number of children for women having at least one child, has remained fairly constant. Thus, in Japan, the secular change in I_f appears to be caused more by I_i than I'_f.

Matsunaga concludes the demographic changes in Japan from 1947 to 1960 may reduce trisomy–21 by one-third, XXY and XXX by less than one-third, Rh–erythroblastosis by more than one-half, and a number of other genetic diseases—including achondroplasia and acrocephalosyndactyla—by something like one-tenth. The reduction in defects due to new mutations and chromosomal abnormalities and the reduction in inbreeding are eugenic. The reduction in some genetic diseases may be dysgenic where selection intensity against deleterious genes is relaxed. There may also be a population reduction in the frequency of genes associated with high fertility.

SUMMARY

Methods are outlined for calculating Crow's index giving the maximum opportunity for natural selection, the components of the index due to differential mortality and fertility, extensions of the index to include prenatal mortality, mortality during the reproductive period, and the effects of family planning on fertility. Data from 57 population samples are presented on the number of women who survive to the start of the reproductive period, the mean number of their live-born offspring, the variance in the number of live-born children, the probability of death before the start of the reproductive period, and the indices for mortality, fertility, and total opportunity for natural selection.

The mean number of children born alive to women with completed fecundity ranges from 1.32 to 9.92 and averages 5.20 in the 57 samples. The variance in fertility ranges from 1.81 to 23.52 with a mean at 8.44. The mortality index ranges from 0.03 to 2.27 with a mean of 0.56. The fertility index range is 0.07–1.68 and its mean is 0.42. The range of the total index is from 0.23 to 3.69 with an average of 1.18. The mortality component is greater than the fertility component in 61.4 percent of the samples.

Information on secular changes in these quantities is presented for six populations. The total index for the Navajo Indians, a rapidly growing population, increased significantly over an 80-year period. Decrease in the total index approaches significance in the nomadic and settled Lapps, who live in an extremely harsh environment, during the period 1841–90. In Great Britain since 1846 fertility, variance in fertility, and mortality have decreased steadily and significantly, while the fertility and total indices (excepting one cohort) have increased steadily and significantly. Similar trends exist in the general populations of Japan and the United States and probably of most industrialized nations.

Although there is a trend toward lower maximum opportunity for genetic change by differential mortality in much of the world population, the maximum opportunity today for natural selection by differential fertility is significantly greater than zero in all peoples and has increased in the last century.

Appendix

NOTES TO TABLE 45

These notes are keyed to the numbers in the first column of Table 45. After the name of the group and the reference(s), the geographical race of the population is given according to the taxonomy of Garn (1961), as well as statements of linguistic affiliation (where not obvious) and type of economy. If appropriate, the exact local group investigated to supply the raw data on fertility and mortality is identified. In a few cases further anthropological information, including common cases of marriage patterns other than monogamy, is noted.

1. *Hutterites* (Eaton and Mayer 1953; especially Tables 10 and 16). European. The Hutterites are an Anabaptist religious sect living mostly as farmers in the western parts of the United States and Canada in small, self-contained colonies. This Protestant sect originated in Switzerland and Bohemia in 1528. Except for the 15-to-19-year age group, the Hutterites are reproducing at close to the maximum level, having increased their population number over nineteenfold between 1880 and 1950, from 443 to 8,542 persons.

2. *Azapa, Chile* (Cruz-Coke et al. 1966). Amerindian. The Azapa are an Aymará-speaking village in the Andean region of Arica. Their agricultural lands are located at an altitude of 300 meters in a semidesert valley. Data on live-born offspring by parity were not included in the report.

3. *Deerfield, Massachusetts,* 1 (Swedlund 1971). European. Deerfield (originally named Pocumtucle), located in northwestern Massachusetts

at the confluence of the Deerfield and Connecticut rivers, was established in 1673 by British colonists and has since remained a rural, largely agricultural community. "Deerfield 1" refers to the married sample, about 6 percent of women in the community never marrying.

4. *Yanomama* (Neel and Chagnon 1968). Amerindian. The Yanomama (Yanomamö) speak a language belonging to the Chirianan family, live in southern Venezuela and northern Brazil, and practice hunting, gathering, and more recently, slash-and-burn agriculture. They had no sustained contacts with Europeans before 1950, about one generation before the data were collected. They, along with the Australian aborigines (note 52), are probably the least contacted and the least acculturated by high civilizations of the populations considered here. Due to the work of Neel and his associates, since 1964 they, with the Xavanti (note 19), have become probably the most intensively and extensively studied tribal population in the world of human biology.

5. *Replacement Man* (Neel and Schull 1972). *Homo sapiens*. Indices are given for a hypothetical stable population with mean fertility just enough to balance mortality before the end of the reproductive period but with a variance in fertility about that of populations in contemporary industrial nations.

6. *San Juan Pueblo* (Aberle 1931; Aberle, Watkins, and Pitney 1940). Amerindian. San Juan is a Tewa-speaking Pueblo village in the northern Rio Grande Valley, New Mexico. They practice agriculture and keep some livestock. Founded about the start of the sixteenth century by Tewa who had lived in the area at least for a few centuries, they have been in contact with Europeans since 1598. Although acculturated in technology and some materials, much of their culture is intact. They have experienced heavy mortality from European diseases.

7. *Molinos, Chile* (Cruz-Coke et al. 1966). Amerindian. Molinos is an Aymará agricultural village located at an altitude of 1,100 meters in a desert valley of Arica, Chile.

8. *Tallensi* (Fortes 1943). African. The Tallensi (Talene, Talni) belong to the Bantu linguistic family and practice a Sudanic-type agricultural economy in the watershed of the Volta River.

9. *Deerfield, 2* (Swedlund 1971). European. The unmarried, although reproductive, subsample of the Deerfield population (see note 3).

10. *Chapiquiña* (Cruz-Coke et al. 1966). Amerindian. An Aymará

agricultural village at an altitude of 3,400 meters in the sierra of Arica, Chile.

11. *Yao* (Mitchell 1949). African. The Yao are a large central Bantu tribe of northern Mozambique, adjacent coastal Tanzania, and southern Nyasaland. The data reported here are from 20 typical agricultural hamlets in the Liwonde district of Nyasaland. Polygyny is common.

12. *Terena* (Salzano and De Oliveira 1970). Amerindian. The Terena are a subgroup of the Arawak-speaking Guaná living in the Mirandu River Basin in the southern part of the state of Mato Grosso, Brazil, whose ancestors inhabited part of the Amazon Basin in pre-Columbian times. Unlike many Indian tribes in the region, the Terena increased in total number from about 3,000 persons in the eighteenth century to about 5,000 in 1960. The data are from the village of Cachoeirinha, one of 12 belonging to the Terena. They are agriculturalists, highly acculturated from 150 years of neo-Brazilian contact.

13. *Belén, Chile* (Cruz-Coke et al. 1966). Amerindian. The Chilean Aymará village of Belén is an agricultural community located at an altitude of 3,200 meters in the sierra of Arica.

14. *Khanna, Punjab* (Wyon and Gordon 1971). Indian. The agricultural villages of the Khanna area are in Ludhiana District of Punjab State in northwestern India. Village populations vary from 100 to 3,000 persons. Agricultural methods, crops, housing, dress, language, and religion are similar for the 11 villages included in the survey.

15. *Arica, Chile* (Cruz-Coke et al. 1966). Amerindian. In the Arica region of Chile, the Andean plateau makes its nearest approach to the Pacific Ocean. This sample is based on civil register data and the census of 1960 and includes the five Aymará agricultural villages surveyed in 1965–66 (notes 2, 7, 10, 13, and 42). The villages are located on a sharp altitudinal gradient from sea level to 5,000 meters at Chapiquiña Pass, located only 80 kilometers from the coast. The agricultural methods are adapted to the different environments of desert valley, sierra, and high plateau. Each zone has been occupied by Amerindians for at least 6,000 years. The villages in the valley are most Westernized.

16. *Yako* (Forde 1939). African. The Yako tribe of southern Nigeria speak a Niger-Congo (Nigritic) language. They probably moved south to their present location with the spread of the Malaysian agricultural complex. Polygyny is favored.

17–18. *Southern Pahira I* and *II* (Basu 1967). Indian. The Pahira, a small tribe of eastern India with a total population of 1,353 individuals in 1963, is divided into three subpopulations: the northern Pahira (note 30), and two branches of the southern Pahira. All are agricultural. Intermarriage between the three groups is rare.

19. *Xavanti* (Salzano, Neel, and Maybury-Lewis 1967). Amerindian. The Xavantes are Gê-speaking Indians who live in the Brazilian Mato Grosso, subsisting by hunting, gathering, and, recently, incipient agriculture. A short period of peaceful contact with the Brazilian colonizers in the late eighteenth century was followed by some fifty years of hostility, with peaceful relations being restored after 1946. Since 1960, acculturation has been rapid through contact with missionaries and government agents. Polygyny is common. The data are from three villages located in the vicinity of the Rio das Mortes.

20. *New South Wales* (Powys 1905). European. This report from New South Wales is one of the early studies on the evolutionary implications of human fertility. In addition to its historical interest, it is included here for comparative purposes because the sample is relatively large and higher birth orders are not pooled. The population was founded in 1788.

21. *!Kung, Farms* (Harpending 1974: personal communication). African. The "farm" !Kung Bushmen (San) speak a Khoisan language and are employed as laborers on European farms.

22. *Bengali Villages* (Aird 1956). Indian. The data are from 667 households in two Muslim agricultural villages on the outskirts of the city of Dacca, Bangladesh.

23. *Nayasaland* (Bettison 1958). African. The sample is from 17 periurban, agricultural villages near Blantyre-Limbe, Nyasaland. The villages include members of several Central Bantu tribes including Lomwe, Ngoni, Chikunda, Nyanja, and the Yao, who constitute 65 percent of the total number of inhabitants. Children tend to be assigned to the tribe of their father.

24. *Karluk Eskimo* (Taylor 1966). Amerindian. Karluk is one of seven Eskimo villages on the Kodiak Island group in the Gulf of Alaska. They derive mostly from the Konyak Eskimo, who inhabited the islands and adjacent mainland from prehistoric times. They are highly acculturated, all villagers learn English as their first language and all are members of the Russian Orthodox Church. The economy is seasonal, with wages from commercial salmon fishing in the summer from June through September

and credit at the company store the rest of the year. During the period from October through May there is some continuance of traditional exploitation of sea mammals, land mammals, birds, and fishes. The sex ratio at the time of the study was unusually high (155:100) with 90 of 148 persons (61 percent) being male.

25. *Hottentot-Boer* (Fischer 1913). African-European hybrids. The Rehoboth Bastaards are a hybrid Boer-Hottentot people living by agriculture and livestock in southwest Africa, numbering some twenty-five hundred persons in 1908, the time of the study. The language of the Hottentots is Khoisan. The "Boers" who entered the mixture were Cape Dutch with some Huguenot admixture, Germans, and British.

26. *U.S. Whites* (Neel and Schull 1972). European. The data are from United States Department of Health, Education, and Welfare, Public Health Service, 1966, Vital Statistics of the United States, 1964, vol. 2, part A (Washington: Government Printing Office).

27. *Ngbaka* (Thomas 1963). African. The Ngbaka, who speak a language of the Eastern branch of the Niger-Congo stock, are an agricultural tribe in the Lobaye region of the Central African Republic. The data were collected in the village of Bobua.

28. *Hirado, Japan* (Neel and Schull 1972). Asiatic. The Japanese island of Hirado lies to the west of Kyushu in the neighborhood of the thirty-third parallel and has been occupied at least from Yayoi times (c. 250 B.C.–c. A.D. 250). In 1960, the population included 40,881 persons living in 60 hamlets, villages, and towns. Agriculture is the main economic activity.

29. *Lesu* (Powdermaker 1931). Melanesian-Papuan. The Lesu are a Melanesian community living on New Ireland in the Bismarck Archipelago. Their economy is based on fishing and gardening.

30. *Northern Pahira* (Basu 1967). Indian. See note 17–18.

31. *!Kung, Ngamiland* (Harpending 1974: personal communication). African. The !Kung Bushmen (San) of Ngamiland in the northwestern part of Botswana are one of the few surviving hunting and gathering cultures. Some families included in the sample subsist entirely on hunting and gathering; others attempt some agriculture in addition.

12. *Ashanti* (Fortes 1953). African. The Ashanti speak a language of the Twi branch of the Niger-Congo linguistic stock. The economy is based on export of cocoa, gold, timber, and kola nuts, supplemented by cultivation of traditional food crops, some hunting, and fishing. The data were collected in the township of Agogo, Ashanti-Akim, Ghana.

33. *Black Carib* (Firschein 1965: personal communication). Amerindian-African. The Black Carib are a Carib Indian–Negro hybrid population founded in 1675 when a cargo of slaves was shipwrecked on St. Vincent Island of the Windward group in the West Indies. To counter their hostility the English moved them in 1795, first to Balliceaux Island and later to Ruatán Island off the coast of Honduras. From there they spread to occupy the entire coastline from Stann Creek in British Honduras to the Black River in the republic of Honduras. The economy is based more on fishing than on agriculture, but hunting is still important.

34. *San Carlos Apache* (Hrdlička 1908). Amerindian. The San Carlos Apache Indians are Western Apache, the name "San Carlos" having no ethnic significance beyond indicating a particular Indian reservation. Their language is Athapascan. They live in an area west of the White Mountains extending almost to Tucson, Arizona. The economy is based on hunting, collecting, and the gardening of corn, beans, and squash. The Apache and Navajo are closely related in biology, language, and culture.

35. *Tsumje, Nepal* (Kawakita 1957). Asiatic. The people of the Nepal Himalayan village of Tsumje are Tibetans (Bhoteas) who speak the Khim dialect of Nepali. The village is located in Shiar Khola Valley of the Upper Buri Gandaki at an altitude of about 3,200 meters. It contains 36 houses, a monastery, and 4 Lamaistic temples. The economy is based on agriculture and animal husbandry. Both fraternal and avuncular polyandry are practiced.

36. *Caingang* (Salzano 1961, 1963). Amerindian. The Caingang are a Gê-speaking agricultural tribe of Indians living in the Brazilian states of Rio Grande do Sul, Santa Catarina, Paraná, and São Paulo. Sample 36 is the pooled data from Nonoai (45), Guarita (46), Ligeiro (49), and Cacique Doble (50).

37. *Rungus-Dasun* (Koblenzer and Carrier 1960). Melanesian-Papuan. The Rungus-Dasun are a Papuan, pagan, agricultural people inhabiting mainly the Kudat Peninsula of Sabah, Malaysia. They are an indigenous tribe thought to be descended from the Muruts of Sabah and Sarawak with a large admixture of Chinese. The data are from the village complex of Maksangkong-Dampirit.

38. *Oglala Sioux* (Hrdlička 1931). Amerindian. The data were collected in the period 1897–1908 from the Oglala Sioux living in the Pine Ridge Reservation, South Dakota. The Sioux (Dakota) are the third

largest and one of the most famous Indian tribes of North America, thanks to their numbers, prowess, and their several wars with the whites. They are farmers and hunters. The earliest known territory of the tribe was on or near the Mississippi River in Minnesota, Wisconsin, and Iowa. Later they spread to the west, reaching the Yellowstone and Platte rivers. At the time of the study they lived mostly on reservations in South and North Dakota. The prereproductive mortality was estimated from the contemporary crude birth and death rates reported by the Indian Service. All the women had passed menopause and had lived in marriage throughout their reproductive periods.

39. *U.S. Nonwhites* (Neel and Schull 1972). African, Asiatic, Indian, and Amerindian. The subjects were mostly American Negroes. See note 26 for source.

40. *Thule Eskimo* (Malaurie, Tabah, and Sutter 1952; Sutter and Tabah 1956). Amerindian. In 1950 and 1951, the Thule Polar Eskimo were living on the northwestern coast of Greenland at 76°–79° north latitude. At that time they were the northernmost human population, although there is archaeological evidence of earlier Eskimo settlements further north in Greenland. Subsistence is based on hunting, fishing, and gathering on land and sea. The Polar Eskimo derive from Old World Mesolithic sources and arrived in Greenland during the twelfth century A.D. The north Greenland tundra is one of the harshest and most dangerous habitats occupied by modern man.

41. *Cocos Island* (Smith 1960). Asiatic. The Cocos Island Malays living on the Cocus or Keeling Islands in the Indian Ocean are one of the more geographically isolated human populations, the nearest land being Christmas Island at 500 miles away, with Australia 1,600 miles and the Asian mainland 800 miles away. Of the 27 coral islands in the group, only Home Island has an enduring human population, consisting of Cocos Malays, Bantamese, and Europeans. Operation of coconut plantations is the main economic activity. The Malay Cocos' diet is based on rice, fish, and coconuts; some vegetables and fruits are grown locally, and sea birds, octopus, crabs, and turtles are occasionally taken for food. The population was founded in 1827 by a Scotch sea captain, his family, and a few score Malays of both sexes. In 1872, they numbered 292, and in 1947 1,802 persons.

42. *Huallatire, Chile* (Cruz-Coke et al. 1966). Amerindian. The Ay-

mará-speaking Indians of the village of Huallatire in the altiplano of Arica, Chile, are seminomadic shepherds living at an altitude of 4,300 meters.

43. *Pima* (Hrdlička 1908). Amerindian. The Pima live in the valleys of the Gila and Salt rivers in Arizona, belong to the Uto-Aztecan linguistic stock, and use irrigation to grow maize, wheat, and cotton as principal crops.

44. *Sioux-Ojibwa, mixed* (Boas 1894). Amerindian-European (see note 38 on the Sioux or Dakota). The Ojibwa (Chippewa) speak an Algonquin language and once occupied the northern shore of Lake Huron, both shores of Lake Superior, and lands westward as far as the Turtle Mountains of North Dakota. Their subsistence was based on hunting, gathering, fishing, sugar making, and some gardening, performed in a region that, although cold and rough, provided a generous food supply. The data were collected by Boas and eight assistants at the World's Columbian Exposition, Chicago, 1893. The numbers of children born to women who had passed menopause were estimated from the contemporary crude birth and death rates reported by the Indian Service for the Sioux reservations.

45. *Nonoai* (Salzano 1961). Amerindian. The Nonoai are one of four Caingang Indian populations of Rio Grande do Sul, Brazil, reported here (see note 36).

46. *Guarita* (Salzano 1961). Amerindian. One of the four Caingang samples (see note 36).

47. *Basoga* (Roscoe 1915). African. The Basoga (Soga) speak Bantu and live in eastern Uganda, north of Lake Victoria. Animal husbandry approaches agriculture in economic importance, with little reliance on hunting or gathering but some on fishing.

48. *Sioux-Ojibwa* (Boas 1894). Amerindian. The unmixed group of the Sioux and Ojibwa Indians studied by Boas (see note 44).

49. *Ligeiro* (Salzano 1961). Amerindian. One of the four Caingang populations (see note 36).

50. *Cacique Doble* (Salzano 1961). Amerindian. Another Caingang sample (see note 36).

51. *Banyoro* (Roscoe 1915). African. The Banyoro (Nyoro) are a Bantu-speaking tribe living to the east of Lake Albert in northwestern Uganda. Their culture and economy closely resemble those of the Basoga (note 47).

52. *Australian Aborigines* (Sharp 1940). Australian. The data on the Australian aborigines were collected between 1933 and 1935 from the Taior, Ngentjin, Yir Yoront, and Yir Mel tribes, Cape York Peninsula, North Queensland, Australia. The total population numbered 376 in 1933 and 370 in 1935. The four tribes occupied about 1,800 square miles and although differentiated linguistically had essentially the same economy, subsisting entirely by fishing, hunting, and gathering. At the time of Sharp's fieldwork, the Taior and Ngentjin had not yet come under any direct, continued European influence.

53. *Peri* (Mead 1930). Melanesian-Papuan. The Melanesian Peri (Pere) is a Manus village on the south coast of the Great Admiralty Island in the Bismarck Archipelago. At the time the data were collected, the Manus population numbered about 30,000 persons. The economy is based on fishing and trading fish for garden products grown by neighboring peoples. Polygamy occurs but is unusual.

NOTES TO TABLE 50

These notes are keyed to the numbers in the first column of Table 50 and follow the format given in the initial paragraph of the notes to Table 45.

54. *Ramah Navajo* (Morgan 1968). Amerindian. The Navajo speak Athapascan and are closely related to the Apache (see note 34). The Ramah group lives off the main Navajo Reservation in an area about 25 by 75 miles in westernmost New Mexico, near the Mormon village of Ramah. Their economy is based on livestock (especially sheep) and corn-bean-squash agriculture but with increasing use of foods and goods from the trading stores. The local population was founded about 1840 by seven families and numbered well over 1,000 by 1960. The Navajo are the largest Indian tribe north of Mexico and probably the fastest-growing ethnic population in the United States. During the period 1960–64 the annual Ramah Navajo growth rate was 3.53 percent. About 16 percent of all Ramah Navajo marriages are polygynous, and among these 57 percent involve sisters, 20 percent stepdaughters, and 23 percent unrelated women.

55. *Lapps, settled* (Barrai and Fraccaro 1965; Fraccaro 1959; Wahlund 1932). Garn (1961) classifies the Lapps as an isolated, local race. Genetically they resemble their European neighbors more than their Asian linguistic relatives. The Lappish language belongs to the Finnish-Lapponic

branch of the Fino-Ugrian family. Wahlund extracted the data from records of the Karesuando, Jukkasjärui, Gällivare, and Jokkmokk parishes in Swedish Lappland. The economy of the settled Lapps is agricultural.

56. *Lapps, nomadic* (references as in note 55). The nomadic Lapps are fishermen and reindeer herders of the tundra and swamps of western Russia, Finland, Sweden, and Norway. The data are from 16 tribes, each consisting of several households and keeping within a geographical area. The nomadic "Mountain Lapps" stay with the herds during the summer in the high mountains and move down during the winter to the forests. The nomadic "Forest Lapps" herd their reindeer in the forests throughout the year and carry on some agriculture. The Mountain Lapps live in an extremely trying environment.

57. *Great Britain* (Glass and Grebenik 1954; Central Statistical Office 1963; Logan 1950). European. The data are from a sample of one-tenth of the married, widowed, and divorced women living in Great Britain on January 7, 1946. Sample response was 87.1 percent. The data used here are restricted to women whose first marriage had not terminated by census date, or, if it had, had not done so before the forty-fifth birthday of the woman concerned, and whose husbands were manual wage earners, including laborers engaged in specific occupations with the exception of agriculture. The data were extracted from Glass and Grebenik (1954), Table A.58, Part II, p. 26, taking into account average age at first marriage (Part I, 102ff.). Higher orders of live births (up to 27) were reported individually. Data on total population numbers and deaths before age 15 for the 1846–62 period are from Logan (1950); those for later periods are from the Central Statistical Office (1963).

58. *Tomisaki, Japan* (Kobayashi 1969). Asiatic. Tomisaki is a fishing community, now included in Tateyama City, on the southern coast of Boso Peninsula, Chiba Perfecture, Honshu Island. The data were collected from official family registers and temple records.

7

Childhood Association, Sexual Attraction, and Fertility in Taiwan

ARTHUR P. WOLF
Department of Anthropology
Stanford University

Through the first three decades of this century Chinese families living in the rural areas of northern Taiwan gave away the majority of their female children shortly after birth and raised in their places wives for their sons.[1] The majority of these "little daughters-in-law" (*sim-pua*) were adopted before they were a year old and eventually married boys who were not more than three or four years old at the time of the adoption. As a result, 40 percent of all first marriages united a boy and girl who had been raised together from early childhood as intimately as any brother and sister.

The purpose of this paper is to report further evidence in support of my contention that the experience of "intimate and prolonged childhood association" lessened sexual attraction and thereby reduced the fertility of couples who were reared in the same family.[2] The paper also discusses alternatives to this hypothesis and outlines the work that remains to be done before the hypothesis can be firmly rejected or accepted. The data reported are again drawn from Japanese household registration records for the period 1905–47 and from field research conducted in the Taipei Basin in 1957–60, 1968, and 1970.[3] The reader who wants further information on the nature of the family life in the villages discussed in this paper should see Margery Wolf, *The House of Lim* (1968) and *Women and the Family in Rural Taiwan* (1972), and Emily Ahern, *The Cult of the Dead in a Chinese Village* (1973).

My strategy in two previous papers was to compare the fertility of women who married housemates with that of women who married into their husband's family as young adults. In the present paper I extend this comparison of what I call minor and major marriages to include the fertility of women whose husbands married against the grain of the Chinese kinship system and became members of their wife's father's household. These uxorilocal marriages usually involved an agreement by which the husband took on certain economic obligations toward his wife's parents and allowed some of his children to take their descent from his wife's father. One arrangement was to assign the firstborn male child to his maternal grandfather's line; another was to alternate the descent of the children regardless of sex.[4]

Continuing work with the Taiwan household registers has led me to recognize that the results reported in my 1970 paper could be spurious. It appears that the recorded fertility of the rural population rose at the same time as the frequency of minor marriages declined. This means that by including in my comparison marriages contracted during this transitional period I may have produced a correlation that only appears to support my hypothesis. Happily, this is not the case, as the data reported below indicate. The fertility of women who married childhood associates is shown to be substantially lower than that of other women in each of seven cohorts born in the years 1881 to 1915. This rules out the possibility that the relationship reported in my 1970 paper is a by-product of rising fertility and a gradual decline in the relative frequency of marriages involving childhood associates.

Before turning to the data and problems of interpretation, I must repeat two points made in my previous papers. The first is that the magnitude of the predicted correlation is limited by cultural and economic constraints as well as by the random character of natural fecundity. In the early decades of this century female children were regarded as "useless things" and were usually given out in adoption at an early age, but male children were highly valued. A couple had to have at least one filial son to support them in their old age and provide for their souls after death, and most people insisted on a minimum of two sons, fearing that one or the other might die or fail to fulfill his filial duties. In addition there were powerful economic incentives to produce as many sons as possible. A tenant farmer with a number of sons could rent more land, increase production, and, by taking advantage of economies of scale, save money to buy land or start a business. Consequently, we cannot expect to find that women who married in the minor fashion bore only one or two children. To rear a minimum of two sons under conditions of high infant mortality, they had to produce five or six children. And if we find the fertility of minor marriages markedly lower than that of major and uxorilocal marriages, the word "aversion" is not too strong to describe the source. A mild sexual dissatisfaction could not have overcome the economic motives favoring high fertility.

My second point concerns the effect of adultery on the predicted relationship between fertility and form of marriage. I have demonstrated elsewhere that women who were forced to marry housemates were more likely to seek sexual satisfaction outside of marriage than those who married men from other families (A. Wolf 1970:511–12). Since the children of a married woman were always registered under the name of her husband, this means that the relative fertility of the three forms of marriage underestimates the effect of childhood association. In other words, by taking recorded fertility as a measure of sexual satisfaction, we risk rejecting the aversion hypothesis for the wrong reason. It could be that those *sim-pua* who were most dissatisfied with their husbands bore as many children as women who married outsiders because, being dissatisfied, they established regular liaisons with other men.

The data reported in this paper take as their universe the first marriages of all women who were born in the years 1881 to 1915 and lived after marriage in one of six "villages" (*li*) on the southwestern side of the Taipei Basin.[5] All but a handful of these women were native speakers of Hokkien, and the great majority were descended from seventeenth- and eighteenth-century immigrants from An-ch'i *hsien* in southern Fukien. Their husbands were farmers, coolies, coal miners, and farm laborers. A few owned the land they cultivated, but no more than a dozen rented land to tenant farmers. Thus it is highly unlikely that any of the differences I report are due to the hidden effects of ethnicity or social class. It is true that the major form of marriage was the prestigious way to marry and the choice of great landlords, wealthy merchants, and officials, but this is not relevant to the data presented in this paper. Within the socioeconomic range represented here wealth did not influence the choice between the major and minor forms of marriage. Whether a man was married to a *sim-pua* or to a girl raised in another family depended primarily on the sex of his next younger sibling. There was little chance of a boy's being matched with a *sim-pua* if his mother's next child was a male who survived the first year of life. Probably because women were unwilling to burden themselves with the care of two or three small children, they only adopted *sim-pua* for their sons if their next child was a girl who could be given away or a boy who died within a few months of birth.[6]

The measure I have used to compare marriages is an age-specific marital fertility rate calculated separately for five-year birth cohorts. The numerator for this rate is the total number of children born to women of a given age and a given cohort; the denominator is the total number of years of marriage experienced by these same women. Women only contribute to this rate from the registered date of their first marriage through termination of that marriage by death, death of husband, or divorce. The experience of women whose families moved is only counted while they were residents of one of the six villages covered by this study. The rate is therefore limited to the most reliable data available and excludes entirely premarital experience, postmarital experience, and all forms of second marriage.

It is important to note that despite these precautions one source of bias remains. Among the women included in the study, the frequency of bridal pregnancies varies from 16.2 percent in the case of major marriages to 21.9 percent in minor marriages to a high of 34.0 percent in uxorilocal marriages. This means that the comparison of major and minor marriages is biased against the hypothesis, while the comparison of uxorilocal and minor marriages is biased in favor of the hypothesis. The reader might well ask why it is that more than 20 percent of all women who married a childhood associate were pregnant at marriage. If these couples were not attracted to one another, why did they sleep together before marriage? The answer is that parents knew young people disliked marrying a childhood associate and therefore delayed registering these marriages until they were sure that they would be accepted. This saved them the embarrassment of a divorce and made it easier for them to find a husband for their "daughter-in-law" if they could not "push" the couple together. The fact is that many minor marriages were never consummated and, as a result, never registered. Had they all been registered when the head of the household decided it was time for the couple to start sleeping together, the fertility of minor marriages would have been considerably lower than is indicated by the data I report.

The factual basis of the present paper is presented in Tables 57, 58, and 59. Table 57 reports the average number of children born per annum; Table 58 lists the numbers on which those averages are based; and Table 59 compares the fertility of minor marriages with that of major and uxorilocal marriages. The reader should note the boldface figures in Tables 57 and 59 and treat them with caution. The Japanese household registration system was initiated in late 1905 and began to deteriorate in the 1940s as World War II moved closer to Taiwan. This makes it difficult to obtain an accurate measure of the early marital fertility of women born in the years 1881–90 and the later marital fertility of those born in the years 1901–15. Many of the former were married before the registration system was set up and may have borne children who did not survive long enough to be included in the registers, while many of the latter may have borne children who were not registered as a result of dislocations caused by the war. It is likely that the boldface figures in Table 57 underestimate actual fertility, and it could be that the comparisons made in Table 59 are biased as a result.

Because of the relatively small number of women involved, the index figures given in Table 59 vary considerably. However, there can be no doubt that the fertility of minor marriages was substantially lower than that of both major and uxorilocal marriages. This was true of all seven cohorts and at all ages. Table 59 makes a total of ninety comparisons, and in all but two of these the index figure exceeds 100. The cumulative magnitude of the differences displayed in Table 59 can best be expressed by calculating the number of children the three forms of marriage would have produced in a population that married at age 15 and survived through age 45. These figures are given in Table 60. The striking fact is that on the average women who married in the minor fashion would have borne 5.71 children as compared with 7.63 children for women married in the major fashion and 7.79 for those married uxorilocally.

Further research may show that these differences in fertility were somewhat larger or somewhat smaller than my data indicate, but it seems un-

TABLE 57
ANNUAL FERTILITY BY AGE, YEAR OF BIRTH, AND TYPE OF MARRIAGE

Year of Birth	*Type of Marriage*	*Age of Wife*					
		15–19	20–24	25–29	30–34	35–39	40–44
1881–1885	Major	**.18**	**.28**	.30	.26	.22	.09
	Minor	**.14**	**.18**	.19	.16	.12	.07
	Ux.	**.23**	**.21**	.24	.17	.16	.11
1886–1890	Major	**.27**	.32	.26	.22	.17	.12
	Minor	**.18**	.25	.22	.21	.14	.07
	Ux.	**.43**	.33	.29	.32	.20	.19
1891–1895	Major	.30	.34	.27	.24	.22	.12
	Minor	.23	.21	.20	.19	.18	.09
	Ux.	.30	.29	.25	.30	.20	.14
1896–1900	Major	.26	.36	.31	.29	.27	.12
	Minor	.24	.26	.23	.21	.16	.10
	Ux.	.42	.26	.26	.24	.21	.11
1901–1905	Major	.33	.34	.32	.29	.22	**.11**
	Minor	.23	.27	.26	.25	.21	**.08**
	Ux.	.36	.32	.32	.32	.22	**.05**
1906–1910	Major	.34	.32	.31	.29	**.20**	—
	Minor	.29	.25	.26	.25	**.19**	—
	Ux.	.47	.33	.35	.29	**.20**	—
1911–1915	Major	.31	.39	.33	**.23**	—	—
	Minor	.27	.27	.23	**.12**	—	—
	Ux.	.49	.31	.33	**.17**	—	—

likely that the conclusion that minor marriages produced fewer children will be overturned. At this point the question is not what but why. I favor the view that intimate childhood association is alone sufficient to arouse sexual aversion and thereby reduce fertility, but alternative interpretations of these data have been suggested by Paul C. Rosenblatt, J. Kirkpatrick, Marvin Harris, and Eugene Hammel. I do not as yet have enough data of the right kind to make conclusive judgments about these alternatives, but I can at least clarify the arguments involved and suggest why I continue to favor the aversion hypothesis.

Let us be clear at the outset as to what an adequate explanation must explain. We have seen that the fertility of minor marriages was lower than that of both major and uxorilocal marriages, that these differences were as strong among women born between 1881 and 1885 as among women born between 1911 and 1915, and that they were as marked among women

TABLE 58
NUMBER OF WOMEN CONTRIBUTING TO FERTILITY RATES IN TABLE 57

Year of Birth	Type of Marriage	Age of Wife					
		15–19	20–24	25–29	30–34	35–39	40–44
1881–1885	Major	62	94	99	97	85	77
	Minor	97	115	111	93	74	66
	Ux.	13	21	21	17	17	15
1886–1890	Major	51	73	76	72	64	56
	Minor	79	90	77	63	56	48
	Ux.	17	29	27	25	20	19
1891–1895	Major	60	79	78	73	65	57
	Minor	65	70	63	55	50	41
	Ux.	32	37	32	29	26	23
1896–1900	Major	79	116	114	105	97	88
	Minor	101	104	90	81	69	63
	Ux.	22	33	31	25	26	22
1901–1905	Major	77	125	118	116	107	97
	Minor	97	107	103	89	77	67
	Ux.	22	33	30	26	25	21
1906–1910	Major	91	132	138	135	130	—
	Minor	112	114	98	79	73	—
	Ux.	22	30	34	28	22	—
1911–1915	Major	97	165	171	156	—	—
	Minor	86	94	79	72	—	—
	Ux.	22	32	31	28	—	—

over forty as among women under twenty. This means that whatever form our explanation takes it must specify a condition or experience that characterized minor marriages but not major or uxorilocal marriages, that persisted from the turn of the century through World War II, and that was capable of influencing a woman's behavior throughout her reproductive career. We cannot be satisfied with an explanation that ignores either of the two alternative forms of marriage, that makes much of the changes initiated in the 1930s, or that explains the behavior of young women but not that of older women.

An explanation I rejected in my 1970 paper demands reconsideration in the light of new evidence. I have since discovered that childhood mortality among adopted daughters was considerably higher than among girls raised as daughters. This lends credence to the native view that adopted daughters were maltreated, overworked, and sometimes deprived of an

TABLE 59
FERTILITY OF MINOR MARRIAGES RELATIVE TO THAT OF MAJOR AND UXORILOCAL MARRIAGES

A. Cohort-Specific Comparison of Major and Minor Marriages
(Major-Marriage Births per 100 Minor-Marriage Births)

Date of Wife's Birth	Age of Wife					
	15–19	20–24	25–29	30–34	35–39	40–44
1881–1885	**126**	**152**	161	156	185	135
1886–1890	**151**	127	121	109	127	173
1891–1895	131	159	134	130	120	139
1896–1900	107	137	136	139	169	118
1901–1905	139	126	122	119	104	**137**
1906–1910	116	131	119	115	**108**	—
1911–1915	116	143	141	**192**	—	—

B. Cohort-Specific Comparison of Uxorilocal and Minor Marriages
(Uxorilocal-Marriage Births per 100 Minor-Marriage Births)

Date of Wife's Birth	Age of Wife					
	15–19	20–24	25–29	30–34	35–39	40–44
1881–1885	**162**	**115**	130	104	139	168
1886–1890	**241**	134	135	154	150	272
1891–1895	131	137	121	160	108	165
1896–1900	176	98	112	115	131	110
1901–1905	152	119	121	129	107	**63**
1906–1910	161	135	133	116	**104**	—
1911–1915	183	116	144	**143**	—	—

adequate diet, suggesting the possibility that the reduced fertility of minor marriages was a consequence of poor health among women who were raised as adopted daughters. Except in the extreme case, a woman's general health does not affect her chances of conceiving, but Dugald Baird's study of the incidence of obstetric abnormalities in Aberdeen indicates that the children of women with poor health have a high perinatal death rate (1965:357–61). Since the Taiwan household registers do not record stillbirths and probably underreport infant deaths, it could be that minor marriages exhibit lower fertility because fewer children survived to be registered. The crucial variable may be the fact that these women were raised as adopted daughters rather than the fact that they married their foster brothers.

TABLE 60
AVERAGE COMPLETED FERTILITY OF A HYPOTHETICAL POPULATION WITH THE AGE-SPECIFIC FERTILITY RATES PRESENTED IN TABLE 57
(Table assumes marriage at age 15 and survival through age 45)

Year of Birth	*Type of Marriage*		
	Major	*Minor*	*Uxorilocal*
1881–1885	6.63	4.32	5.68
1886–1890	6.85	5.29	8.85
1891–1895	7.42	5.48	7.35
1896–1900	8.02	5.99	7.47
1901–1905	8.04	6.52	7.93
1906–1910	7.35	6.21	8.20
1911–1915	6.27	4.44	6.52

This is an appealing explanation because it is direct, simple, and does not involve such admittedly fuzzy concepts as sexual aversion. Nonetheless, it is wrong. Many girls who were raised as adopted daughters married out of their natal families or were used as the means of bringing a man into the family by way of an uxorilocal marriage. If the lower fertility of minor marriages was a result of the treatment these women were subjected to as children, adopted daughters should show low fertility regardless of how they married. Tables 61 through 64 prove conclusively that this is not the case. The fertility of adopted daughters who married in the major fashion or uxorilocally was nearly as high as that of women raised as daughters. Adopted daughters only experienced substantially lower fertility when they married in the minor fashion.

A second explanation concerned with the health of adopted daughters was suggested by Paul C. Rosenblatt.[7] Rosenblatt accepts my contention that the conjugal relationship created by the minor form of marriage was less satisfactory than that created by the other two forms of marriage but fears that relative fertility is a poor measure of this difference. If couples married in the minor fashion were more likely to look for sexual satisfaction outside of marriage, with many husbands seeking the company of prostitutes, it could be that the relatively low fertility of minor marriages reflects a comparatively high incidence of venereal diseases. Venereal diseases might have affected fertility directly through lower conception rates

TABLE 61
ANNUAL FERTILITY BY AGE, YEAR OF BIRTH, TYPE OF MARRIAGE, AND EXPERIENCE OF ADOPTION

Year of Birth	*Marriage and Adoption**	*Age of Wife* 15–19	20–24	25–29	30–34	35–39	40–44
1881–1885	No Adoption	**.19**	**.28**	.31	.25	.21	.09
	Adoption A	**.14**	**.18**	.19	.16	.12	.07
	Adoption B	**.21**	**.22**	.23	.19	.21	.12
1886–1890	No Adoption	**.27**	.30	.27	.22	.16	.12
	Adoption A	**.18**	.25	.22	.21	.14	.07
	Adoption B	**.42**	.36	.28	.33	.26	.22
1891–1895	No Adoption	.34	.35	.28	.24	.18	.13
	Adoption A	.23	.21	.20	.19	.18	.09
	Adoption B	.25	.28	.25	.29	.25	.12
1896–1900	No Adoption	.28	.35	.30	.30	.26	.12
	Adoption A	.24	.26	.23	.21	.16	.10
	Adoption B	.30	.32	.29	.26	.27	.12
1901–1905	No Adoption	.38	.31	.33	.31	.23	**.11**
	Adoption A	.23	.27	.26	.25	.21	**.08**
	Adoption B	.27	.38	.31	.27	.21	**.09**
1906–1910	No Adoption	.39	.35	.33	.30	**.22**	—
	Adoption A	.29	.25	.26	.25	**.19**	—
	Adoption B	.32	.29	.31	.27	**.15**	—
1911–1916	No Adoption	.33	.38	.34	**.22**	—	—
	Adoption A	.27	.27	.23	**.12**	—	—
	Adoption B	.35	.36	.32	**.22**	—	—

* "A" indicates adopted daughters in minor marriages, "B" adopted daughters in major and uxorilocal marriages.

or higher infant mortality rates or indirectly by making the husband less attractive to the wife.

Two of the facts we have discovered suggest that this argument is probably incorrect. For one thing, we have seen that fertility differences were as marked among women aged fifteen to nineteen as among older women. Since the likelihood of a couple's contracting a disease would have increased with exposure to the source of the disease and hence with age, consistency across ages argues that variation by form of marriage was not the result of venereal diseases. For another, the evidence says that uxorilocal marriages produced as many children as major marriages and far more than minor marriages. This is relevant because many women who married uxorilocally worked as prostitutes before marriage. A family that

TABLE 62
NUMBER OF WOMEN CONTRIBUTING TO FERTILITY RATES IN TABLE 61

Year of Birth	Marriage and Adoption*	Age of Wife					
		15–19	20–24	25–29	30–34	35–39	40–44
1881–1885	No Adoption	60	93	96	94	82	76
	Adoption A	97	115	111	93	74	66
	Adoption B	15	22	24	20	20	16
1886–1890	No Adoption	51	69	74	68	64	58
	Adoption A	79	90	77	63	56	48
	Adoption B	17	33	29	29	20	17
1891–1895	No Adoption	48	65	64	62	54	48
	Adoption A	65	70	63	55	50	41
	Adoption B	44	51	46	40	37	32
1896–1900	No Adoption	53	84	82	77	70	64
	Adoption A	101	104	90	81	69	63
	Adoption B	48	65	63	53	53	46
1901–1905	No Adoption	59	93	84	81	73	68
	Adoption A	97	107	103	89	77	67
	Adoption B	40	65	64	61	59	50
1906–1910	No Adoption	63	97	110	107	102	—
	Adoption A	112	114	98	79	73	—
	Adoption B	50	65	62	56	50	—
1911–1915	No Adoption	68	124	135	127	—	—
	Adoption A	86	94	79	72	—	—
	Adoption B	51	73	67	57	—	—

* "A" indicates adopted daughters in minor marriages, "B" adopted daughters in major and uxorilocal marriages.

had no male children or whose only sons were too young to support their elderly parents usually attempted to arrange an uxorilocal marriage for a daughter or an adopted daughter, but because it was always difficult to find an able man who was willing to marry into his wife's family, marriage was often delayed and the family was forced to send the girl to work as a prostitute in the meantime. This difference in the premarital experience of women who married uxorilocally is clearly reflected in illegitimacy rates. Only 93 (9.3 percent) of 1,001 women who married virilocally bore a child before marriage as compared with 57 (34.8 percent) of 164 women who married uxorilocally. It appears that the incidence of venereal diseases in the population was either too low to affect fertility or so high that varying degrees of exposure to prostitution did not make much difference.

TABLE 63
FERTILITY OF ADOPTED DAUGHTERS IN MAJOR AND UXORILOCAL MARRIAGES (A) RELATIVE TO THAT OF ADOPTED DAUGHTERS IN MINOR MARRIAGES (B) AND DAUGHTERS IN MAJOR AND UXORILOCAL MARRIAGES (C)

A. Cohort-Specific Comparison of A and B
(B Births per 100 A Births)

Date of Wife's Birth	*Age of Wife* 15–19	20–24	25–29	30–34	35–39	40–44
1881–1885	**68**	**83**	81	86	57	56
1886–1890	**42**	69	79	63	53	33
1891–1895	91	75	82	65	72	71
1896–1900	80	82	78	81	61	85
1901–1905	88	72	86	90	98	93
1906–1910	90	85	86	95	123	—
1911–1915	76	75	73	55	—	—

B. Cohort-Specific Comparison of A and C
(C Births per 100 A Births)

Date of Wife's Birth	*Age of Wife* 15–19	20–24	25–29	30–34	35–39	40–44
1881–1885	**87**	**126**	132	133	100	74
1886–1890	**63**	84	97	66	62	54
1891–1895	134	126	112	84	73	106
1896–1900	95	112	104	115	96	99
1901–1905	143	83	108	115	105	**124**
1906–1910	120	120	108	113	**143**	—
1911–1915	95	105	106	**102**	—	—

Rosenblatt also suggests that "couples in minor marriages may lack the commitment that stems from the element of personal choice present in major marriages." But in fact it was not until economic changes initiated in the late 1920s precipitated a gradual deterioration of parental authority that major marriages allowed more freedom of choice than minor marriages. Until that time all marriages were arranged by the senior generation with reference to their needs and the needs of the family. The young people involved were seldom consulted and ordinarily did not meet until the day of the wedding. Consequently, we cannot attribute the variation in

TABLE 64
AVERAGE COMPLETED FERTILITY OF A HYPOTHETICAL POPULATION WITH THE AGE-SPECIFIC FERTILITY RATES PRESENTED IN TABLE 61
(Table assumes marriage at age 15 and survival through age 45.)

Year of Birth	*Daughters in Major & Uxorilocal Marriages*	*Adopted Daughters in Minor Marriages*	*Adopted Daughters in Major & Uxorilocal Marriages*
1881–1885	6.60	4.32	5.92
1886–1890	6.67	5.29	9.32
1891–1895	7.60	5.48	7.19
1896–1900	8.04	5.99	7.73
1901–1905	8.33	6.52	7.61
1906–1910	7.95	6.21	6.70
1911–1915	6.34	4.44	6.22

fertility among women born between 1881 and 1900 to varying degrees of personal commitment. Moreover, we must conclude that personal commitment stemming from choice did not affect fertility, since the difference in fertility did not increase with the change in relative freedom of choice. Rosenblatt's argument is an attractive one but does not fit the facts as well as the aversion hypothesis.

A third explanation offered by Rosenblatt is based on a different set of assumptions. After noting that many adopted daughters were treated like servants and were deprived of the glamour associated with a bridal procession and a grand wedding, he suggests that it may have been their Cinderella-like status that made them unattractive to their husbands. It was one thing to marry a girl whose entry into the family was a celebrated event and who came dressed in imperial finery; it was quite another to be told that the drudge who helped mother in the kitchen was now your wife. There may have been something like aversion involved, but its source was the bride's lowly status rather than intimate association.

One objection to this argument is that however glamorous she may have appeared on her wedding day, the wife who married in the major fashion was quickly reduced to the status of a household drudge. Regardless of whether she was raised in the family or entered as a young adult, a Chinese daughter-in-law was treated like a servant by her husband's parents and only achieved a position of dignity when she herself became a mother-in-law. I can accept the thought that the first impressions made by the two kinds of brides might have affected fertility during the early years of marriage, but the difference was too short-lived to have influenced fertility for forty years. The variable we are looking for must be a continuing condition or an experience potent enough to leave an indelible imprint on the conjugal relationship.

A second counterargument is suggested by the comparison between major and uxorilocal marriages. If a man who was forced to marry his foster sister was put off by her low status, so must the woman whose parents insisted on her marrying uxorilocally have been put off by her spouse. Ordinarily these husbands were poor men who could not afford a bride price, and by marrying uxorilocally they were ipso facto inferior human beings. It was axiomatic that no principled man would "desert his parents" to reside with his wife's family. In the old days uxorilocally married men were commonly referred to as *huana-gu*, "barbarians' cows," "because their wife's family worked them to death and gave them nothing." Thus, given the premises of Rosenblatt's argument, we should find lower fertility among uxorilocal marriages than among major marriages; in fact, the fertility of uxorilocal marriages was slightly higher than that of major marriages.

The same argument applies to Marvin Harris's criticism of my 1966 paper. Harris argues that the data presented in that article "are more readily intelligible as examples of the frustration and discontent that many junior members of extended families experience in their subordinate and dependent relationship. This frustration was especially marked in the case under consideration since infant betrothals were traditionally regarded as an inferior form of marriage" (1971:293). The emphasis Harris lays on the subordinate position of the junior generation is misleading because irrelevant. Junior members of Chinese families were subordinate regardless of how they married. The only relevant fact is the inferior status of the minor form of marriage, and it appears that this was not as critical as Harris takes it to be. Uxorilocal marriages were also markedly inferior, but they produced as many, even more, children than socially superior major marriages.

Where Rosenblatt and Harris emphasize the inferior status of the minor form of marriage, J. Kirkpatrick suggests that the critical variable may have been the resentment adopted daughters felt as a result of the prejudicial treatment they received in their foster homes. "In the minor marriage, the adopted daughter married her 'brother', that is, one of the favored persons in the family menage for whose benefit the adopted daughter is less well fed, and presumably, is discriminated against in other ways as well. Imagine, then, the negative attitudes such a woman would form toward the entire family, but especially toward that privileged person, her erstwhile 'brother' and future spouse" (1972:783–84).

I find it difficult to deal with these criticisms in a fair-handed manner as Kirkpatrick concludes by suggesting that I leave off analyzing household registers and pay some attention to "the subjective responses of women as well as men," thereby leaving the reader with the impression that I have yet to discover the relevance of women's feelings to the study of conjugal relationships. I have not only interviewed many women on this subject (as well as others) but have in fact published an account of what women say about the treatment they received in their foster families (A. Wolf 1968:871–72). In brief, my conclusion was that, while adopted daughters were commonly mistreated, they directed their resentment at their parents and clung to their ties with their foster parents, a point that is confirmed by Margery Wolf's analysis in *Women and the Family in Rural Taiwan* (1972:175–80). I have also noted that both men and women objected to the minor form of marriage because they found it "embarrassing" and "uninteresting" (A. Wolf 1966:890–91). There is nothing in what either sex says to suggest that they were motivated by resentment, jealousy, or bitterness. One *woman* told me that she and her foster brother discussed their marriage in bed one night, decided that their relationship was "uninteresting," and devised a plan to obtain a divorce while their father was out of town.

The last alternative I take up was suggested to me by Eugene Hammel, who attended the Santa Fe conference and served as discussant for an earlier version of this paper. Hammel guessed, and correctly, as the data in Table 65 indicate, that women who married in the minor fashion were on the average closer in age to their husbands than those who married in the major fashion or uxorilocally. Beginning then with the assumption that women wanted fewer children than their husbands, Hammel argued that the lower fertility of minor marriages might reflect a more nearly balanced conjugal relationship. The essence of his argument was that women who were close to their husbands in age were in a relatively more powerful position and therefore better able to reject sexual demands than those who were much younger than their husbands. The implication is that women who were older than their husbands bore the fewest children, those who were ten or more years younger the most.

TABLE 65
RELATIVE AGE OF HUSBAND AND WIFE BY TYPE OF MARRIAGE
(All marriages of women born 1881–1915)

		Percentage of Marriages with Specified Age Difference			
Type of Marriage	*Number of Marriages*	*Wife 5 or More Years Younger*	*Wife More than 2 but Less than 5 Years Younger*	*Difference in Age Less than 2 Years*	*Wife More than 2 Years Older*
Major	974	31.00	40.24	26.89	1.84
Minor	795	19.24	56.10	17.23	7.42
Uxorilocal	275	39.63	40.72	17.81	1.81

Hammel and I are now working to test this possibility and will publish the results as soon as they are known. At this point all I can say is that I doubt that the difference in the relative ages of husband and wife will account for more than a small percentage of the variation in fertility. Put more generally, Hammel's hypothesis is that anything that shifted the balance of conjugal power in favor of the wife reduced fertility. If this were the case, uxorilocal marriages would exhibit far lower fertility than any other form of marriage. The man who married into his wife's family lost status by marrying in this fashion and at the same time placed himself in a dependent position. When his wife's father died the family's land was registered in the name of the wife or in the names of those sons who took their descent from their mother. The husband could claim nothing. And while the considerable authority that was granted by custom to Chinese husbands was thus undercut, the wife gained the advantage of remaining in her native community and among her closest relatives. The fact that these marriages were the most fertile of all argues that one or more of Hammel's assumptions is mistaken. Perhaps women were not motivated to limit their fertility because children were the basis of their power. Alternatively, there is a possibility that the conjugal balance of power did not decide the positions husband and wife assumed in the bedroom.

I am not entirely satisfied with the counterarguments advanced in this chapter and do not feel that the aversion hypothesis has been proved beyond any reasonable doubt. All I can say at this point is that it still appears to be the best explanation of the facts. Whether or not it is the right explanation is another matter. I think it is highly unlikely that families who raised their sons' wives were markedly wealthier or poorer than other families, but this must be demonstrated directly rather than on the basis of the indirect evidence offered to date. An analysis of land records now under way will give me a reasonably good measure of socioeconomic status, but the effects of wealth and social status can probably be best tested by comparing the fertility of women who married brothers. It was not uncommon for one brother to marry in the major fashion while another married a girl raised to be his wife. Clear evidence that men who married childhood associates produced fewer children than their brothers who married outsiders would prove that childhood association reduced fertility regardless of wealth and social standing.

The existence of major and minor marriages in the same family also offers us an opportunity to evaluate further the ideas suggested by Rosenblatt and Harris. The essence of their argument is that the lower fertility of minor marriages was the result, not of sexual dissatisfaction, but of dissatisfaction with an inferior form of marriage. Suppose, then, that we were to compare minor marriages involving men all of whose brothers had also married in the minor fashion with minor marriages involving men whose brothers had made major marriages. Given the competitive character of the fraternal relationship in Chinese society, it is reasonable to assume that men who saw their marriage as inferior to a brother's marriage would be more dissatisfied with their lot than those who did not have such an immediate comparison. Thus the Rosenblatt-Harris interpretation implies that the fertility of the former class of marriages was lower than that of the latter class. Evidence to the contrary would argue stoutly that people did not care very much about the relative status of the two forms of marriage or that such dissatisfaction as was aroused by the inferior status of minor marriages was not keen enough to reduce fertility.

By far the most important task remaining is to enlarge the population under study to the point that it is possible to investigate the effects of varying degrees of childhood association. Although the great majority of all *sim-pua* were adopted within a year of birth and matched with boys who were not more than three or four years old at the time, age of adoption and the age of the husband on first meeting his future wife did vary. Some couples were brought together before they were a year old; others did not meet until they were eight or nine years of age. A clear demonstration that those couples who were matched as infants bore fewer children than those who were matched a little later in life would provide powerful support for my contention that childhood association aroused an aversion and thereby reduced fertility. Given such evidence one could fairly say that the burden of proof rests with those whose assumptions about human behavior led them to reject the aversion hypothesis.

NOTES

1. Collection of the data reported in this paper was supported by grants from the China Program at Cornell University and the Center for Research in International Studies at Stanford University; the analysis was financed by a grant from the National Science Foundation (GS-3041).

2. My previous work was reported in a series of three articles in the *American Anthropologist* (A. Wolf 1966, 1968, and 1970).

3. A brief description of the format and content of the Japanese household registers is contained in my essay in *Women in Chinese Society* (A. Wolf 1975); a more detailed description and an evaluation of the registers is being prepared.

4. The institutional aspects of these three forms of marriage are discussed in detail in my essay entitled "Marriage and Adoption in Northern Taiwan" (A. Wolf 1974).

5. Four of the six are part of what is now known as San-hsia *chen*; the other two are part of neighboring Pan-ch'iao *chen*.

6. The evidence supporting this argument will be presented in a book I am preparing in collaboration with Huang Chieh-shan.

7. My summary of Rosenblatt's points is based on personal correspondence; the reader should consult his essay in Ted L. Huston's *Foundations of Interpersonal Attraction* (Rosenblatt 1974). I take this opportunity to thank Professor Rosenblatt for his perceptive comments and his encouragement. His contribution to this paper is gratefully acknowledged.

8

Stability and Instability: A Problem in Long-Term Regional Growth

EZRA B. W. ZUBROW

Department of Anthropology,
Stanford University

INTRODUCTION

The problem of growth is fundamental to archaeology. The cultural phenomena which this discipline attempts to explain and observe change through time in a patterned manner. A basic question that has been asked is whether this growth process is discontinuous. Two positions have been taken: that growth is an anomalous unstable condition or, conversely, that it is a continual condition. Each has its own proponents. Both sides of the problem were broached by Braidwood and Willey (1962:351) in their pioneer discussion of the Urban Revolution. They suggest that the difference between the courses of development in Mesoamerica and Mesopotamia is the difference between a single, long-term, smooth growth process and a series of short-term, abrupt growth processes. Their metaphors were to compare a "ramp" with a "step" function.

The question of stability is neither heuristic nor dependent upon the level of temporal resolution. One contention of this paper is that the degree of stability of growth processes is measurable and the results are not a matter of scale. A second contention is that both stable and unstable growth processes can operate simultaneously and complementarily on the same domain. To expect a cultural system a priori to exhibit solely stable or unstable growth processes is insufficient, analogous to the position taken prior to Le Broglie that light must show either wave or particle properties but not both.

This paper examines cultural and regional growth processes using economic models and prehistoric data. It will be argued that the pattern of economic growth (stable or unstable) is expressed in the changing regional structure of settlements and thus in the population. Several themes will be briefly developed. First, I wish to consider the archaeological definition of culture as a systemic phenomenon providing the theoretical framework for examining systemic growth. Economic growth and the growth of the regional structure of settlements will be considered as specific examples of systemic growth. Second, two economic development models will be suggested that are both systemic and that contrast stable and unstable growth. Third, the nature of regions and the structure of regional settlement systems will be considered. Following the development of these themes, the expected effects of stable and unstable growth on regional settlement structure will be delineated, and a methodology as well as data from two regions comprising 1,577 sites will be presented. Neither model individually is sufficient to explain the total growth within each region; in conjunction, they are sufficient. The results are more elegant for the stable model than for the unstable model for both prehistoric regions.

CULTURE AS A SYSTEMIC PHENOMENON

Recently archaeologists have perceived culture as a system. This viewpoint is critical in changing archaeology from a historical discipline studying the statistics of particular events to a processual science studying such dynamics as the stability of growth processes. Systems theory has the advantage of allowing theoretical model building between the levels of the highly generalized constructions of pure mathematics and the specific theories of specialized disciplines. Since it has both inductive and deductive derivations and applications, it allows one to transcend the boundaries between the biological, physical, and social sciences. In short, systems theory was designed to provide a theoretical bridge between diverse disciplines and domains. In this case it is used to combine economics and archaeology, growth and structure, as well as prehistoric settlements and regions.

Presently archaeologists use two distinct systemic definitions of culture; one ultimately derived from information theory, the other from biological ecology and energistics. Clarke (1968) presents culture as a system in which the component interrelationships as well as the positive and negative feedback processes are defined through information flows, variety, equivocation, and redundancy. Binford (1968:328) has defined culture as an extrasomatic adaptive system that integrates a society with its environment. Whereas the Clarke system calculates information flows, the Binford system uses energy or economic flows. For Clarke the equilibrium states exist within the cultural system; for Binford equilibriums exist between the environment and the culture. Although I prefer Binford's definition, an examination of the nature of systemic growth will be productive in discussing aspects of cultural growth for either definition.

SYSTEMIC GROWTH

What is *growth?* The usual definition is "a process of gradual increase"; however, it is also possible to define growth in an evolutionary framework as "the movement of the phenomenon under consideration from one state to another." This latter definition implies structural change and is often termed developmental. Growth is a form of expansion that brings out the capabilities or possibilities inherent within a system. Its characteristics, including increased size, increased number, increased range, and increased variation, need not be mutually exclusive. It is a gross oversimplification to think of growth simply as development by accumulation.

So far we have discussed the definition of culture as a system without actually defining a *system* or answering the question of how it grows. A system may be defined at various levels of sophistication. At an informal level it is a set of inputs, outputs, components, and interrelationships within an environment.[1] On this level, systemic growth may take the form of increased numbers and size of components, increased numbers of relationships among components, increased numbers of inputs and/or outputs to the environment, or increased size of the environment.

If one considers regional growth or economic production from a systemic viewpoint, it is clear that growth of these cultural phenomena cannot be looked at simply as an aggregate. Components should be defined. Depending upon the level of analysis and the system under consideration, one may be analyzing such diverse phenomena as individuals, cohorts, settlements, consumers, households, or agricultural production. Their size, interrelationships, numbers, environment, and input and output functions are all relevant aspects of growth. Many regional and economic models (e.g., Forrester's model of urban dynamics [1969]) explicitly or implicitly make use of this systemic structure.

The next sections of this paper examine two economic growth models for which one may define the systemic components, interrelationships, and so forth. The unstable model employs innovation, production cost, production value, consumption, labor, capital, and investment as components; the stable model uses capital, investment, savings, and real output. A regional model is then discussed that incorporates a spatial component (size, location, distances), a functional component, and a structural component.

ECONOMIC MODELS

Every culture must face economic goals, the outcome of which is critical for economic growth. On the one hand, a culture must satisfy the material wants of the population using current technology and the available limited quantities of natural resources, labor, and capital. This may be called the optimization problem: it speaks to current needs with limited resources. It is also necessary, however, to consider the developmental problem. A culture must increase its production through time in order to satisfy the increasing demand for consumption, which may be the result of either an increasing population with the same demands, or the same population with increasing demands, or both. The trade-off occurs because the investment of scarce resources into future needs (development) diminishes the amount available for current needs (optimization).[2]

As previously noted, the problem of stable versus unstable economic growth is neither a heuristic problem nor one of resolution or scale. It is not heuristic because when resources are scarce, mutually exclusive decisions must be made between a society's current needs and future needs. How the growth process is perceived will affect this decision process. If growth is viewed as an anomalous condition, then relatively more decisions will be made opting for current needs. Current needs are the more frequent and better-known condition; thus prediction and decision making are easier. If, on the other hand, growth is seen as a continual condition, then the importance of future needs will be emphasized. In situations of continual growth, decisions must take into account the expected differences between present and future demands, consumptions, and productions. This is the same process by which the present was predicted from the past.

The question of stable or unstable growth is also not one of resolution or scale. For example, it has been argued that a stable growth pattern is simply an unstable growth pattern analyzed at an inappropriately gross scale. Imagine a regularized step pattern of growth, of real output, that is measured on a 300-year scale divided into 50-year intervals (Fig. 15). If, instead, one measures this same process extracting information every 100 years (Fig. 16), it is possible to interpret the data as a continual growth process (Fig. 17). However, when two sets of data from the same data base show differing degrees of discontinuity on the same scale (Fig. 18), the scale cannot be the cause of the differences. Instead, they signify differing growth patterns. In short, growth may be abstracted analytically

FIGURE 15. Unstable growth (50-year scale)

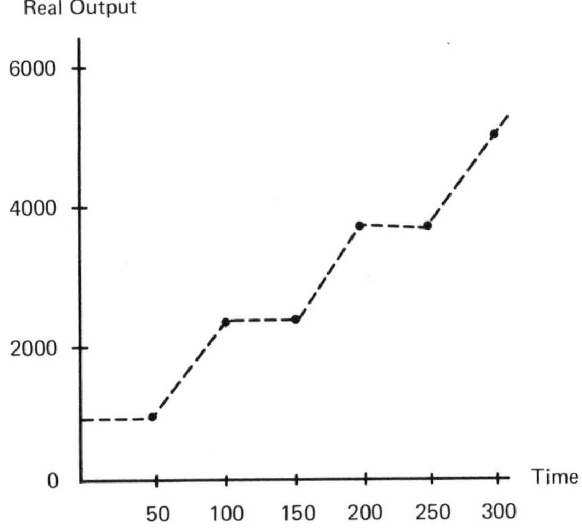

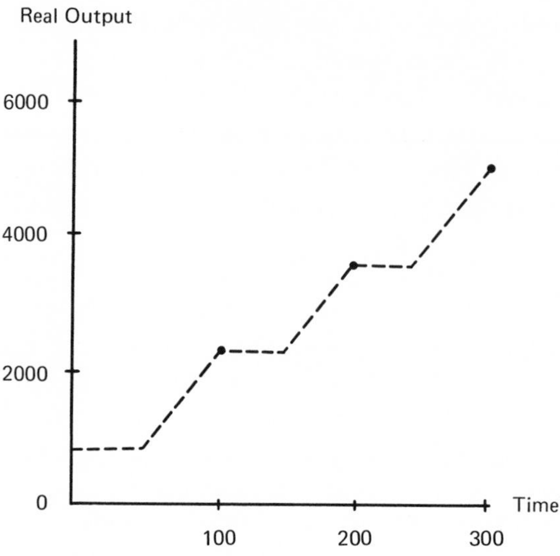

FIGURE 16. Unstable growth (100-year scale). Abstracted data (points) may be interpreted as stable growth.

FIGURE 17. Data plotted in Figures 15 and 16 interpreted as stable growth

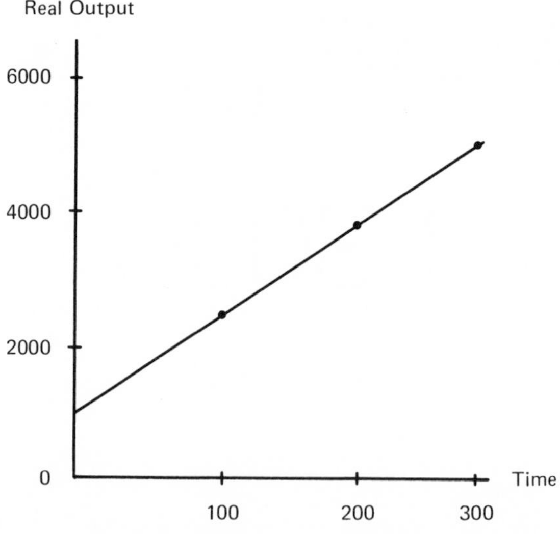

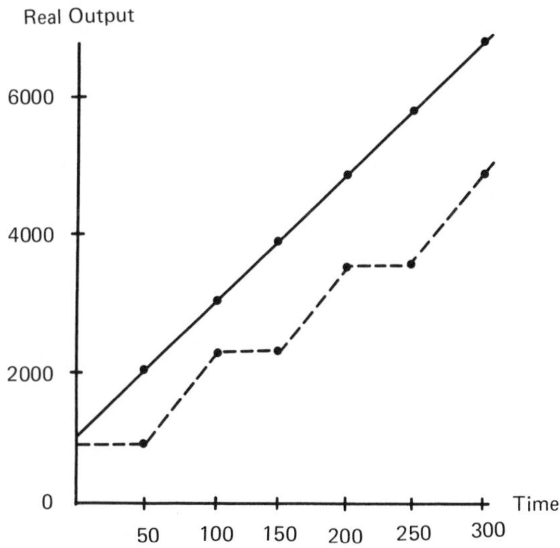

FIGURE 18. Stable and unstable growth at the same scale signifying differing growth patterns.

in order to make comparisons, provided we are careful that the context or scale is equivalent.

Unstable Growth

Schumpeter (1911) has put forth a model of unstable economic growth that begins with the economy of the society in stationary equilibrium. A balanced circular flow exists in which costs of production, value of production, value of labor for production, and demand for consuming the product are equal. Development, or the permanent change of the values of these variables, is the change from one equilibrium to another. After the new equilibrium is reached the variables continue to equal each other, but their absolute values have increased. This change is caused by a discontinuous disturbance of the circular flow in the form of an innovation, by which Schumpeter means either a "technical or resource discovery." The innovation may disturb the circular flow through four factors that increase production and output. First, it may increase the efficiency of production. Second, it may render previous equipment obsolete. In the short run, this raises the production costs while the new, more efficient equipment replaces the old equipment; in the long run, however, the increased efficiency reduces production costs. Third, an innovation may lead to the expectation of monopoly benefits, as well as creating competitive advantages in its marketing or use. Fourth, the product or innovation becomes so attractive or valuable that demand for consumption increases as the consumer is willing to expend savings. This increased demand then requires increased production (Higgens 1968:101). In short, innovations bring about an increase in output through increased production.

Historically, Schumpeter argues, most innovations are produced and marketed by new firms, as it is too expensive to retool old firms. Generalizing, then, we may state that new innovations require new production and redistribution mechanisms that in turn require new social and economic institutions. Once the success of the new innovation is shown, however, there are clusters of followers who are willing to attempt production. This swarming effect includes the retooling of old and related industries in order to maintain their competitive advantage as well as to take into account changing patterns of demand. This gestation period often includes a series of related innovations.

In fact, according to Schumpeter, significant innovations must occur in clusters. A single innovation does not have a major effect upon production unless it is backed up by a series of reinforcing innovations. For example, the introduction of the internal combustion engine needed a vast number of reinforcing innovations. Before the automobile industry could cause an effective difference in the national product, an expansion of the highway system and of the petroleum and rubber industries was necessary. Or, to use a prehistoric example, irrigation had no long-term effect upon agricultural productivity until the necessary social innovations took place allowing the maintenance of canals, the distribution of water, and the allocation of the surplus product. Once a cluster of innovations has been introduced, they become a competitive necessity and diffuse widely.

After the period of disequilibrium and innovation development, a new equilibrium is reached. As new institutions complete the development of new production facilities, the rate of investment decreases because the costs of maintenance are considerably less than the costs of original production of the innovation. With the increased production resulting from the swarming effect, the value of the new product is decreased. A new equilibrium state has been reached.[3]

Stability and Instability

Schumpeter's theory of innovation implies that economic growth is discontinuous, while a state of nongrowth is normal. If we could measure growth output over long periods of time, we would see a growth curve represented by a series of stages or plateaus connected by short periods of growth. In short, the result of the model is a traditional stage system of development (see Fig. 15).

Stable Growth

What kind of model is necessary to generate a process of continual growth, one whose equilibrium state is growth and whose disequilibrium is the status quo?

One steady-state model of economic growth is postulated by Harrod (1948) and Domar (1957). A simplified model devised to explain modern economic development, it has been described as a parable of an economy because of its assumptions: (1) the model economy produces only one composite commodity, which may be either consumed after production or accumulated as a stock of capital; and (2) there is a homogeneous labor supply which, combined with the stock of capital available from past accumulation, is an input to current production. Although this model is highly simplified for modern industrial societies, there is less discrepancy when it is applied to prehistoric economies. In comparison to the large number of commodities modern economies produce, hunting-gathering economies are basically two-commodity systems—they produce hunted products and gathered products. Peasants use a three-commodity system comprising hunted products, gathered products, and agricultural products. The labor force for both is homogeneous and the stock of capital is available only from past accumulation.

What broad facts about economic growth is the Harrod-Domar model attempting to reproduce? In 1958 Nicholas Kaldor summed these up as a set of developmental facts, of which four are relevant here: (1) productivity is increasing through time; (2) the amount of capital has been growing at a faster rate than the labor supply; (3) the rate of growth of real output and that of capital goods are approximately equal; and (4) the rate of growth of real output per capita is culturally specific and variable. An economy growing according to these rules is defined as being in a steady state.

Under what circumstances is an economy capable of such growth?

Harrod and Domar answer this question with their famous consistency condition. In order to define their model they make three specific assumptions. First, the population and the labor force grow at a constant proportional rate, called N, that is independent of other economic factors. Second, savings and investment are a fixed fraction, called S, of output at any instant of time.[4] Third, technology may be defined on the basis of two coefficients that are constants: first, the capital requirement per unit of output, called V; second, the labor requirement per unit of output. These are constants in that they cannot be varied at any moment in time but will change when there is a major transition in the technology. The question is how to combine these variables in order to have a model economy capable of generating steady-state growth. The theoretical answer given by Harrod and Domar is that an economy will grow steadily if and only if $S = VN$, or the saving rate is the product of the capital-output ratio and the rate of growth of the labor force. This famous point can be made in many ways; for example, the savings rate must be just equal to the required ratio of investment to output for a steady state to be possible.[5] There are strong homeostatic forces that tend to drive the system back into balance when disequilibriums occur.[6]

What makes this model interesting is that the probability that $S = VN$ would be very small if it occurred by accident. However, the empirical reality of the Kaldor stylized facts indicates to a certain extent that these conditions are actually met.

REGIONS

Any traveler moving through an area notes differences among the cultures and the populations. All cultures and populations have spatial components. If one classifies a population by its spatial cultural units, a hierarchy is defined. Whether one uses the sequence house–settlement–culture area or household-town-state-nation, one has the feeling that there is a missing level, bigger than the town or settlement but smaller than the culture or state. This level is usually called the *region*.

The theoretical construction of the properties of regions was initiated by Losch (1954) and Christaller (1966) and has had wide circulation through their students, including Isard (1960) and Leontieff (1966).

Stability and Instability

What is a region? It may be characterized by three criteria. First, a region has spatial definition: it is an areal unit. Second, it has an inherent uniformity differentiating it from other regions and surrounding areas; this uniformity may be along an economic, demographic, cultural, or any of a number of other axes. Third, regions are systems with structure: settlement size, location, type, and so forth are not random phenomena but are located as a result of processes. The components of the system are not only indentifiable but are connected to each other by a series of interrelationships, such that when changes affect part of the system, the results may be felt throughout.

The Spatial Definition

Space need not be perceived in a traditional Euclidean framework. Regional geographers often see it as a "field of action"—a functional space. For example, one may add or replace axes, calculate coefficients, and map new types of space, including a "cost space," a "production space," or a "mortality space." We shall be interested in a "structural space": in other words, how does the hierarchical organization of settlements vary across space and time?

Inherent Uniformity

The uniformity of a region often is used to characterize it. The term "agricultural region" evokes pictures in the mind of large alluvial valleys with meandering rivers and perhaps slightly rolling hills, a far cry from the mountainous, rugged terrain of a mining region. Expert writers are able to distinguish fine subtleties. For example, "it may be the quiet mood of the hop fields of Kent, or even that of our own backyard; it may be the gemutlich air of Southern Germany, with its dark forests and solid homes, which marks it off from the bright, denuded Cézanne landscapes of Southern France" (Yi-Fu Tuan 1972:535).

A region may be uniform along one axis, however, without being uniform along others. Consider the San Francisco Bay Area, in which the population and transportation distributions do not exactly correspond to each other. The uniformity of a region may also change through time, as will be seen in one of the prehistoric examples analyzed later.

Structure and System

As has already been pointed out, regions are systems with structure. The hierarchical structure of a region and its systemic organization are not mutually exclusive. In general, the greater the number of components a system has, the greater the number of echelons in the hierarchy.

Prior to turning to the hierarchical structure of settlements within a region, we shall consider briefly the attributes of the ideal hierarchy and two examples of potential hierarchical organizations within a region. Figure 19 shows a general hierarchy that subdivides the phenomenon A into 14 additional categories. Each category is differentiated by the binary presence or absence of one of four attributes—the three letters *B, C, D,* and the "′". Each level or echelon of this particular hierarchy is represented by the addition of a letter. For example, the difference between the second and third echelons is the addition of the *C* division, which may take the two forms *C* and *C′*. It is possible to determine general equations for the number of categories, for the hierarchy, and for each echelon. In addition, one may generate the categories themselves.

Regions are often ecological systems and thus hierarchically organized with regard to numbers of organisms, energy transfer, biomass, and so on. For example, the food chain determining the energy flow has a hierarchical structure reflected in the relative amounts of energy, biomass, or numbers at each trophic level.

Populations within regions can also be hierarchically arranged. Consider for a moment the structure of a population. One of the usual techniques of a demographic analyst is to divide the population into cohorts and consider these both separately and jointly. Population pyramids are hierarchical structurings of the population by age or sex. Given that the environments and populations of regions may be hierarchically organized, it is no surprise to find settlements similarly organized.

The Regional Distribution of Settlements

The details of the spatial location, uniform characteristics, and structure of the distribution of settlements in regions have been the focus of considerable effort. Berry, Barnum, and Tennant (1962) have used functional units and trade areas in Iowa; Woldenberg (1967) has looked at market examples from Finland, Germany, and Nigeria. Again we shall

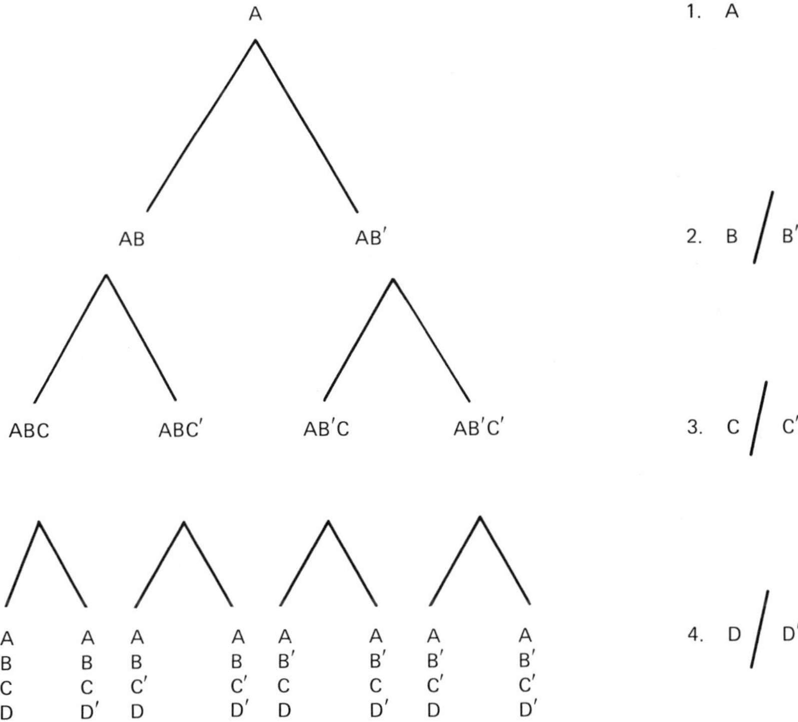

FIGURE 19. A general hierarchy

consider space, uniformity, and structure in turn. Theoretically, the ideas were originally put forth by Christaller and Losch, who asked the spatial question, What would be the optimal spatial division of an undifferentiated resource landscape among a group of settlements? If the settlements use evenly distributed resources to optimize their use, the settlements will be located at a maximal distance from each other. The shape of the polygon formed by attempting to space maximally a series of points in a plane is a series of hexagons.

Next let us introduce the notions of the uniform characteristics and the structured hierarchy of settlements. There are two "additional" axes upon which settlements within regions may be measured. One is an axis of centrality. This is essentially a spatial measure, but instead of measuring space in some absolute sense it is a relative measure, indicating the relationship between a settlement and other settlements.[7] The other is an axis of production. Imagine, as did Christaller and Losch, that there are at least two types of settlement: central places and dependent places. Central places would be the larger trade centers, where commerce and consumption are more important than primary production based upon natural resources. Dependent places are the smaller primary production centers, in which primary production is relatively large but consumption and commerce are small. These dependent places are located peripherally to the central place.

Central places and dependent places represent two different echelons in a structured hierarchy of the types noted previously. These echelon divisions may be extended so that the central places for one group of settlements are the peripheral settlements for another group of larger settlements. Thus, a town such as Maidenhead may be central to a group of smaller villages such as Marlowe and yet at the same time be peripheral to a more central city such as London.

There are a variety of ways in which central and dependent places can be located in relation to each other and still maintain the hexagonal nets. Figures 20, 21, and 22 show three of the smaller hexagonal territories in a Loschian landscape,[8] each diagram representing a different system of hexagonal nesting. The differences are caused by the orientation of the hexagonal net and the size of each hexagon. For example, in the $K = 3$ system, or *Versorgungsprinzip* model, this value is made up of the central place itself and a one-third share in the six border settlements. Each dependent place is shared among three central places. For $K = 4$, the *Verkehrsprinzip* model, the dependent place is shared by only two central places; therefore, the value $K = 4$ is made up of a one-half share of six dependent centers plus the central place. The K value is dependent upon the packing order.[9]

Two other aspects of the theory are relevant for us. First, the probabilities of the various K systems actually existing are not equal. Christaller noted that when $K = 3$ the number of market towns is conserved; when $K = 4$ the transportation rates are economized because so many major cities lie on straight roads. When $K = 7$, $K = 13$, or $K = 19$ the control of dependent settlements is maximized because there are no divided or shared central places; hence this configuration should be politically and economically stable. An example of an inefficient K is $K = 12$. In this case, the ratio of the number of dependent places served by a central place to the maximum distance necessary to travel from a central place to the farthest dependent place is very low.

Second, what will be the statistical distribution of the various places? (For example, what are the relationships of central places of different echelons to each other and to dependent places?) Figure 20 shows the $K = 3$ model emphasizing the size of the different towns. It is possible to calculate the ratio of central places to dependent places for each order of magnitude or echelon. For example, for a $K = 3$ system there would be 1 central city for every 2 towns, 2 towns for every 6 villages, 6 villages for every 18 hamlets, and so forth. The ratio of the numbers is $A{:}B{:}C{:}D{:}E{:}F{:}\ldots = 1{:}2{:}6{:}18{:}54{:}162 \ldots$ where A represents the most central places, or highest echelon, B the next highest echelon, and so on. This represents numerically a hierarchical pyramid following the echelon structure. It

FIGURE 20. Christaller's *Versorgungsprinzip* model ($K = 3$)

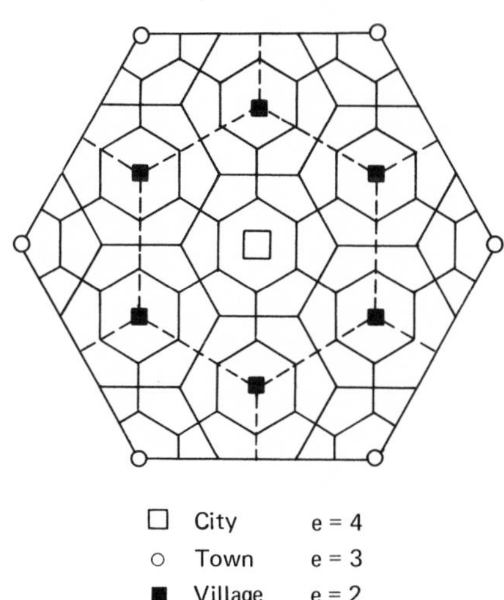

should be noted, however, that the above ratio counts only the number of centers functioning at the stated level, and does not include centers at a higher level. If one counts each center not only at its highest level but also at all lower levels, the numeric series is cumulative: A:*B*:*C*:*D*:*E*:*F*: . . . = 1:3:9:27:81:243. . . . The general equation $N_e = K^e$ summarizes these numbers.[10] This latter series suggests that A not only operates as an A central place but also provides the production, services, and trade of a B central place, of a C central place, and so on.

The $K = 4$ model with the size of the towns differentiated is presented in Figure 21. The numerical ratio for this type of hierarchy is A:*B*:*C*:*D*:*E*: . . . = 1:3:12:48:192: . . . or, alternatively, the accumulative form has centers in the ratio of A:*B*:*C*:*D*:*E*: . . . = 1:4:16:64:256: . . . . Figure 22 shows the $K = 7$ model, again with the size of the towns differentiated.

FIGURE 21. Christaller's *Verkehrsprinzip* model $(K = 4)$

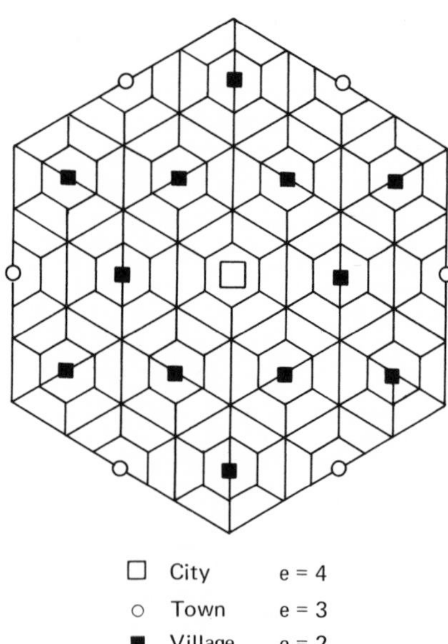

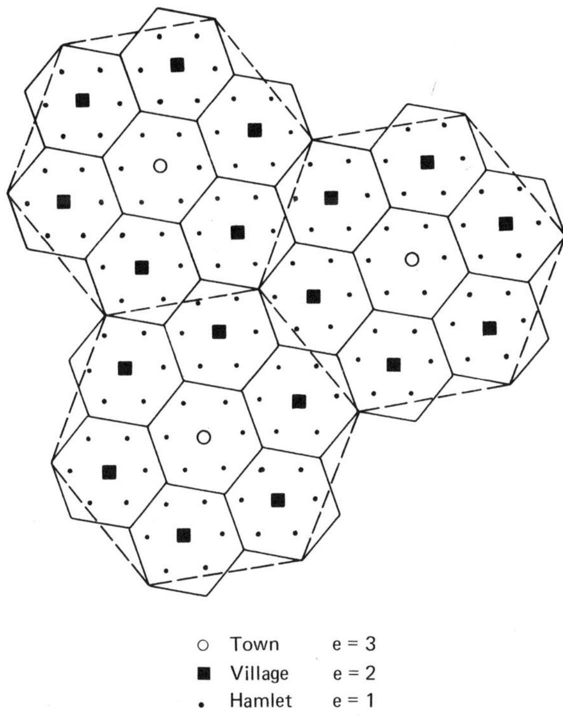

FIGURE 22. A model satisfying Christaller's *Absonderungsprinzip* conditions ($K = 7$)

The two sequences of relative frequencies of centers in this case are A:B:C:D:E: . . . = 1:6:42:294:2,058 . . . as an exclusive numerical ratio and A:B:C:D:E: . . . = 1:7:49:343:2,401 . . . as the inclusive sequence of the numbers of central places.

TEST IMPLICATIONS

What are the implications for regional settlement growth of each of the economic development models? If the Harrod-Domar model were operating, one would expect a steady filling of the region with hierarchically arranged settlements over time. This filling may follow any of the K patterns, and should correspond to the saving and investment patterns of the economic models. One might wish to argue that the probabilities are in favor of a configuration of settlements that would follow one of the more economically efficient patterns, namely, $K = 3, 4,$ or 7. However, this is not necessary. In addition, one could hypothesize that once a pattern has been established it will continue because it is more efficient to maintain a single pattern than to change patterns. Thus, if one were to trace the filling of a region across time, the following sequence would be expected. If a perfect $K = 3$ pattern were being followed, at time 1 there would be one settlement in echelon 1, that is, hamlet size. As capital and labor increase in a continual process, we would expect three settlements in echelon 1 and one village (echelon 2). Similarly for time 3, the expectations are nine settlements in echelon 1, three settlements in echelon 2, and one town (echelon 3). This progression would continue, following the ratio through the subsequent time periods. The other ratios for the $K = 4$ or $K = 7$ systems could be placed in a temporal sequence powered by continual growth.

On the other hand, if the nonstable growth model of Schumpeter were operating, one would expect an unstable, discontinuous rate in filling the region with settlements. Periods of growth would be initiated by clusters of innovations. Growth would follow the expected ratios for short periods of time, but for other periods there would be equilibrium states of nongrowth. For example, at time 1 there might be one settlement in echelon 1; at time 2, three in echelon 1 and one in echelon 2. However, for times 3, 4, and 5 there might be no change whatsoever. Growth powered by innovations might reoccur at time 6 and echelons 1 to 3 would then have nine, three, and one settlements, respectively. The ratios from any Loschian landscape may be used across time.

If the economic growth pattern, whether stable or unstable, reversed because of increasing pressure on resources or for other reasons, one would expect that the filling pattern would also reverse.

DESCRIPTIVE METHODOLOGY AND DATA

There is a methodological problem in describing the data. We need to indicate that the economic models produce different patterns of growth as well as represent the changing ratios over time of the number of villages per level of central place. Our methodology is to graph logarithmically the number of settlements per "central-place echelon size" across time. The essential problem is the representation in two dimensions of the shape of the growth curve, time, number of settlements in each echelon, and number of echelons. Our solution of comparing the expected to the observed logarithmic echelon values and curves warrants discussion. One way of representing the growth expectations is to construct settlement pyramids and compare these pyramids across time. These are similar to population pyramids, which relate the number of people to the age of each subgrouping of people. The settlement pyramid relates the number of settlements to the echelon level. Figure 23 shows the expected settlement pyramids for a $K = 3$ model growing during times 1 through 4 and decreasing during time 5. At time 1 there are 3 settlements in the lowest echelon, indicated on the axis by $e = 1$. At time 2, the number of settlements has grown to a total of 12, 9 of which are at the lowest echelon and 3 at the next higher echelon ($e = 2$). These latter 3 settlements are larger and more central to the other nine. Times 3, 4, and 5 are similar.

It is clear that we can separate out of these pyramids the number of settlements per echelon. This is indicated in Figure 24 in which the pyra-

FIGURE 23. Settlement pyramids through five time periods

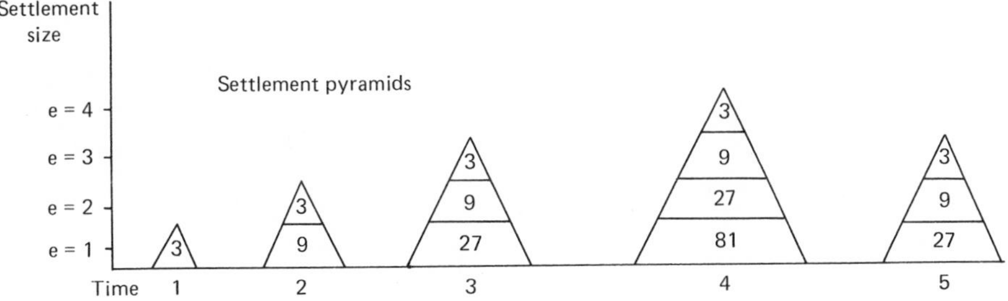

FIGURE 24. Settlement echelons represented by settlement pyramids

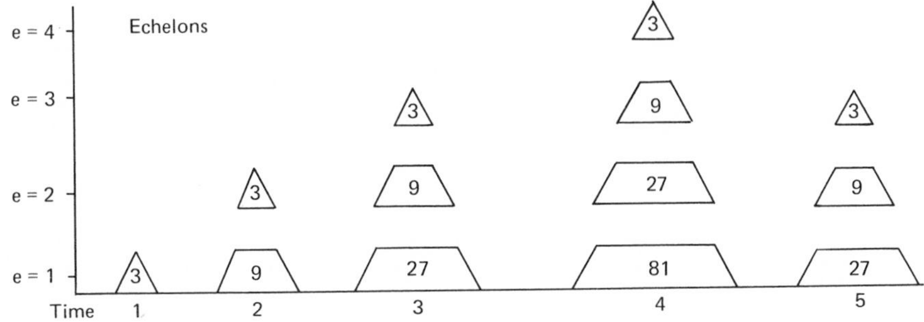

mid is divided so that the echelons are clear. Table 66 shows the same data as Figures 23 and 24. The number of settlements per echelon per time appears as a number with its logarithm following in parentheses. Since our expected growth functions are exponential series, logarithms are an appropriate scale. Figure 25 presents the actual number of expected settlements for a $K = 3$ model across time by echelon. In this figure each line labeled $e = 1, 2, 3 \ldots$ represents the graph of the number of settlements in that echelon by time; Figure 26 is the same graph displayed logarithmically.

This method of graphic representation has various advantages. If the growth pattern is equivalent to the theoretically predicted exponential function for steady filling, the graph of each echelon will be a straight line, and that for the entire region will represent a series of parallel lines. The lowest echelon ($e = 1$) should have the earliest settlements, then the next echelon ($e = 2$), then the third ($e = 3$), and so forth. The number of settlements should be inversely related to the height of the echelon according to the predicted ratios (that is, the lowest echelons should have the most settlements). This gives us the instrument for testing the application of economic models on the growth of settlement patterns in actual regions and then examining the relationships between the predicted theoretical models and the real data.

Between 1967 and 1971 I worked with the Southwestern Archaeological Expedition of the Field Museum of Natural History in the Hay Hollow Valley (Arizona). During its fifteen years or so of operation, this expedition put together one of the most massive systemic surveys of a small

TABLE 66
NUMBER OF SETTLEMENTS BY SIZE (ECHELON) AND BY TIME IN BOTH NONLOGARITHMIC AND LOGARITHMIC FORMS

	Time				
Echelon (e)	1	2	3	4	5
4	0	0	0	3(.48)	0
3	0	0	3(.48)	9(.95)	3(.48)
2	0	3(.48)	9(.95)	27(1.43)	9(.95)
1	3(.48)	9(.95)	27(1.43)	81(1.91)	27(1.43)

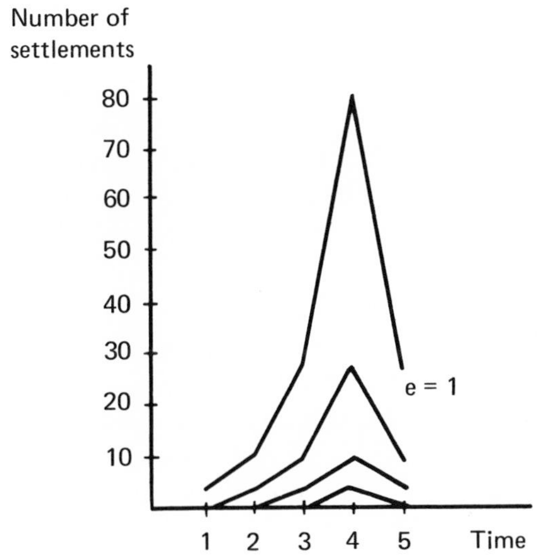

Number of settlements
80
70
60
50
40
30
20
10
e = 1
1
2
3
4
5
Time

FIGURE 25. Graph of the number of settlements by echelon by time

Log N
1.90
1.80
1.70
1.60
1.50
1.40
1.30
1.20
1.10
1.00
.90
.80
.70
.60
.50
.40
.30
.20
.10
1
2
3
4
5
Time

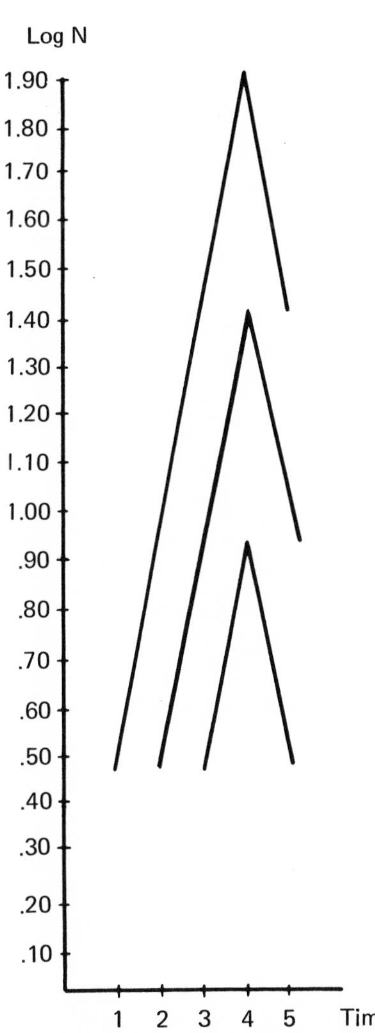

FIGURE 26. Graph of the number of settlements by echelon by time logarithmically

region, approximately twenty square miles. The dates and sizes of 671 prehistoric settlements were determined. The distribution of settlements by numbers of rooms across time is one set of data used in the comparison with the models' expectations.

The second set of data is based upon the Wetherill Mesa (Colorado) survey, which corresponds in approximate time span, cultural manifestation, and survey technique to the Hay Hollow survey; 906 sites were found, analyzed, and dated. The two sets of data were grouped identically.

Figure 27 shows the relationship between predicted models and actual data for the three lowest echelons across time in the Hay Hollow Valley. Several points should be noted. (1) There is a high degree of correlation between the expected models, based on a steady-state economic growth theory, and the real data. Pearson product-moment correlation coefficients were calculated: .99 and .97 for the lowest echelon; .99 and .93 for the second echelon; and .97 and .96 for the third echelon.[11] Needless to say, all of these are significant at the .05 and .01 levels. In other words, there is a close fit between the expected number of settlements in each echelon at each time and the observed number of settlements. (2) The relative order and size of the echelons are equivalent to the expectation from the theoretical model. The lower the echelon, the earlier it appears and the larger the number of sites per time period. (3) All three observed echelons closely fit the $K = 3$ model.

Figure 28 shows the theoretically predicted fourth echelon versus the real data for the Hay Hollow survey. Clearly, there is no correlation: a stable model of growth is not being met. A different set of processes is obviously at work here.

Turning to the 826 usable sites from the Wetherill Mesa survey, one finds again for three echelons a high degree of correspondence between prediction and observation. These are echelons 2, 4, and 5 in Figure 29. They have Pearson product-moment regression coefficients of $r = .99$, .99, and .94, respectively, across the entire time sequence. It is important to note here that the K values during the growth phase differ from the K values during the decline phase: $K = 7$ during the growth, $K = 3$ during the decline. This exemplifies a change in the uniformity characteristics of the region. The size and order of the observed echelons for the periods of growth and decline are appropriate from the perspective of the theoretical stable growth model. Once again, the lowest echelons appear earliest,

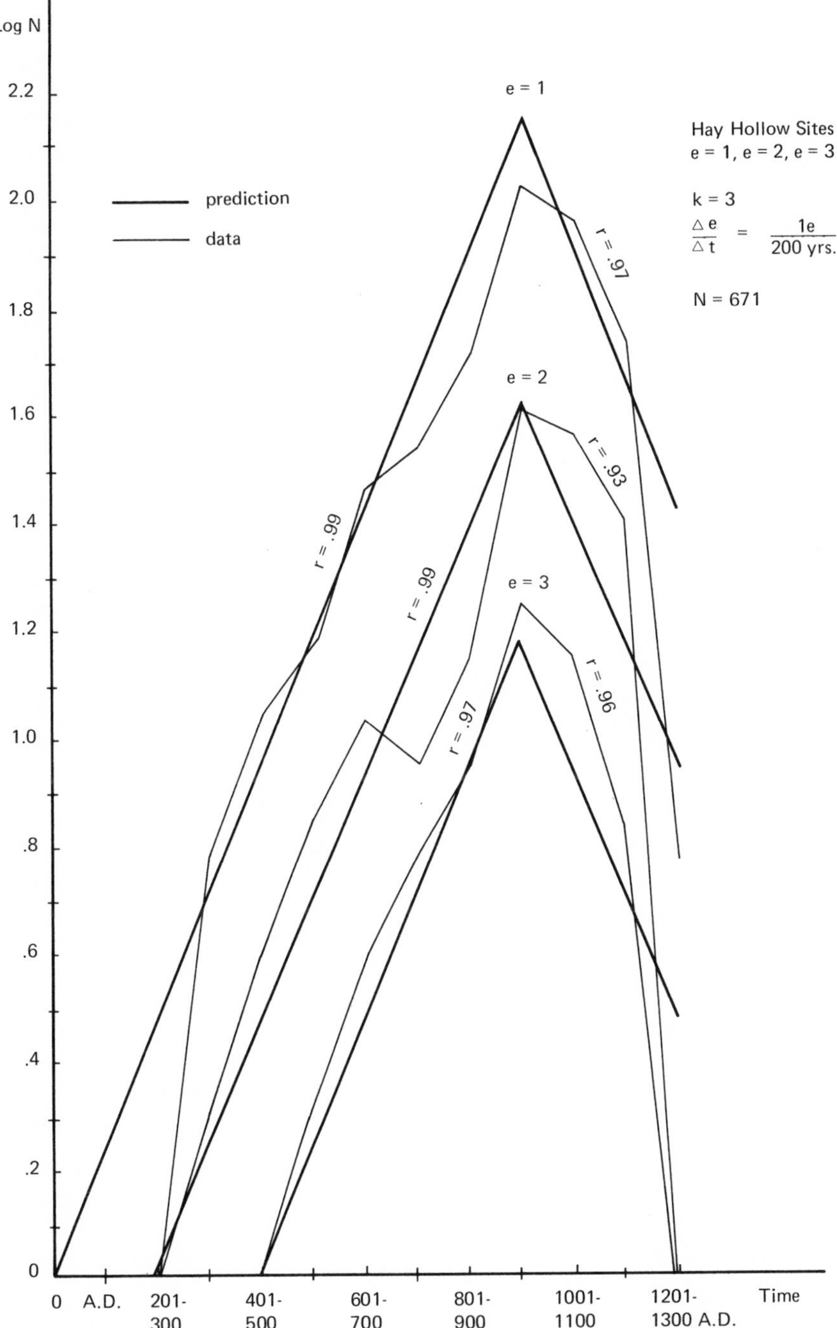

FIGURE 27. A comparison of the expected and observed numbers of settlements by echelon by time for the Hay Hollow Valley. Data for echelons 1, 2, and 3 are presented logarithmically.

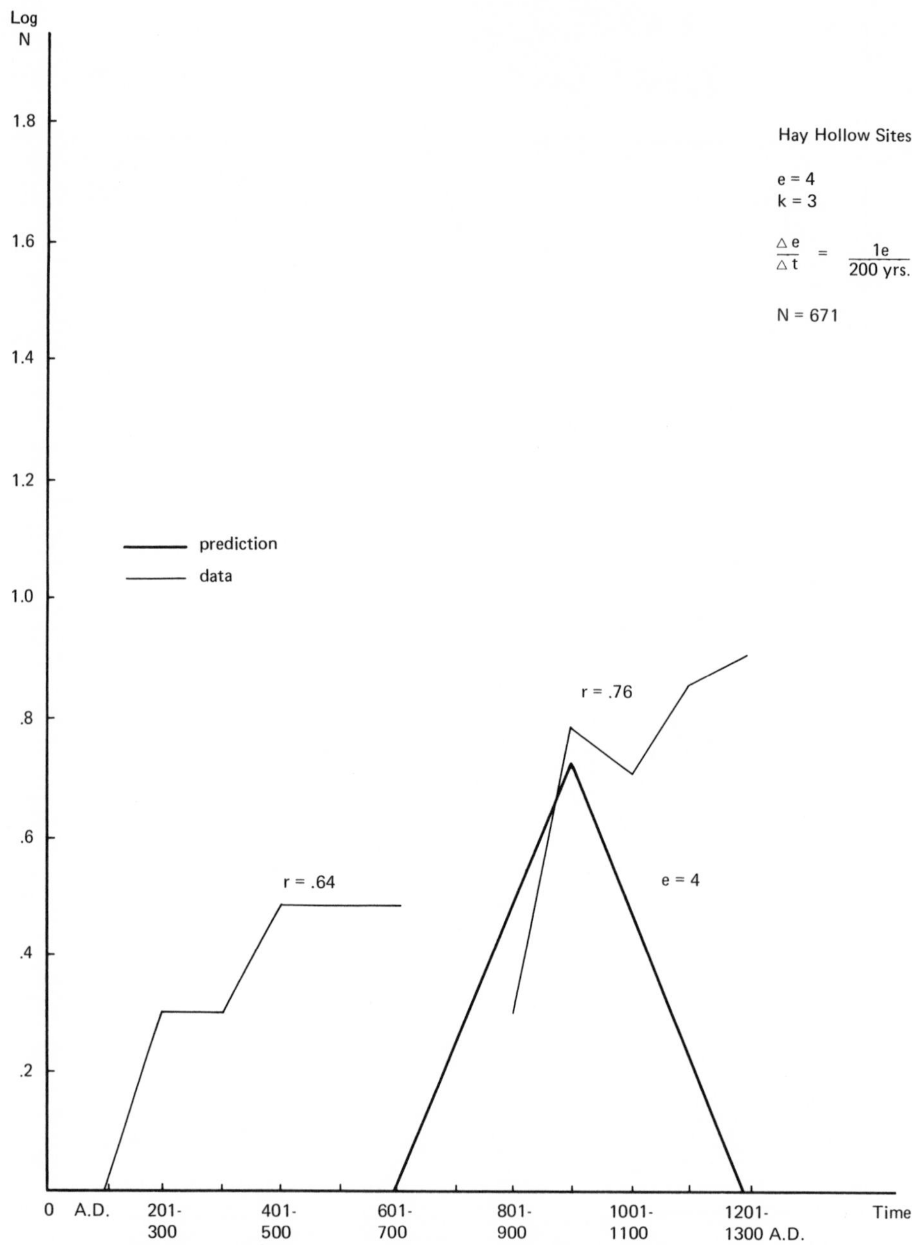

FIGURE 28. A comparison of the expected and observed numbers of settlements by echelon by time for the Hay Hollow Valley. Data for echelon 4 are presented logarithmically.

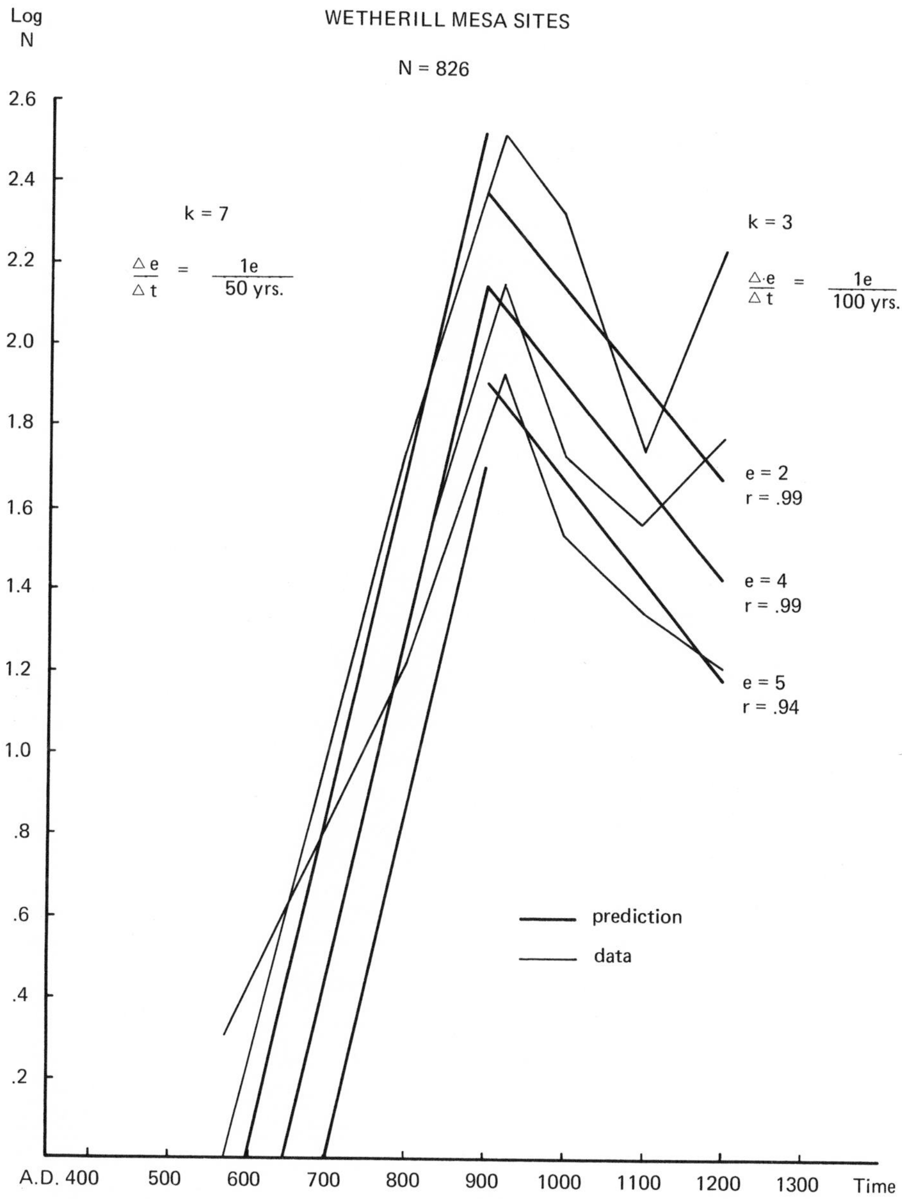

FIGURE 29. A comparison of the expected and observed numbers of settlements by echelon by time for Wetherill Mesa. Data for echelons 2, 4, and 5 are presented logarithmically.

disappear latest, and have the most sites. However, the echelon order is not as sequential as in Figure 28, as it omits echelons 1 and 3.

Figure 30 shows the remaining echelons over time for the Wetherill Mesa sites. Like the fourth echelon of the Hay Hollow data, this figure shows a nonstable process operating. There is no high correlation nor is there a clear sense of relationship. Furthermore, one should note that the order of these echelons is reversed in relation to the previous diagrams; in this case higher echelons with smaller numbers of sites grew first, then lower echelons with larger numbers of places.

SUMMARY AND CONCLUSIONS

This paper has

1. suggested that cultural growth processes such as economic or regional growth be examined as specific examples of systemic growth;
2. presented models for stable and unstable economic growth;
3. defined some characteristic criteria of regions;
4. predicted the effects of stable and unstable economic growth on the distribution of settlements within a variety of regions;
5. compared the predicted growth patterns from both models to the observed patterns for two prehistoric regions comprising approximately fifteen hundred sites between A.D. 0 and A.D. 1300; and
6. shown that both stable and unstable growth were taking place simultaneously in each region within different echelons.

Clearly, neither stable nor unstable growth is sufficient by itself to explain the data. Stable models only explain three-fourths of the Hay Hollow data and one-half of the Wetherill Mesa data; the rest are unstable. The fact that settlements of different sizes, centralities, and locations (that is, of different echelons) grow differently raises a series of interesting issues that should be explored further. First, the existence of differential growth processes implies that over time the inequality between settlements in a region is a foregone conclusion, even if the settlements are originally approximately equal. Second, this inequality implies that, organizationally, growth may be sectored. Thus, third, although the evidence is not totally clear, larger, more central settlements (that is, higher echelons) seem to have a tendency to grow unstably, while smaller, more peripheral settlements (lower echelons) grow more stably. One may

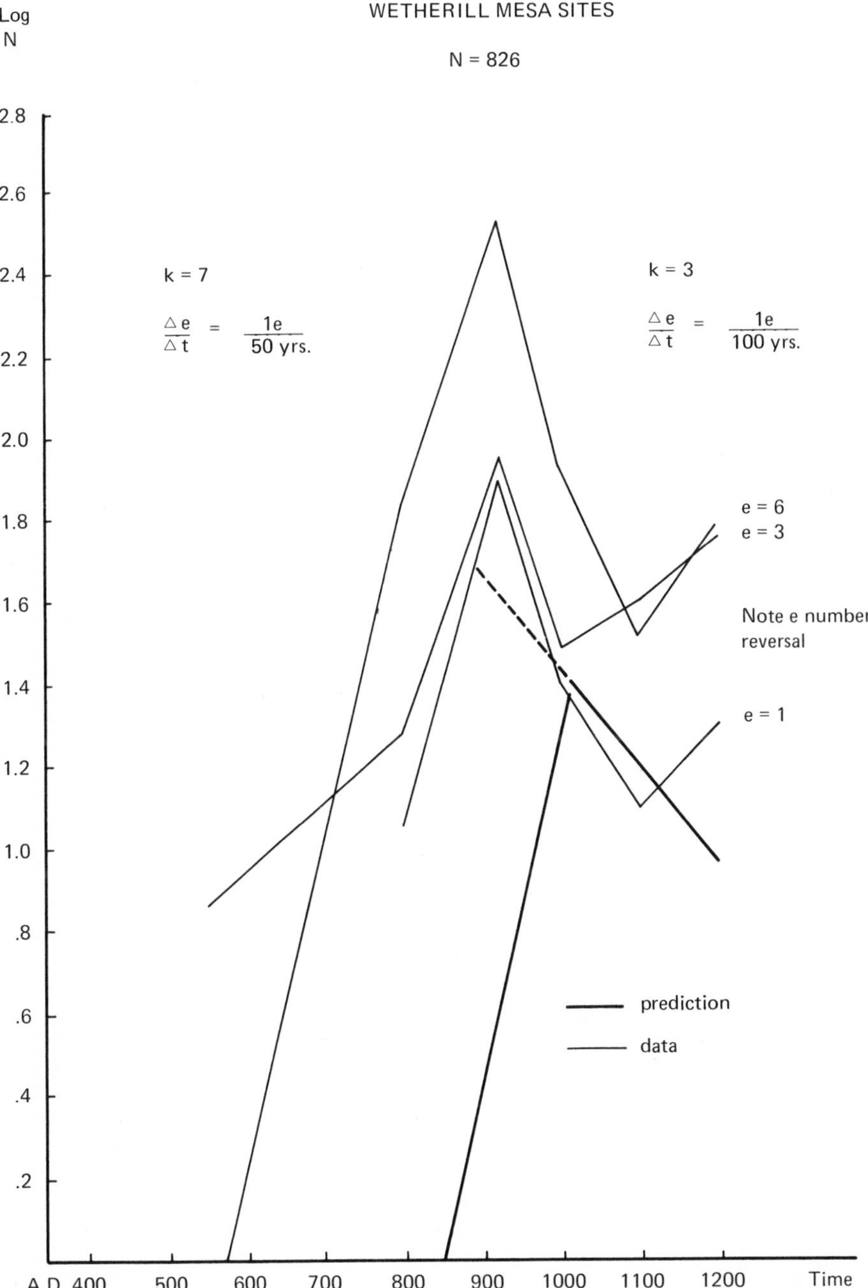

FIGURE 30. A simplified comparison of the expected and observed numbers of settlements by echelon by time for Wetherill Mesa. Data for echelons 1, 3, and 6 are presented logarithmically.

note that the highest echelons in both the Hay Hollow and the Wetherill Mesa regions do not follow stable growth processes.

In conclusion, as light has both particle and wave characteristics, growth has simultaneously both stable and unstable forms.

NOTES

1. A more sophisticated definition may be found in Hall and Fagan (1968:81–82) and, for the connoisseur, a mathematical definition is presented in Wymore (1967).

2. This is a formalist argument. Unlike the substantivists, I accept the reality of scarce resources and the optimization principle with man's concomitant rationality.

3. Critical to the above theory is the rationale for why innovations occur and are favored by the equilibrium state. First, the stability of the economic system results in a minimal risk of failure, while the small margin of resource surplus and small profits result in a maximum pressure to innovate. As the intensification of the rate of innovation increases, the economy becomes more disequilibrated, and larger margins of surplus and larger profits reduce the pressure to innovate.

One reason why stability and equilibrium increase the rate of innovation is that the marginal efficiency or the marginal cost of investment is small. Thus it is possible to argue that the cost of investment and the risk of failure are two causes of the innovation rate. This has interesting implications. For example, if one sets up these variables in a two-by-two table with the squares measuring rate of innovation, the expectations are the following:

Risk of Failure ↓ / Cost of Investment ⟶		
	high	medium
	medium	low

The Rate of Innovations

4. *S* is more accurately defined as the sum of net savings and investment divided by net output.

5. One way to understand the model is by an example originally conceived by Merida Blanco. Imagine a village of 50 people with a labor force of 25 (population equals twice the labor). The labor force needs to put 1 person in the field for every bushel of corn produced; in addition, it requires $1.00 of capital for seed per bushel. The village begins with $25.00, puts 25 people into the field, and thus grows 25 bushels of corn. The total output of 25 bushels is sold at the market for $76.00. After paying out expenses of $25.00 to the labor force ($1.00 per person) and $25.00 for the cost of the seed, there is $26.00 left over. The village inhabitants now have two options. They can save $1.00 and invest $25.00 in new seed, which would be a steady economy without change, except in the saving sector. However, if $26.00 is invested in new seed, then it is necessary for one more person to work in the field. If the cycle goes around another time with $26.00 invested in corn seed, 26 people working in the field, and the corn sold for $79.00, there is $26.00 to pay the laborers, $26.00 for the seed cost, and $27.00 left over. Simultaneously note that the price of corn can go

down: in the first cycle it was \$3.040 per bushel and in the second cycle \$3.038 per bushel. It is the growth in saving and investment per output unit (for example, the \$1.00 increase between \$25.00 and \$26.00 at the end of the first cycle being invested in corn) that must equal the increase in population being used in the labor force.

6. What happens if *S* exceeds *VN*? If the unemployment rate is held constant, so that employment grows as fast as the labor force, each year's saving and investment must be more than enough to provide capital for the annual increment to employment. Every year the economy is adding to its excess capacity over and above the normal excess capacity already included in V. In other words, instead of a \$1.00 increase per annual cycle, as in note 5, there might be a \$2.00 or \$3.00 increase per annual cycle. While this could be used to buy more seed, soon there will not be the labor force with which to plant it. Alternatively, the economy may insist on using all the capacity created by the investment of the \$2.00 or \$4.00. It can do so only by increasing employment faster than the growth of the labor force, for example by child labor, old age labor, and so on. Eventually the economy will run out of labor. When the labor force cannot be expanded, the situation reverts to the first state of affairs. In other words, if S exceeds VN, either the supply of labor is inadequate to man the actual capacity or, if the capacity is manned, the labor force eventually will be completely depleted.

If *S* is less than *VN*, then there will be an extra person without any seeds to plant, because if the economy tries to keep the unemployment rate constant, it runs out of capacity. On the other hand, if the society tries to keep the capacity fixed, the unemployment rate will gradually rise toward 100 percent. This occurs as one person after another is unable to get seeds, as there is only \$1.00 that is being held in excess capacity. They cannot work in the fields and are idle. In other words, the economy is saving and investing so little that it fails to create enough capital to provide employment for the annual increment to the labor force.

7. The now famous nearest-neighbor statistic is an example of this relative spatial measure.

8. Hudson and Dacey have generated other Loschian landscapes. Dacey generates them using the formula

$Q = u^2 + uv + v^2$ where
Q = set of market sizes and
u and v are non negative integers,
so that uv and $v = 1, 2, 3, n$,

while Hudson shows that most of the Loschian landscapes are reducible by factoring to combinations of $K = 3, 4, 7$. Hagget's *Locational Analysis in Human Geography* (1966) has diagrams of the nine simple Loschian landscapes.

9. In general, $K = b + s$, where b is the number of settlements within the boundary and s is the sum of the shared fraction of each site that is located on the boundary. Another equation for K is based on relative relationships among the hexagon areas. The number of dependent places dominated by a central place is given by the formula $N_e = K^e$, where N is the number of dependent places and e is the echelon of the hierarchy.

10. An important question concerns the relationship between increased production and the formation of new settlements or the shifting of a settlement from one echelon to another. It would require another article to present the processes in any detail, so I

shall only examine some generalities here that provide the direction of the argument.

In preindustrial societies, production is a function of labor, land, and capital. Although capital exists in minimum quantities, it plays a critical role. In hunting and gathering societies, capital equipment consists of tools of bone, stone, and wood. In agricultural societies, there is considerably more capital expenditure expressed in seed stocks, fertilizers, milling and processing equipment, storage facilities, irrigation systems, transportation systems, and a wide variety of agricultural tools from digging sticks to plows.

Only by foregoing present consumption can a society shift its resources to the production of capital equipment. Agricultural savings are low due to low per capita income; this is aggravated by the way relatively large expenditures of saved resources are often spent in religion (ceremonies and temples) and construction. Since transportation systems are primitive if they exist at all, a large proportion of capital equipment must be kept in inventories. In fact, any preindustrial settlement must keep its inventories in much higher proportion to current production than any industrial society. These inventories (buffers against famine, etc.) are a form of investment or capital accumulation. They have more of a stabilizing character and less of a developmental character.

Inventories have a secondary attribute, which may be called redundancy. Preindustrial capital accumulation has a high redundancy factor. In other words, once needs are met without trade, surpluses are redundant. For example, if a field needs 1,000 pounds of fertilizer, an inventory of 2,000 pounds will not increase production. As population increases, there are also redundancies in labor; in areas with low population densities, there may also be redundancies in land.

The essential argument is that, under conditions of production growth, the proportion of settlements that develop (that is, change echelon) in relation to the proportion of settlements that are replicated at the same level (that is, more settlements at the same echelon) is a function of the proportion of capital, labor, and land that is developmental and not redundant to the proportions that are stabilizing and redundant.

11. For the Hay Hollow data, two sets of correlation coefficients were calculated for each echelon: one for the period of increase or growth, A.D. 0–1000, and one for the period of decline or negative growth, A.D. 1000–1300.

References

ABERLE, S.
1931 "Frequency of Pregnancies and Birth Interval among Pueblo Indians," *American Journal of Physical Anthropology* 16:63–80.

ABERLE, S., J. H. WATKINS, AND E. H. PITNEY
1940 "The Vital History of San Juan Pueblo," *Human Biology* 12(2):184–87.

ACSADI, G. Y., AND J. NEMESKERI
1970 *History of Human Life Span and Mortality* (Budapest: Akademiai Kiado).

ADAMS, ROBERT McC.
1965 *Land behind Baghdad* (Chicago: University of Chicago Press).

ADAMS, ROBERT McC., AND HANS J. NISSEN
1972 *The Uruk Countryside* (Chicago: University of Chicago Press).

AHERN, EMILY M.
1973 *The Cult of the Dead in a Chinese Village* (Stanford: Stanford University Press).

AIRD, JOHN S.
1956 "Fertility Levels and Differentials in Two Bengali Villages," Ph.D. Diss., University of Michigan.

AMERICAN ASSOCIATION FOR THE ADVANCEMENT OF SCIENCE
1974 *Culture and Population Change* (Washington, D.C.: AAAS).

AMMERMAN, ALBERT J., AND L. L. CAVALLI-SFORZA
1971 "Measuring the Rate of Spread of Early Farming in Europe," *Man* 6:674–88.
1973 "A Population Model for the Diffusion of Early Farming in Europe," in *The Explanation of Culture Change*, ed. Colin Renfrew (London: Duckworth & Co.).

AMSDEN, CHARLES
1972 "But What Happened in between? Nunamiut Settlement and Exploitative Patterns—1900 to 1970," paper presented at the Symposium on the Late Prehistoric/Historic Eskimos of Interior Alaska, Thirty-Seventh Annual Meeting of the Society for American Archaeology, Miami.

ANGEL, J. L.

1969 "The Bases of Paleodemography," *American Journal of Physical Anthropology* 30:427–37.

1971 "Early Neolithic Skeletons from Çatal Hüyük: Demography and Pathology," *Anatolian Studies* 21:77–98.

1972 "Ecology and Population in the Eastern Mediterranean," *World Archaeology* 4:88–105.

ARMSTRONG, ALEXANDER

1857 *A Personal Narrative of the Discovery of the Northwest Passage* (London: Hurst & Blackett).

BACON, FRANCIS

1620 "Novum Organum," in *The Works of Francis Bacon*, 1819 ed. (London: C. & J. Rivington et al.), 8:1–217.

BAIRD, DUGALD

1965 "Variations in Fertility associated with Changes in Health," in *Public Health and Population Change*, ed. Mindel C. Sheps and Jeanne Clare Ridley (Pittsburgh: University of Pittsburgh Press).

BAKER, PAUL T., AND WILLIAM T. SANDERS

1971 "Demographic Studies in Anthropology," *Annual Review of Anthropology* 1:151–78.

BARRAI, I., L. L. CAVALLI-SFORZA, AND A. MORONI

1962 "Frequencies of Pedigrees of Consanguineous Marriages and Mating Structure of the Population," *Annals of Human Genetics* 25:347–76.

BARRAI, I., AND M. FRACCARO

1965 "Intensities of Selection in Nomadic and Settled Lapps," *Folia Hereditaria et Pathologica* (Milan) 14:1–6.

BASU, A.

1967 "Selection Intensity in the Pahiras," *Eugenics Quarterly* 14(3):241–42.

BERELSON, B.

1967 "A Review of Major Governmental Programmes," *United Nations World Population Conference*, 1965, 2:253–56.

1969 "National Family Planning Programs: Where We Stand," in *Fertility and Family Planning*, ed. S. J. Behrman et al. (Ann Arbor: University of Michigan Press), pp. 341–87.

BERRY, B. J. L., H. G. BARNUM, AND R. J. TENNANT

1962 "Retail Location and Consumer Behavior," *Regional Science Association Papers and Proceedings* 9:65–106.

BETTISON, DAVID G.

1958 *The Social and Economic Structure of Seventeen Villages, Glantyre-Limbe, Nyasaland*, Communication of the Lusaka, Rhodes-Livingstone Institute no. 12.

BINFORD, LEWIS R.

1964 "A Consideration of Archaeological Research Design," *American Antiquity* 29(4):425–41.

1968 "Post-Pleistocene Adaptations," in *New Perspectives in Archaeology*, ed. Sally R. Binford and L. R. Binford (Chicago: Aldine Publishing Co.), pp. 313–41.

1971 *Mortuary Practices: Their Study and Their Potential,* Social Dimensions of Mortuary Practices, memoir no. 25, Society for American Archaeology.

n.d. *The Ecology of Hunters and Gatherers* (New York and London: Academic Press), anticipated in 1976.

BINFORD, SALLY R., AND LEWIS R. BINFORD, EDS.

1968 *New Perspectives in Archaeology* (Chicago: Aldine Publishing Co.).

BIRKET-SMITH, KAJ

1959 *The Eskimos* (London: Methuen and Co.).

BLAKE, J.

1969 "Population Problems for Americans," *Science* 164:522–29.

BOAS, F.

1894 "The Half-Blood Indian: An Anthropometric Study," *Popular Science Monthly* 45:761–70.

BOSERUP, ESTER

1965 *The Conditions of Agricultural Growth* (London: George Allen and Unwin; and Chicago: Aldine Publishing Co.).

BOURGEOIS-PICHAT, J.

1965 "Les facteurs de la fécondité non dirigée," *Population* 20:383–424.

1967 "Relation between Foetal-Infant Mortality and Fertility," *United Nations World Population Conference, 1965,* 2:68–72.

BRAIDWOOD, ROBERT J., HALET CAMBEL, CHARLES L. REDMAN, AND PATTY JO WATSON

1971 "Beginnings of Village-Farming Communities in Southeastern Turkey," *Proceedings of the National Academy of Science* 68:1236–40.

BRAIDWOOD, ROBERT J., AND BRUCE HOWE

1960 *Prehistoric Invesitgations in Iraqi Kurdistan* (Chicago: Oriental Institute of the University of Chicago).

BRAIDWOOD, ROBERT J., AND CHARLES A. REED

1957 "The Achievement and Early Consequences of Food Production: A Consideration of the Archaeological and Natural-Historical Evidence," *Cold Spring Harbor Symposia on Quantitative Biology* 22:10–31.

BRAIDWOOD, ROBERT J., AND GORDON R. WILLEY, EDS.

1962 "Conclusions and Afterthoughts," in *Courses toward Urban Life,* Viking Fund Publications in Anthropology, no. 32 (New York: Wenner-Gren Foundation for Anthropological Research), pp. 331–59.

BROTHWELL, D. R.

1971 "Palaeodemography," in *Biological Aspects of Demography,* ed. W. Brass (London: Taylor and Francis).

BUMPASS, L., AND C. F. WESTOFF

1970 "The 'Perfect Contraceptive' Population," *Science* 169:1177–82.

BURCH, ERNEST S., JR.

1972 "The Caribou Wild Reindeer as a Human Resource," *American Antiquity* 37(3):339–68.

CARNEIRO, ROBERT L.

1960 "Slash-and-Burn Agriculture: A Closer Look at Its Implications for Settlement

Patterns," in *Men and Cultures: Selected Papers of the Fifth International Congress of Anthropological and Ethnological Sciences,* ed. A. F. C. Wallace, pp. 229–34.

1972 "From Autonomous Villages to the State: a Numerical Estimation," in *Population Growth: Anthropological Implications,* ed. Brian Spooner (Cambridge, Mass.: M.I.T. Press).

CARNEIRO, ROBERT L., AND DAISY F. HILSE

1966 "On Determining the Probable Rate of Population Growth during the Neolithic," *American Anthropologist* 68:177–81.

CAVALLI-SFORZA, L. L., AND W. B. BODMER

1971 *The Genetics of Human Populations* (San Francisco: W. H. Freeman).

CAVALLI-SFORZA, L. L., M. KIMURA, AND I. BARRAI

1966 "The Probability of Consanguineous Marriages," *Genetics* 54:37–60.

CENTRAL STATISTICAL OFFICE

1963 *Annual Abstract of Statistics,* no. 100 (London: Her Majesty's Stationery Office).

CHANG, K. C.

1958 "Study of the Neolithic Social Groupings: Examples from the New World," *American Anthropologist* 60:298–334.

CHRISTALLER, WALTER

1966 *Central Place Theory in Southern Germany,* Baskin translation (Englewood Cliffs, N.J.: Prentice-Hall).

CLARK, COLIN

1951 *The Conditions of Economic Progress,* 2d ed. (London: Macmillan & Co.).

CLARK, GEOFFREY A.

1969 "A Preliminary Analysis of Burial Clusters at the Grasshopper Site, East-Central Arizona," *The Kiva* 35(2):57–86.

CLARKE, DAVID L.

1968 *Analytical Archaeology* (London: Methuen & Co.).

COALE, ANSLEY J.

1956 "The Effects of Changes in Mortality and Fertility on Age Composition," *Milban Memorial Fund Quarterly* 34(1):79–114.

1972 *The Growth and Structure of Human Populations* (Princeton: Princeton University Press).

COALE, ANSLEY J., AND P. DEMENY

1966 *Regional Model Life Tables and Stable Populations* (Princeton: Princeton University Press).

COLTON, HAROLD S.

1936 "The Rise and Fall of the Prehistoric Population of Northern Arizona," *Science* 84:337–43.

1949 "The Prehistoric Population of the Flagstaff Area," *Plateau* 22(1):21–25.

COOK, SHERBURNE F.

1972a *Prehistoric Demography* (Reading, Mass.: Addison-Wesley Publishing Co.).

1972b "Can Pottery Residues Be Used as an Index to Population?," *Contributions of the University of California Archaeological Research Facility,* no. 14 (Berkeley), pp. 17–40.

COOK, SHERBURNE F. AND ROBERT F. HEIZER

1965 *The Quantitative Approach to the Relation between Population and Settlement Size,* Contributions of the University of California Archaeological Research Facility, no. 64 (Berkeley).

1968 "Relationship among Houses, Settlement Areas, and Population in Aboriginal California," in *Settlement Archaeology,* ed. K. C. Chang (Palo Alto, Calif.: National Press), pp. 76–116.

COWGILL, GEORGE L.

1964 "The Selection of Samples from Large Sherd Collections," *American Antiquity* 29:467–73.

1970 "Some Sampling and Reliability Problems in Archaeology," in *Archéologie et Calculateurs, Problèmes Semiologiques et Mathematiques* (Paris: Centre National de la Recherche Scientifique), pp. 161–72.

CROW, JAMES F.

1958 *Some Possibilities for Measuring Selection Intensities in Man,* American Anthropological Association Memoir 86 (Washington, D.C.).

1973 "Some Effects of Relaxed Selection," in *Proceedings of the International Congress of Human Genetics, Paris, 1971,* pp. 155–66.

CRUZ-COKE, R., A. P. CRISTOFFANINI, M. ASPILLAGA, AND F. BIANCANI

1966 "Evolutionary Forces in Human Populations in an Environmental Gradient in Arica, Chile," *Human Biology* 38(4):421–38.

DAHLBERG, G.

1948 *Mathematical Methods for Population Genetics* (New York: Interscience Publishers).

DAVIS, K.

1963 "The Theory of Change and Response in Modern Demographic History," *Population Index* 29:345–66.

1967 "Population Policy: Will Current Programs Succeed?" *Science* 158:730–39.

DeCASTRO, J.

1952 *The Geography of Hunger* (Boston: Little, Brown and Co.).

DEETZ, JAMES

1965 *The Dynamics of Stylistic Change in Arikara Ceramics,* Illinois Studies in Anthropology, no. 4 (Urbana: University of Illinois Press).

DOMAR, EVSEY D.

1957 *Essays in the Theory of Economic Growth* (Fairlawn, N.J.: Oxford University Press).

DORN, HAROLD F.

1959 "Mortality," in *The Study of Population,* ed. Philip M. Hauser and Otis Dudley Duncan (Chicago: University of Chicago Press), pp. 437–71.

DUMOND, D. E.

1965 "Population Growth and Culture Change," *Southwestern Journal of Anthropology* 21(4):302–24.

DUNN, FREDERICK L.

1968 "Epidemiological Factors: Health and Disease in Hunter-Gatherers," in *Man the Hunter,* ed. Richard B. Lee and Irven DeVore (Chicago: Aldine Publishing Co.), pp. 221–28.

EATON, J. W., AND A. J. MAYER
1953 "The Social Biology of Very High Fertility among the Hutterites: the Demography of a Unique Population," *Human Biology* 25(3):206–64.

EVANS, JOHN D.
1971 "Neolithic Knossos: The Growth of a Settlement," *Proceedings of the Prehistoric Society* 37(2):95–117.

FALLERS, LLOYD
1954 "A Note on the Trickle Effect," *Public Opinion Quarterly* 18:314–21.

FISCHER, E.
1913 *Die Rehobother Bastards* (Jena: G. Fischer).

FISHER, R. A.
1958 *The Genetical Theory of Natural Selection*, 2d ed. (New York: Dover Publications).

FORDE, C. D.
1939 *Marriage and Family among the Yakö*, Monograph of Social Anthropology no. 5 (London: Lund and Humphries).

FORRESTER, JAY W.
1969 *Urban Dynamics* (Cambridge, Mass.: M.I.T. Press).

FORTES, M.
1943 "A Note on Fertility among the Tallensi of the Gold Coast," *Sociological Review* 35:99–113.
1953 "A Demographic Field Study in Ashanti," in *Culture and Human Fertility*, ed. Frank Lorimer (New York: UNESCO).

FRACCARO, MARIO
1959 "Fertility Differential in Two Lappish Populations," *American Journal of Human Genetics* 11:92.

FREEMAN, MILTON M. R.
1971 "The Significance of Demographic Changes Occurring in the Canadian East Arctic," *Anthropologica* 13:215–36.

FRENCH, F. E., AND J. M. BIERMAN
1962 "Probabilities of Fetal Mortality," *Public Health Reports* 77:835–47.

GANGULEE, N.
1939 *Health and Nutrition in India* (London: Faber and Faber).

GARN, S. M.
1961 *Human Races* (Springfield, Ill.: Charles C. Thomas).

GILBERT, JOHN P., AND E. A. HAMMEL
1963 "Computer Simulation of Problems in Kinship and Social Structure," paper presented at the Annual Meeting of the American Anthropological Association, San Francisco.
1966 "Computer Simulation of Problems in Kinship and Social Structure," *American Anthropologist* 68:71–93.

GLASS, D. V., AND E. GREBENIK
1954 *The Trend and Pattern of Fertility in Great Britain. A Report on the Family Census of 1946*, Papers of the Royal Commission on Population, 2 parts (London: Her Majesty's Stationery Office).

References

GOODALE, JANE C.
1959 "The Tiwi Women of Melville Island, North Australia," Ph.D. diss., University of Pennsylvania.

GRAUNT, JOHN
1662 *Natural and Political Observations upon the Bills of Mortality*, ed. Walter F. Willcox, 1939 ed. (Baltimore: Johns Hopkins University Press).

GRIFFIN, P. BION
1967 "A High Status Burial from Grasshopper Ruin, Arizona," *The Kiva* 33(2): 37–53.
1969 "Late Mogollon Readaptation in East-central Arizona," Ph.D. diss., University of Arizona.

GUBSER, N. J.
1965 *The Nunamiut Eskimos: Hunters of Caribou* (New Haven: Yale University Press).

GUMERMAN, GEORGE J., ED.
1971 *The Distribution of Prehistoric Population Aggregates*, Prescott College Anthropological Reports, no. 1 (Prescott, Ariz.: Prescott College Press).
1972 *Proceedings of Second Annual Meeting of the Southwestern Anthropological Research Group*, Prescott College Anthropological Reports, no. 3 (Prescott, Ariz.: Prescott College Press).

HAGGET, PETER
1966 *Locational Analysis in Human Geography* (New York: St. Martin's Press).

HAJNAL, J.
1963 "Concepts of Random Mating and the Frequency of Consanguineous Marriage," *Proceedings of the Royal Society, B* 159:125–77.

HALDANE, J. B. S.
1932 *The Causes of Evolution* (New York: Harper & Brothers).

HALL, A. D., AND R. E. FAGAN
1968 "Definition of System," in *Modern Systems Research for the Behavioral Scientist*, ed. W. Buckley (Chicago: Aldine Publishing Co.), pp. 81–82.

HAMMEL, E. A.
1964 "Culture as an Information System," *Papers of the Kroeber Anthropological Society* 16:47–54.

HAMMEL, E. A., AND DAVID HUTCHINSON
1972 "Two Tests of Computer Microsimulation: The Effect of an Incest Tabu on Population Viability, and the Effect of Age Differences between Spouses on the Skewing of Consanguineal Relationships between Them," in *Proceedings of the Conference on Uses of Computer Simulation in Human Population Studies*, ed. Bennett Dyke (New York: Seminar Press), in press.

HANSON, W. C.
1969 *Anaktuvuk Pass, Alaska Village Census*, A.E.C. Research and Development Report BNWL-1242 UC-48 (Springfield, Va.).

HARPENDING, HENRY
n.d. "Genetic and Demographic Variation in Zu/Wasi Populations," in press.

HARRIS, MARVIN
1971 *Culture, Man, and Nature* (New York: Thomas Y. Crowell Co.).

HARROD, R. F.

1948 *Toward a Dynamic Economics* (London: MacMillan & Co.).

HAWTHORN, G.

1970 *The Sociology of Fertility* (London: MacMillan).

HENRY, L.

1953 *Fécondité des mariages* (Paris: Institut National D'Etudes Démographiques).

1961 "Some Data on Natural Fertility," *Eugenics Quarterly* 8:81–91.

HENRY, L., AND C. LEVY

1960 "Ducs et pairs sous l'Ancien Régime: Caractèristiques démographiques d'une caste," *Population* 15:807–30.

HIGGENS, BENJAMIN

1968 *Economic Development: Problems, Principles, and Policies* (New York: W. W. Norton & Co.).

HILL. JAMES N.

1967 "Random Sampling: A Tool for Discovery," paper presented at the annual meeting of the Society for American Archaeology.

1970 *Broken K. Pueblo: Prehistoric Social Organization in the American Southwest,* Anthropological Papers of the University of Arizona, no. 18 (Tucson).

HIMES, N. E.

1936 *Medical History of Contraception* (Baltimore: Williams and Wilkins).

HOLE, FRANK, KENT V. FLANNERY, AND JAMES A. NEELY

1969 *Prehistory and Human Ecology of the Deh Luran Plain,* Memoirs of the Museum of Anthropology, University of Michigan, no. 1 (Ann Arbor).

HOOTON, E. A.

1930 *The Indians of Pecos Pueblo: A Study of Their Skeletal Remains* (New Haven, Conn.).

HOTCHKISS, ROBERT S.

1944 *Fertility in Men: A Clinical Study of the Causes, Diagnosis, and Treatment of Impaired Fertility in Men* (Philadelphia: J. B. Lippincott Co.).

HOWELLS, W. W.

1960 "Estimating Population Numbers through Archaeological and Skeletal Remains," in *The Application of Quantitative Methods in Archaeology,* ed. Robert F. Heizer and Sherburne F. Cook, Viking Fund Publications in Anthropology, no. 28 (New York: Viking Fund), pp. 158–85.

HRDLIČKA, A.

1908 *Physiological and Medical Observations among the Indians of Southwestern United States and Northern Mexico,* Bureau of American Ethnology Bulletin 34.

1931 "Fecundity in the Sioux Women," *American Journal of Physical Anthropology* 16:81–90.

INGSTAD, HELGE

1954 *Nunamiut* (London: George Allen and Unwin).

ISARD, WALTER

1960 *Methods of Regional Analysis: An Introduction to Regional Science* (New York: M.I.T. Press and John Wiley & Sons).

References

JACQUARD, ALBERT

1970 *Structures génétiques des populations* (Paris: Masson et cie.).

JAPANESE CENSUS

1960 Bureau of Statistics, Office of Prime Minister 3(1).

JOHNSON, ALFRED E.

1965 *The Development of Western Pueblo Culture,* Ph.D. diss. University of Arizona.

JOHNSTON, F. E., AND K. M. KENSINGER

1971 "Fertility and Mortality Differentials and Their Implications for Micro-Evolutionary Change among the Cashinahua," *Human Biology* 43:356–64.

KATZ, SOLOMON H.

1972 "Biological Factors in Population Control," in *Population Growth: Anthropological Implications,* ed. Brian Spooner (Cambridge, Mass.: M.I.T. Press), pp. 351–69

KAWAKITA, J.

1957 "Ethno-Geographical Observations of the Nepal Himalaya," in *Peoples of Nepal Himalaya,* ed. H. Kihara (Kyoto: Fauna and Flora Research Society), 3:1–362.

KAY, PAUL

1965 "A Generalization of the Cross/Parallel Distinction," *American Anthropologist* 67:30–43.

1966 "Comment on Colby," *Current Anthropology* 7:20–23.

1967 "On the Multiplicity of Cross/Parallel Distinctions," *American Anthropologist* 69:83–85.

1968 "Correctional Notes on Cross/Parallel," *American Anthropologist* 70:106–7.

KENDALL, M. G., AND A. STUART

1958 *The Advanced Theory of Statistics,* vol. 1, *Distribution Theory* (London: Charles Griffin).

KEYFITZ, NATHAN

1971 "How Birth Control Affects Birth," *Social Biology* 18(2):109–21.

KIRK, D.

1968 "Patterns of Survival and Reproduction in the United States: Implications for Selection," *Proceedings of the National Academy of Sciences* 59:13–21.

KIRKPATRICK, J.

1972 "Some Unexamined Aspects of Childhood Association and Sexual Attraction in the Chinese Minor Marriage," *American Anthropologist* 74(3):783–84.

KOBAYASHI, KAYUMASA

1969 "Changing Patterns of Differential Fertility in the Population of Japan," in *Proceedings of the Eighth International Congress of Anthropological and Ethnological Sciences* (Tokyo: Science Council of Japan), pp. 345–47.

KOBLENZER, P. J., AND N. H. CARRIER

1960 "The Fertility, Mortality, and Nuptiality of the Rungus Dasun," *Population Studies* 13(3):266–77.

KREBS, CHARLES J.

1972 *Ecology—The Experimental Analysis of Distribution and Abundance* (New York: Harper & Row).

KRZYWICKI, LUDWIK
1934 *Primitive Society and Its Vital Statistics* (London: Macmillan & Co.).

LANDA, BISHOP DIEGO DE
1566 *Relación de las cosas de Yucatán*, ed. Alfred Tozzer, Papers of the Peabody Museum, vol. 18, 1941 ed. (Cambridge, Mass.).

LANE, REBECCA A., AND A. J. SUBLETT
1972 "Osteology of Social Organization: Residence Pattern," *American Antiquity* 37(2):186–201.

LEACH, EDMUND R.
1951 "The Structural Implications of Matrilineal Cross-Cousin Marriage," *Journal of the Royal Anthropological Institute* 81:23–55.
1957 "On Asymmetrical Marriage Systems," *American Anthropologist* 59:343.
1965 "Unilateral Cross-Cousin Marriage—Reply to Rose," *Man*, no. 12.

LE BLANC, STEVEN
1971 "An Addition to Naroll's Suggested Floor Area and Settlement Population Relationship," *American Antiquity* 36(2):210–11.

LEE, B. M., AND J. ISBISTER
1966 "The Impact of Birth Control on Fertility," in *Family Planning and Population Programs*, ed. B. Berelson et al. (Chicago: University of Chicago Press), pp. 737–58.

LEE, RICHARD B.
1968 "What Hunters Do for a Living, or, How to Make Out on Scarce Resources," in *Man the Hunter*, ed. Richard B. Lee and Irven DeVore (Chicago: Aldine Publishing Co.), pp. 30–48.

LEONTIEFF, WASSILY
1966 *Input-Output Economics* (Fairlawn, N.J.: Oxford University Press).

LEVI-STRAUSS, CLAUDE
1949 *Les Structures élémentaires de la parenté* (Paris: Presses Universitaires de France).

LOGAN, W. P. D.
1950 "Mortality in England and Wales from 1848 to 1947," *Population Studies* 4:132–78.

LONGACRE, WILLIAM A.
1964 "A Synthesis of Upper Little Colorado Prehistory, Eastern Arizona," in *Chapters in the Prehistory of Eastern Arizona, II, Fieldiana: Anthropology*, vol. 55 (Chicago: Chicago Natural History Museum), pp. 201–15.
1970a *Archaeology as Anthropology: A Case Study*, Anthropological Papers of the University of Arizona, no. 17 (Tucson).
1970b *Reconstructing Prehistoric Pueblo Societies*, School of American Research Advanced Seminar Series (Albuquerque: University of New Mexico Press).

LONGACRE, WILLIAM A., AND J. J. REID
1971 "Research Strategy for Locational Analysis: An Outline," in *The Distribution of Prehistoric Population Aggregates*, ed. George J. Gumerman, Prescott College Anthropological Reports, no. 1 (Prescott, Ariz.: Prescott College Press), pp. 103–10.

LOSCH, AUGUST
1954 *The Economics of Location,* Woglum-Stopler translation (New Haven: Yale University Press).

MacCLUER, J., AND W. SCHULL
1970 "Frequencies of Consanguineous Marriage and Accumulation of Inbreeding in an Artificial Population," *American Journal of Human Genetics* 22:160–75.

McKEOWN, THOMAS, R. G. BROWN, AND R. G. RECORD
1972 "An Interpretation of the Modern Rise of Population in Europe," *Population Studies* 26:345–82.

MALAURIE, J., L. TABAH, AND J. SÛTTER
1952 "L'Isolat equimau de Thulé (Groenland)," *Population* 7:675–712.

MARTIN, PAUL S.
1971 "The Revolution in Archaeology," *American Antiquity* 36(1):1–18.

MATRAS, J.
1965 "The Social Strategy of Family Formation: Some Variations in Time and Space," *Demography* 2:349–62.

MATSUNAGA, E.
1966 "Possible Genetic Consequences of Family Planning," *Journal of the American Medical Association* 198:533–40.
1967 "Measures Affecting Population Trends and Possible Genetic Consequences," in *United Nations World Population Conference, 1965,* 2:481–85.

MAYNARD, JAMES
1967 "Eskimo Infant Deaths Twice Indians," *Medical Tribune,* February 25–26.

MEAD, MARGARET
1930 *Growing Up in New Guinea* (New York: William Morrow and Co.).

MILAN, F. A.
1970 "Demography of an Alaskan Eskimo Village," *Arctic Anthropology* 7(1).

MITCHELL, J. C.
1949 "An Estimate of Fertility in Some Yao Hamlets," *Africa* 29:293–308.

MORGAN, K.
1968 "The Genetic Demography of a Small Navajo Community," Ph.D. diss., University of Michigan.

MORTON, N. E.
1970 "Genetic Structure of Northeastern Brazilian Populations," in *The Ongoing Evolution of Latin American Populations,* ed. F. M. Salzano (Springfield, Ill.: Charles C. Thomas), pp. 251–76.

MURDOCH, JOHN
1892 *Ethnological Results of the Point Barrow Expedition,* Ninth Annual Report of the Bureau of American Ethnology, Part 1 (Washington, D.C.: Smithsonian Institution).

NAG, MONI
1962 *Factors Affecting Human Fertility in Nonindustrial Societies: A Cross-Cultural Study,* Yale University Publications in Anthropology, no. 66 (New Haven, Conn.).

NAPIER, J. R., AND P. H. NAPIER
1967 *A Handbook of Living Primates* (London: Academic Press).

NAROLL, RAOUL
1962 "Floor Area and Settlement Population," *American Antiquity* 27:587–89.

NEEDHAM, RODNEY
1959 "The Formal Analysis of Prescriptive Patrilineal Cross-Cousin Marriage," *Southwestern Journal of Anthropology* 14:199–219.

NEEL, J. V., AND N. A. CHAGNON
1968 "The Demography of Two Tribes of Primitive, Relatively Unacculturated American Indians," *Proceedings of the National Academy of Sciences* 59(3): 680–89.

NEEL, J. V., AND W. J. SCHULL
1972 "Differential Fertility and Human Evolution," in *Evolutionary Biology*, ed. T. Dobzhansky, M. K. Hecht, and W. C. Steere (New York: Appleton-Century-Crofts), 6:363–78.

NELSON, EDWARD W.
1899 *The Eskimo about Bering Strait*, Eighteenth Annual Report of the Bureau of American Ethnology, Part 1 (Washington, D.C.: Smithsonian Institution).

NEWTON, ISAAC
1687 *The Mathematical Principles of Natural Philosophy*, trans. by Andrew Motte (1729), rev. by Florian Cajori (1946) (Berkeley: University of California Press).

PETERS, CHARLES R.
1970 "Introduction Topics in Probability Sampling Theory for Archaeology," *Anthropology UCLA* 2(2):33–50.

PETROFF, I.
1884 "Report on the Population, Industries, and Resources of Alaska," in *Tenth Census U.S.*, vol. 8 (Washington, D.C.: Government Printing Office).

POLGAR, STEPHEN
1971 *Culture and Population: A Collection of Current Studies* (Chapel Hill, N.C.: Carolina Population Center).

POSPISIL, LEOPOLD
1964 "Law and Societal Structure among the Nunamiut Eskimo," in *Explorations in Cultural Anthropology*, ed. Ward H. Goodenough (New York: McGraw-Hill), pp. 395–431.

POTTER, R. G., JR.
1969 "Estimating Births Averted in a Family Planning Program," in *Fertility and Family Planning*, ed. S. J. Behrman et al. (Ann Arbor: University of Michigan Press).

POWDERMAKER, H.
1931 "Vital Statistics of New Ireland (Bismarck Archipelago) as Revealed in Genealogies," *Human Biology* 3(2):351–75.

POWYS, A. O.
1905 "On Fertility, Duration of Life, and Reproductive Selection," *Biometrika* 4:233–85.

References

RAGIR, SONIA

1967 "A Review of Techniques for Archaeological Sampling," in *A Guide to Field Methods in Archaeology*, ed. Robert F. Heizer and J. A. Graham (Palo Alto, Calif.: National Press), pp. 181–97.

RAUSCH, ROBERT

1951 "Notes on the Nunamiut Eskimo and Mammals of the Anaktuvuk Pass Region, Brooks Range, Alaska," *Arctic* 4(3):147–95.

RAY, P. H.

1885 *Report of the International Polar Expedition to Point Barrow, Alaska* (Washington, D.C.).

REDMAN, CHARLES L., AND PATTY-JO WATSON

1970 "Systematic, Intensive Surface Collection," *American Antiquity* 35(3): 279–91.

REED, ERIK L.

1948 "The Western Pueblo Archaeological Complex," *El Palacio* 55(1):1–15.

1950 "Eastern-Central Arizona Archaeology in Relation to the Western Pueblos," *Southwestern Journal of Anthropology* 6(2):120–33.

REID, J. JEFFERSON, AND I. SHIMADA

n.d. "Pueblo Growth at Grasshopper: Methods and Models," in *Multi-Disciplinary Research at Grasshopper*, Anthropological Papers of the University of Arizona (Tucson), in press.

RENFREW, COLIN

1972a *The Emergence of Civilization: The Cyclades and the Aegean in the Third Millennium B.C.* (London: Methuen & Co.).

1972b "Patterns of Population Growth in the Prehistoric Aegean," in *Man, Settlement and Urbanism*, ed. P. J. Ucko, R. Tringham, and G. W. Dimbleby (London: Duckworth & Co.), pp. 383–99.

RINALDO, JOHN B.

1964 "Notes on the Origins of Historic Zuni Culture," *The Kiva* 29(4):86–98.

RODDEN, ROBERT J.

1965 "An Early Neolithic Village in Greece," *Scientific American* 222(4):82–92.

ROOTENBERG, S.

1964 "Archaeological Field Sampling," *American Antiquity* 30(2):181–88.

ROSCOE, JOHN

1915 *The Northern Bantu* (Cambridge: Cambridge University Press).

ROSE, FREDERICK G. G.

1960 *Classification of Kin, Age Structure, and Marriage amongst the Groote Eylandt Aborigines* (Berlin: Akademie Verlag).

1965 "Unilateral Cross-Cousin Marriage," *Man* 16(11):24.

ROSENBLATT, PAUL C.

1974 "Cross-Cultural Perspective on Attraction," in *Foundations of Interpersonal Attraction*, ed. Ted L. Huston (New York: Academic Press).

RYDER, N. B., AND C. F. WESTOFF

1967 "Oral Contraception and American Birth Rates," in *Family and Fertility*, ed. W. T. Lin (South Bend, Ind.: University of Notre Dame Press).

SALISBURY, RICHARD

1956 "Asymmetrical Marriage Systems," *American Anthropologist* 58:639–55.

SALZANO, F. M.

1961 "Studies on the Caingang Indians. I. Demography," *Human Biology* 33:110–30.

1963 "Selection Intensity in Brazilian Caingang Indians," *Nature* 199:514.

SALZANO, F. M., AND R. DE OLIVEIRA

1970 "Genetic Aspects of the Demography of Brazilian Terena Indians," *Social Biology* 17:217–23.

SALZANO, F. M., J. V. NEEL, AND D. MAYBURY-LEWIS

1967 "Further Studies on the Xavante Indians. 1. Demographic Data on Two Additional Villages; Genetic Structure of the Tribe," *American Journal of Human Genetics* 9:299–309.

SCHAEFER, OTTO

1971 "When the Eskimo Comes to Town," *Nutrition Today* 6:8–16.

SCHNEIDER, DAVID M.

1965 "Some Muddles in the Models: or, How the System Really Works," in *The Relevance of Models for Social Anthropology*, A.S.A. Monographs, no. 1, M. Banton, general editor (London: Tavistock Publications).

SCHOENWETTER, JAMES, AND A. E. DITTERT

1968 "An Ecological Interpretation of Anasazi Settlement Patterns," in *Anthropological Archaeology in the Americas*, ed. Betty J. Meggers (Washington, D.C.: Anthropological Society of Washington), pp. 41–66.

SCHUMPETER, JOSEPH

1911 *The Theory of Economic Development*, 1934 translation (Cambridge, Mass.: Harvard University Press).

SCHWARTZ, DOUGLAS

1963 "Survey of Nankoweap Canyon," *American Antiquity* 28(2):296–97.

SHARP, R. L.

1940 "An Australian Aboriginal Population," *Human Biology* 12:481–507.

SLONAKER, MARIAM K.

1928 "The Effect of Different Percents of Protein in the Diet on Successive Generations," *American Journal of Physiology* 123:526–40.

SMITH, PHILIP E. L., AND T. C. YOUNG

1972 "The Evolution of Early Agriculture and Culture in Greater Mesopotamia: A Trial Model," in *Population Growth: Anthropological Implications*, ed. Brian Spooner (Cambridge, Mass.: M.I.T. Press).

SMITH, T. E.

1960 "The Cocos-Keeling Islands: A Demographic Study," *Population Studies* 14:94–130.

SPUHLER, J. N.

1962 "Empirical Studies on Quantitative Human Genetics," in *Proceedings of the UN/WHO Seminar on the Use of Vital and Health Statistics for Genetic and Radiation Studies, Geneva, 5–9 September* 1960 (New York: United Nations).

1963 "The Scope for Natural Selection in Man," in *Genetic Selection in Man*, ed. W. J. Schull (Ann Arbor: University of Michigan Press), pp. 1–111.

SUTTER, J., AND L. TABAH

1956 "Méthode mécanographique pour établir la généalogie d'une population," *Population* 11:507–30.

SWEDLUND, ALAN C.

1971 *The Genetic Structure of an Historical Population: A Study of Marriage and Fertility in Old Deerfield, Massachusetts*, Research Reports of the Department of Anthropology, University of Massachusetts, Amherst, no. 7.

TAEUBER, I. B.

1958 *The Population of Japan* (Princeton: Princeton University Press).

TAYLOR, KENNETH

1966 "A Demographic Study of Karluk, Kodiak Island, Alaska, 1962–1964," *Arctic Anthropology* 3(2):211–40.

TEXTOR, ROBERT

1967 *A Cross-Cultural Summary* (New Haven: Human Relations Area File Press).

THOMAS, J. M. C.

1963 *Les Ngbaka de la Lobaye* (Paris: Mouton & Co.).

TIETZE, C.

1967 "Effectiveness, Acceptability, and Safety of Modern Contraceptive Methods," in *United Nations World Population Conference, 1965*, 2:305–8.

TRIGGER, BRUCE G.

1965 *History and Settlement in Lower Nubia*, Yale University Publications in Anthropology, no. 69 (New Haven, Conn.).

TUAN, YI-FU

1972 "Discrepancies between Environmental Attitude and Behavior: Examples from Europe and China," in *Man, Space, and Environment*, ed. Paul Ward English and Robert C. Mayfield (New York: Oxford University Press), pp. 68–81.

TUGGLE, H. DAVID

1970 "Prehistoric Community Relationships in East-Central Arizona," Ph.D. diss., University of Arizona.

TURNBULL, COLIN M.

1965 *Wayward Servants: The Two Worlds of the African Pygmies* (New York: Doubleday & Co., Natural History Press).

TURNER, CHRISTY G., II, AND L. LOFGREN

1966 "Household Size of Prehistoric Western Pueblo Indians," *Southwestern Journal of Anthropology* 22(1):117–32.

TYLER, S. A.

1966 "Parallel/Cross: An Evaluation of Definitions," *Southwestern Journal of Anthropology* 22:416–32.

UDRY, J. RICHARD, AND NAOMI M. MORRIS

1967 "Seasonality of Coitus and Seasonality of Birth," *Demography* 4(2):673–79.

UNDERWOOD, JANE H.

1969 *Human Skeletal Remains from Sand Dune Site (H1), South Point (Ka Lae), Hawaii: A Preliminary Examination*, Pacific Anthropological Records, no. 9 Honolulu: Bernice P. Bishop Museum).

UNITED NATIONS
1954 *Demographic Yearbook of Statistical Office of the United Nations.*
1973 *The Determinants and Consequences of Population Trends,* vol. 1, rev. ed.

VALLEE, F. G.
1967 *Kabloona and Eskimo in the Central Keewatin* (Ottawa: Canadian Research Centre for Anthropology).

VESCELIUS, G. S.
1960 "Archaeological Sampling: A Problem of Statistical Inference," in *Essays in the Science of Culture in Honor of Leslie A. White,* ed. G. E. Dole and R. L. Carneiro (New York: Thomas Y. Crowell Co.), pp. 457–70.

WAGNER, ROY
1972 "Incest and Identity: A Critique and Theory on the Subject of Exogamy and Incest Prohibition," *Man* 7:601–13.

WAHLUND, S.
1932 *Demographic Studies in the Nomadic and Settled Populations of Northern Lappland* (Uppsala: Almqvist & Wiksells).

WARBURTON, D., AND F. C. FRASER
1964 "Spontaneous Abortion Risks in Man," *American Journal of Human Genetics* 16:1–25.

WEISS, KENNETH M.
1973 *Demographic Models in Anthropology,* memoir no. 27, Society for American Archaeology (Washington, D.C.).

WESTOFF, C. F., R. G. POTTER, JR., P. C. SAGI, AND E. G. MISHLER
1961 *Family Growth in Metropolitan America* (Princeton: Princeton University Press).

WEYER, EDWARD M., JR.
1962 *The Eskimos: Their Environment and Folkways* (Hamden, Conn.: Archon Books).

WILCOX, DAVID R.
1975 "A Strategy for Perceiving Social Groups in Puebloan Sites," in *Chapters in the Prehistory of Eastern Arizona, IV, Fieldiana: Anthropology* (Chicago: Chicago Natural History Museum), 65:120–65.
n.d. "Sampling Pueblos: The Implications of Room-Set Additions at Grasshopper Pueblo," in *Multi-Disciplinary Research at Grasshopper,* Anthropological Papers of the University of Arizona (Tucson: University of Arizona Press), in press.

WILSON, E. B., AND N. M. HILFERTY
1935 "Size of Completed Families," *Journal of the American Statistical Association* 30(suppl.):577–80.

WILSON, EDWARD O., AND WILLIAM H. BOSSERT
1971 *A Primer of Population Biology* (Stamford, Conn.: Sinauer).

WOLDENBERG, MICHAEL J.
1967 *The Identification of Mixed Hexagonal Central Place Hierarchies with Examples from Finland, Germany, Ghana, and Nigeria,* Harvard Papers in Theoretical Geography, Geography and Properties of Surfaces Series, no. 5. Fifth Technical Report, Office for Naval Research, Contract no. 0014–67A–0298.

WOLF, ARTHUR P.

1966 "Childhood Association, Sexual Attraction, and the Incest Taboo: A Chinese Case," *American Anthropologist* 68(4)883–98.

1968 "Adopt a Daughter-in-Law, Marry a Sister: A Chinese Solution to the Problem of the Incest Taboo," *American Anthropologist* 70(5):864–74.

1970 "Childhood Association and Sexual Attraction: A Further Test of the Westermarck Hypothesis," *American Anthropologist* 72(3):503–15.

1974 "Marriage and Adoption in Northern Taiwan," in *Social Organization and the Applications of Anthropology,* ed. Robert J. Smith (Ithaca, N.Y.: Cornell University Press).

1975 "The Women of Hai-shan: A Demographic Portrait," in *Women in Chinese Society,* ed. Margery Wolf and Roxane Witke (Stanford: Stanford University Press).

WOLF, MARGERY

1968 *The House of Lim* (New York: Appleton-Century-Crofts).

1972 *Women and the Family in Rural Taiwan* (Stanford: Stanford University Press).

WRIGHT, HENRY T.

1969 *The Administration of Rural Production in an Early Mesopatamian Town,* University of Michigan Anthropological Papers, no. 38 (Ann Arbor).

WYMORE, A. WAYNE

1967 *A Mathematical Theory of Systems Engineering: The Elements* (New York: John Wiley & Sons).

WYON, J. B. , AND J. E. GORDON

1971 *The Khanna Study: Population Problems in the Rural Punjab* (Cambridge, Mass.: Harvard University Press).

ZUBROW, EZRA B. W.

1971 "Carrying Capacity and Dynamic Equilibrium in the Prehistoric Southwest," *American Antiquity* 36(2):127–38.

ZUCKERMAN, SALLY

1962 *The Ovary* (New York: Academic Press).

Index